The Dead Duke,
His Secret Wife, and the Missing Corpse

The Dead Duke, His Secret Wife, and the Missing Corpse

*An Extraordinary Edwardian Case of
Deception and Intrigue*

PIU MARIE EATWELL

Liveright Publishing Corporation

A Division of W. W. Norton & Company

NEW YORK • LONDON

For information about permission to reproduce selections
from this book,
write to Permissions, Liveright Publishing Corporation,
a division of W. W. Norton & Company, Inc.,
500 Fifth Avenue, New York, NY 10110

For information about special discounts for bulk purchases, please
contact W. W. Norton Special Sales at specialsales@wwnorton.com
or 800-233-4830

Manufacturing by RR Donnelley Westford
Production manager: Louise Mattarelliano

ISBN 978-1-63149-123-8

Liveright Publishing Corporation
500 Fifth Avenue, New York, N.Y. 10110
www.wwnorton.com

W. W. Norton & Company Ltd.
Castle House, 75/76 Wells Street, London W1T 3QT

1 2 3 4 5 6 7 8 9 0

To my sister Pieta Dalglish,
for whom, as for me, the past is always present

Welbeck Abbey, 1889

CONTENTS

CONTENTS

DRAMATIS PERSONAE

ATHERLEY-JONES, LLEWELLYN

Barrister representing George Hollamby Druce / the prosecution in the perjury trial of *R. v. Herbert Druce*.

AVORY, HORACE

Barrister representing Herbert Druce / the defence in the perjury trial of *R. v. Herbert Druce*.

BAILEY, HORSEMAN

Solicitor at Baileys, Shaw & Gillett, legal representatives of the Dukes of Portland.

BARNES, MR JUSTICE

Judge on the probate action brought by Anna Maria Druce to set aside the will of T. C. Druce in 1898.

BAYLY, CATHERINE

Long-serving nurse to the Druce family; testified to the death of T. C. Druce in legal proceedings.

CALDWELL, ROBERT

Witness for the prosecution / George Hollamby Druce in the perjury trial of *R. v. Herbert Druce*.

CAVENDISH-BENTINCK, CHRISTINA ANNE JESSICA, LATER LADY TATTON SYKES

Descended from the 3rd Duke of Portland. Married Sir Tatton Sykes, Baronet of Sledmere House, Sledmere, Yorkshire in 1874.

CAVENDISH-BENTINCK, WILLIAM JOHN ARTHUR
CHARLES JAMES, 6TH DUKE OF PORTLAND
A cousin of the 5th Duke of Portland, inherited the dukedom when
the 5th Duke died in December 1879. Died in 1943.

CAVENDISH-BENTINCK, WINIFRED ANNA,
DUCHESS OF PORTLAND
Wife of the 6th Duke of Portland.

CAVENDISH-BENTINCK-SCOTT, WILLIAM JOHN,
5TH DUKE OF PORTLAND
*referred to as 'the 5th Duke', 'Marquess of Titchfield' or
'Lord John'*

The second of four sons to the 4th Duke of Portland, previously the
Marquess of Titchfield, inherited the dukedom in 1854. Notorious
eccentric. Alleged to have led a double life as T. C. Druce of the
Baker Street Bazaar. Died in December 1879.

CAVENDISH-BENTINCK-SCOTT, GEORGE FREDERICK, LORD
referred to as 'Lord George'

Younger brother of the 5th Duke of Portland. English Conservative
politician and racehorse owner, notable for his role with Disraeli in
unseating the prime minister, Sir Robert Peel, over the Corn Laws.
Died in mysterious circumstances in 1848 at the age of forty-six.

COBURN, THOMAS KENNEDY VERNON
Australian barrister, legal advisor and confederate of George
Hollamby Druce.

COOPER-MATHIESON, VENI
see Amanda Gibson, below

Australian novelist, mystic and self-help guru extraordinaire.
Worked in 1907 as secretary to the Druce-Portland Company.

CUFFE, HAMILTON JOHN AGMONDESHAM,
5TH EARL OF DESART
referred to as 'Lord Desart'

Treasury Solicitor and Director of Public Prosecutions.

DEW, WALTER, DETECTIVE CHIEF INSPECTOR
A leading detective at Scotland Yard CID, in charge of the Druce case at a late stage of the proceedings.

DRUCE, ANNA MARIA
Daughter-in-law to Thomas Charles Druce, married his son Walter Thomas in 1872.

DRUCE, FRANCES ELIZABETH ('FANNY')
The first daughter of T. C. Druce, generally regarded as his favourite.

DRUCE, CHARLES EDGAR
Great-grandson of T. C. Druce and cousin of George Hollamby Druce. Lived in Sydney.

DRUCE, GEORGE
The second son of T. C. Druce; emigrated to Australia.

DRUCE, GEORGE HOLLAMBY
Son of George Druce; came from Melbourne, Australia.

DRUCE, HERBERT
Eldest son of T. C. Druce and Annie May. Inherited the business at the Baker Street Bazaar. Refused to give permission for T. C. Druce's grave to be opened.

DRUCE, SIDNEY
Eldest surviving son of Anna Maria Druce; emigrated to Australia.

DRUCE, THOMAS CHARLES
London businessman who made a fortune from the department store the Baker Street Bazaar. Ostensibly died in December 1864. Alleged to have been the 5th Duke of Portland in disguise.

DRUCE, WALTER THOMAS
Son of T. C. Druce, married Anna Maria Druce in 1872.

FRESHFIELD, EDWIN

Senior partner at the firm of Freshfield and Williams, legal advisor to Herbert Druce; in charge of the Druce case.

GIBSON, AMANDA

later known as Veni Cooper-Mathieson

Australian novelist, mystic and self-help guru extraordinaire. Worked in 1907 as secretary to the Druce-Portland Company.

HAMILTON, MARGARET LOUISE JANE

Witness for the prosecution/George Hollamby Druce in the perjury trial of *R. v. Herbert Druce*. Known as the 'Veiled Lady'.

HENDERSON, KENNETH

Grandson of Fanny Druce, T. C. Druce's daughter. Managing editor of *The Idler*, which produced a series of pamphlets advertising the Druce case.

JEUNE, SIR FRANCIS

President of the probate division of the High Court.

KIMBER, EDMUND

Solicitor; legal representative of George Hollamby Druce.

MARLOW, THOMAS AND HENRY

Brothers; shady figures on the fringes of the London underworld.

MAY, ANNIE

Wife of T. C. Druce and mother of Herbert Druce.

PLOWDEN, ALFRED CHICHELE

Police magistrate, acting magistrate at the preliminary hearing of *R. v. Herbert Druce*.

ROBINSON, MARY ANN, ALSO KNOWN AS MARY ROBINSON

Witness for the prosecution/George Hollamby Druce in the perjury trial of *R. v. Herbert Druce*.

SHERIDAN, JOHN
Journalist for *Lloyd's Weekly Newspaper*.

STATHAM, ARNOLD
Barrister representing Anna Maria Druce.

SYKES, LADY TATTON, NÉE CHRISTINA ANNE JESSICA
CAVENDISH-BENTINCK
Descended from the 3rd Duke of Portland. Married Sir Tatton
Sykes, baronet of Sledmere House, Sledmere, Yorkshire in 1874.

SYKES, SIR TATTON, 5TH BARONET
Landowner, racehorse-breeder, flower-hater and church-going
eccentric. Seat at Sledmere House, Yorkshire. Married Jessica
Cavendish-Bentinck in 1874.

TRISTRAM, THOMAS HUTCHINSON, CHANCELLOR
Judge at the hearing of Anna Maria's case in the church court/
consistory court at St Paul's Cathedral. Twice granted a faculty for
the opening of the Druce vault.

TURNER, THOMAS WARNER
Land agent for the 6th Duke of Portland, placed in charge of
much of the evidence-gathering in the Druce case. His father,
J. F. Turner, was land agent to both the 5th and 6th Dukes.

YOUNG, ALEXANDER
Accountant, old friend of T. C. Druce and executor of Druce's will.
Defendant to proceedings brought in the probate division of the
High Court by Anna Maria, *Druce* v. *Young*.

All the world's a stage,
And all the men and women merely players;
They have their exits and their entrances,
And one man in his time plays many parts, . . .

WILLIAM SHAKESPEARE,
As You Like It, ACT II, SCENE VII

Act One

BURIAL

*I set forth to pave the way for discovery —
the dark and doubtful way.*

WILKIE COLLINS, *The Woman in White*

Mrs Druce at T. C. Druce's grave in Highgate Cemetery
(the *Penny Illustrated Paper*, 18 March 1899)

Welbeck Abbey

December 1879

Eccentric men have peculiar habits; they do not
seem to move in the same sphere with other mortals,
but are actuated by different influences from those
which affect the bulk of mankind.

GEORGE FREDERICK GRAHAM
English Synonyms Classified and Explained (1857)

I t was a dark, windy winter evening a few days before
Christmas 1879. The occupants of the saloon carriage of
the train of the Great Central Railway Company that rat-
tled from King's Cross Station in the direction of Sheffield were
tense and silent. In the carriage sat a young man of twenty-two.
He was pale, with a high forehead and heavily hooded eyes.
Also in the carriage sat five other people: two younger men,
a sickly boy, a pensive and alert-looking little girl of six years
old, and an older woman who regarded the other occupants
with anxious attention. All the party were dressed in sombre
black, the garb of deep mourning. Every so often, the countryside bordering the line would light up as the train approached
a town: Luton, Northampton, Leicester or Nottingham. In the
wells of shadow in between, nothing was discernible from the
carriage window, save – as the train toiled further north – the
dark mass of Sherwood Forest.

After about three hours, the train came to a screeching

halt at the small station of Worksop, about fifteen miles from Sheffield. Worksop Station was a newish building constructed some thirty years previously for the Great Central Railway Company (then known as the Manchester, Sheffield and Lincolnshire Railway). It was a somewhat preposterous affair, with its mock-Jacobean pinnacles, rustications, scrolls, scraps, lozenges and other whatnots. A small market town for much of its history, Worksop had seen a burst of growth with the construction of the Chesterfield Canal in 1777 and the arrival of the railway in 1849, both of which ran through the settlement. The discovery of a sizeable coal seam had brought a rush of new inhabitants to what had been a sleepy country town, nestled in the shadow of Sherwood Forest.

Other occupants of the train might have been surprised to see the saloon carriage party – who were clearly of a well-to-do sort – descend at such a humble spot as Worksop. Nevertheless, it appeared that they were expected, as an inquisitive crowd enveloped the group as soon as they emerged from the train, their white faces and dark clothes catching the light of the oil lamps as they made their way across the platform to the old-fashioned carriage that awaited them. 'The young duke! Did you see him?' was the excited whisper that went round.

After a long and dreary drive through wet country lanes, the party that included the 'young duke' – for that was the identity of the pale and heavy-eyed young man of twenty-two – arrived at its destination. Welbeck Abbey, like the nearby town of Worksop, was situated near the northern end of Sherwood Forest. The area was known as 'the Dukeries' – there being no fewer than four ducal seats within a few miles' radius. Welbeck Abbey had been the principal seat of the Dukes of Portland since 1809, but by 1879 there was little to be found of the original 'Abbey', apart from the name. The abbey had been founded as the chief seat of the white-cassocked Premonstratensian monastic Order in the twelfth century. During the Dissolution, the house had been handed by Henry VIII to his prominent administrator, Richard Whalley of Screveton. Afterwards, it had passed to Whalley's son, then through a series of sales and transfers to Lord Talbot, heir to the Earl of Shrewsbury, and finally in 1607 to Sir Charles Cavendish, a son of one of the best-known figures of the Elizabethan age, Bess of Hardwick.

Bess was a friend of Queen Elizabeth I, but while she shared many of her characteristics – including her first name and shrewd personality – she did not, like her, live and die a maiden. Quite to the contrary; by the end of her career, she had married no fewer than four times, and accumulated a fortune in landed estates across the country. She was also, by her many marriages and complex network of family connections, a remote ancestor of most of England's nobility, and even boasted royal connections.

The portrait of Bess that hung in the great hall of Welbeck in 1879 – and remains in the abbey to this day – reveals a woman with a broad forehead and a determined line to her mouth. She is handsome as opposed to beautiful, and her hands are shapely. Most importantly of all, the huge wealth acquired from her marriages is symbolized in the quadruple string of pearls that dangles around her neck, down to her waist. Bess had a passion for building, which amounted almost to the pathological. One biographer says of her:

All her life she was surrounded by masons, carpenters, brick-dust. She could not cease building, and her workmen were still busy when she died. It was said that she believed a prediction that she could not die as long as she was building.

We have reason to be grateful for Bess' building mania, for she built some of the finest houses to be seen in England today. It is also possible that she passed on her fetish for construction work to at least one of her descendants, who was to occupy the abbey in later years.

Welbeck Abbey reached the Dukes of Portland through the marriage of Lady Margaret Cavendish Holles-Harley to the 2nd Duke of Portland in 1734. The Portland dukedom was a relatively new title. Back in 1689, an earldom had been bestowed on the Bentinck family in recognition of the close friendship between William III and his protégé, the Dutchman Hans-Willem Bentinck. Hans-Willem had been one of the principal organizers of William's invasion of England in 1688, and had sailed to England with the Prince of Orange. The Portland dukedom was created for Hans-Willem's eldest son in 1716. In 1801, William Henry Cavendish-Bentinck, the 3rd Duke of Portland, changed the family name from plain Bentinck to Cavendish-Bentinck, in recognition of the alliance between the Bentinck and the Cavendish families that dated back to the 2nd Duke's marriage to Lady Margaret. The latest incumbent of Welbeck Abbey had been William John Cavendish-Bentinck-Scott, the 5th Duke of Portland, commonly referred to as 'Lord John', who had died on 6 December 1879, ostensibly without issue. As a result, the Portland title had devolved on to a cousin — twenty-two-year-old

William John Arthur Charles James Cavendish-Bentinck, the new 6th Duke of Portland. He was the pale young man travelling to Welbeck on the winter day of which we speak.

William was only a second cousin of the 5th Duke. His father was Lieutenant-General A. C. Cavendish-Bentinck, whose descent was through the 3rd Duke. William had been born on 28 December 1857, and it must have then seemed a remote possibility that, in less than twenty-five years, he would succeed to one of the greatest dukedoms in the land. The other members of the party arriving at Welbeck that evening were the new duke's half-brothers and sisters and his beloved stepmother: his mother having died when he was a few days old, they were his closest family. The pensive, alert-looking little girl, the new duke's half-sister, was to be famous in later life as the socialite and Bloomsbury Group hostess Lady Ottoline Morrell.

The entrance to Welbeck Abbey was then one of the most unusual of any stately home in England. Before reaching the lodge at the entrance to the estate, the new visitors drove through glorious woodland. The silhouettes of native oaks, elms and yews, dotted with more exotic specimens in the form of cedars and Himalayan firs, clustered in black shadows at the side of the track, the frosty silence interrupted only by the occasional whirring of a pheasant's wings or the rustle of a squirrel scampering through the frozen bracken. However, as soon as the carriage reached the lodge, it was plunged into a black-mouthed tunnel that cut through the side of a slope beside the lodge gates. The tunnel was not entirely dark, however; periodically, shafts of pale light entered through circular skylights in its roof, and gas jets set along its walls glowed with incandescent blue. The extraordinary underground entrance to Welbeck Abbey had been created by the 5th Duke of Portland. As they travelled through the darkness, the people in the carriage must have wondered what could have induced the duke to create such a sepulchral and cavernous subterranean entrance to his estate, when he could have driven to his front door entirely above ground, and through some of the most beautiful woods in England.

After a few minutes the coach party was abruptly catapulted into daylight as the tunnel opened onto a gravelled driveway leading to the abbey. The great house itself was imposing enough: a Palladian-style building with turrets and an elaborate façade that seemed to yearn for a clear blue Italian sky, rather than the leaden English cloudscape that weighed upon it. The mansion was perched on the edge of a huge ornamental lake that stretched to the horizon. As the carriage drew closer, however, it was clear that the place was deserted and unkempt. The driveway at the entrance was covered in wild grass and builders' rubble, and temporary planks had been placed to enable the carriage to reach the front door. The hall inside had no floor, and again temporary boards had been laid to allow the new residents to walk on it. The new duke and his party were met at the door by anxious estate staff: the agent, house steward, clerk of works and some others.

Upon closer inspection, it seemed that the only habitable part of Welbeck Abbey was the suite of rooms in the west wing of the house. These were the rooms that had lately been occupied by the bachelor 5th Duke. They were sparsely furnished: each room had double sets of brass letter boxes on the doors, one for letters in, and one for letters out. It was explained to the puzzled visitors that this was how the late duke preferred to communicate with his staff, choosing to send and receive written messages, rather than speak directly to his servants. It was this obsessive need for privacy, and a desire not to be seen about his daily movements, that had led the 5th Duke to dig the underground roadway from the lodge to the abbey; and when he travelled in his carriage, it was always with the green silk blind tightly drawn. The duke's carriage was unmarked, with no coat of arms or ducal coronet. Even when he arrived at the station to travel to and from London, he never left his own carriage, but had it lifted directly onto the goods wagon. The secrecy of the duke's presence in the carriage was so complete that one day his coachman offloaded the coach from the train at the station in London and, thinking it empty, stopped at a local inn for a drink. He was startled out of his senses to hear his Grace's impatient voice from inside the carriage, asking him if he did not think it time to drive on.

Scandalous rumours circulated about the 5th Duke of Portland. It was said, for instance, that his Grace had a dead body housed in a box on the roof of his flat at Hyde Park Gardens. The rumours were so persistent that the local health-and-safety officials actually came to inspect the flat. In the event, they found nothing but a great glass enclosure on the roof, apparently built for the purposes of enjoying the view. If he went out at all, the duke mainly travelled at night, a lantern strapped to his belt; and when he did venture forth during the daytime, he usually wore two or even three overcoats (whatever the weather), a very tall hat and high collar, and carried a vast umbrella, behind which he would attempt to hide if addressed by anyone (the duke was extremely attached to umbrellas, and never travelled without one under his arm, rain or shine). Staff at Welbeck were ordered not to greet the duke personally if they encountered him on the estate, or even acknowledge his presence unless spoken to first, on pain of immediate dismissal. They were to pay no more attention to him than as if 'he were a tree'.

And yet, despite such eccentricities, the 5th Duke was known as a kindly and generous employer, always willing to assist any of the many workmen on his premises. He provided them with donkeys to carry them to and from work, and umbrellas to take shelter from the rain. He also had a large skating rink built in the pleasure garden, and encouraged the housemaids to skate. If he encountered one of them sweeping the rooms or the stairs, he would send the terrified girl out to skate — whether she wanted to or not. An elderly worker on the Welbeck estate recalled how, if the men worked overtime after 5.20 p.m., the duke would give them bread, cheese and beer, tobacco and cigars. Sometimes his Grace would bring the tobacco out himself. Sometimes he would stop a little way off, quietly listening to the men singing. It was said that he preferred the company of servants to his social equals.

Thoroughly exhausted by their long journey, the members of the new duke's party retired to bed, Charlie, the sickly half-brother, being accommodated as best he could in the chilly rooms. When the party embarked on a full exploration of the house the next day, they found that — apart from the ducal suite — it was entirely empty. All the rooms were painted pink, with parquet floors, bare of any furniture save that each had a 'convenience' in the corner — completely exposed to public view. In one room lay a huge stack of paintings: Old Masters, and other priceless treasures. Many were cut out of their frames, and all were dusty and neglected. In the great kitchen there was a large cooking spit, where a chicken used to be kept permanently roasting for the 5th Duke. He would eat one half in the morning, and the other in the evening. Rare Gobelins tapestries tumbled out of long tin boxes, preserved with peppercorns. One room was lined with stacks of green boxes, in each of which was a dark brown wig. In other cupboards were boxes of cream Balbriggan socks and white silk handkerchiefs. Some of the handkerchiefs were embroidered with the initials 'SP' for 'Scott Portland', others with the ducal coronet. Yet others carried mysterious initials, such as 'LL', 'HH' or 'T'. These were thought, at the time, to be the locations in which they were kept.

Most extraordinary of all, however, was the vast network of underground tunnels, passages and rooms that the 5th Duke had constructed. These criss-crossed beneath the abbey in a vast labyrinth, like a Nottinghamshire Palace of Knossos. The 5th Duke seemed to have inherited more than a share of the mania for building that characterized his distant ancestor, Bess of Hardwick. In his case, however, the results were below, rather than above, ground. There was a tunnel over one thousand yards in length, leading from the house to the colossal riding school that the duke had built. This was wide enough for several people to walk side by side. A longer and more elaborate tunnel, one and a half miles long and intended as a carriage drive broad enough for two carriages to pass, led towards Worksop, although this had been abandoned a few years before. Railway lines ran along some of the tunnels between the kitchen and dining rooms, so that food could be conveyed in heated trucks.

Radiating out from the tunnels was a network of underground rooms. Three of these were very large and the third was truly immense, being a hundred and sixty feet long and sixty feet wide. The underground rooms were painted pink like the rooms above them, with skylights in the roof to let in the daylight. These skylights could be seen above ground, where they appeared as circular glass windows set at the edge of the paths that tracked over the estate. The skylights had been installed, at intervals of twenty feet, to light and ventilate the underground rooms and tunnels. Even today, both tunnels and skylights are marked on Ordnance Survey maps of the area.

The largest underground room, which had been intended originally as a church, was later used as a ballroom. And yet the 5th Duke never entertained. The whole place was a construction site: shovels, wheelbarrows and builders' rubble lay everywhere. For the child Ottoline, there was 'no beauty in these rooms – they were just vast, rather bare, empty rooms, and except for the top lighting, one would not have been aware that they were sunk into the earth.' The only relief from the endless miles of pink walls was the ceiling of the old riding school, which the 5th Duke – in what must have been an unaccustomed fit of gaiety – had painted in soft and rosy sunset hues, before lining the walls with mirrors, 'leaving the mock sunset to shine on the lonely figure reflected a hundred times in the mirrors around him'.

The new duke shuddered at the chilly emptiness of the cavernous space that he had inherited, and was minded simply to shut it up and leave. However, his stepmother – a kindly but formidable lady – persuaded him to stay and do his duty. She then set about making something approaching a normal home out of the vast mausoleum of Welbeck Abbey, ordering furniture from London, trawling through attic rooms and chests, beginning the immense task of cataloguing the abandoned treasures of the neglected mansion.

Nobody knew why the 5th Duke had lived the extraordinary life that he had led, or the cause of his extreme shyness and withdrawal from the world. It was known for him to disappear, for months at a time, in his network of underground warrens. It was true that he did suffer from a mysterious skin complaint, a disfiguring condition that was possibly one reason for his retirement from public view. Some spoke of madness inherited from his mother Henrietta (modern psychological analysis might point to a form of autism). Others said his desire to hide away was in some way connected with the sudden death of his younger brother, Lord George Bentinck.

A marked contrast to his introverted elder brother, Lord George had been a flamboyant figure in public life and politics. He had been both a notable racehorse owner, and prominent supporter of the Conservative politician, Benjamin Disraeli. Disraeli had been engaged, during the 1840s, in a battle with the then prime minister, Sir Robert Peel, over the controversial proposed repeal of the protectionist Corn Laws. It was due to the campaigning of Lord George that a large number of peers were persuaded to oppose Peel, winning the support of country gentlemen who would otherwise have been deeply suspicious of Disraeli – an Anglicized Sephardic

Jew and novelist-turned-politician. Lord George's untimely death at the age of forty-six in September 1848 – officially from a heart attack in a field near Welbeck on his way to a dinner at a neighbouring estate – had long been the subject of colourful rumour. There were those who speculated that his involvement in horseracing had led to a quarrel with William Palmer, also known as the 'Rugeley Poisoner', and that he was poisoned by Palmer as a result. Palmer was a doctor who poisoned a number of victims with strychnine in the 1840s and 1850s, for their insurance policies and to feed his gambling habit. The idea that he had murdered Lord George was fanciful to say the least, but the whispers circulated even among the highest circles.

Even more persistent, however, was the rumour that the 5th Duke, then the Marquess of Titchfield, was somehow involved in his younger brother's death. The rumour was fuelled by whispers that the Marquess of Titchfield had been at or near the scene of Lord George's collapse. The exact whereabouts of the marquess at the time of his brother's death was never definitively established, and several eye-witnesses at the inquest testified that he might have been present at the time and place where Lord George died. A labourer named John Evans, his son and a woodman named John Mee, all said that they saw someone at the spot, and that they thought it was the Marquess of Titchfield.

Madness, guilt, eccentricity, subterfuge: whatever lay behind the 5th Duke's peculiar behaviour, the person least likely to know the truth of the matter was his successor William, the 6th Duke. William had never met his eccentric forebear in life, and only set eyes on him when he was called to see the 5th Duke's body laid out after his death. The new duke was perfectly content to accept his distant cousin's behaviour as a harmless, if expensive, eccentricity: a peculiar fetish for burrowing which any Englishman was entitled to indulge in his own home, if he had the means and inclination to do so. The 6th Duke had the reputation, among his contemporaries, of being a 'good fellow' – a phrase that, at the time, carried with it a specific set of connotations. Like most men of his class and generation, he asked few questions and simply got on with the job of settling into his strange new home, transforming its echoing underground vaults into buzzing reception rooms and ballrooms to entertain the highest of high society. Under William's regime, the old house crept out of the shadows: Welbeck Abbey began to look less like a building site and more like a stately home.

In 1889 – at the age of thirty-two, ten years after he inherited the dukedom – the 6th Duke married Winifred Dallas-Yorke. Although she came from an ancient Lincolnshire family, Winifred was not among the obvious, titled candidates for the 6th Duke's hand. 'Willy and Winnie', as they were known to their friends, entertained in lavish style at Welbeck, which was now to play host to some of the most famous people of the age. Both Queen Victoria and Edward, Prince of Wales, were guests there, as were the Duke and Duchess of Sparta, the Crown Prince and Princess of Greece and – a quarter-century later – the Archduke Franz Ferdinand, shortly before his assassination in Sarajevo in 1914. As Master of the Horse under Lord Salisbury's government, William was an important member of the Royal household staff. He masterminded, among other great ceremonial events, the arrangements for Queen Victoria's Diamond Jubilee.

Winifred, the new Duchess of Portland, was nearly six feet in height and considered one of the great beauties of her generation. The artist John Singer Sargent memorably captured her in a portrait of 1902 – a full-length canvas in which Winnie is revealed standing against a Corinthian column. The scale of the painting emphasizes her statuesque height, and the evening light heightens the dramatic contrast of her black hair against her crimson cloak and white gown. Winnie concentrated on supporting her husband in his role as a great landowner, throwing herself into charitable work and the life of the estate. It was a time of glittering balls, weekend parties and rifle shoots, the heyday of the English country house. Exchanges were organized between the house parties at Welbeck and the neighbouring 'Dukeries' estate of Clumber, owned by the Duke of Newcastle. Autumn and winter were the seasons for fox-hunting and shooting, when the valley echoed with gunshots and the abbey dining tables were loaded with pheasants, partridges, hare and rabbit. Summer was the season for lawn tennis and croquet, when gentlemen in boaters and ladies with parasols idled the hours away to the lazy strains of a gramophone. They were waited on by the abbey servants at picnic tables spread with a delicious array of exotic delicacies such as caviar, truffles and foie gras. Winnie herself presided over her guests with dignity, ignoring the fickleness of fashion by choosing to stick to her favourite fan-shaped Medici lace collar, paired with a spray of Malmaison carnations. She had an innate sense of the grandeur of her position. Once, when lost in London, she was obliged to ask her way of a policeman. On being given directions, she said: 'The City? I have only been here in processions.' Willy and

Winnie's first child, Lady Victoria, was followed by a son, William Arthur Henry, who became the new Marquess of Titchfield. The future of the Portland dukedom seemed to be assured.

Until, that is, some twenty years after the 6th Duke's accession, when he was informed by his lawyers of a most fantastical set of assertions being made by an obscure widow in the church courts of London. A set of assertions that, if true, would call into question not only his entire inheritance, but the very future of Welbeck Abbey.

SCENE TWO

St Paul's Cathedral

March 1898

A grave's a fine and private place…

ANDREW MARVELL
'To His Coy Mistress'

C hancellor Tristram could not believe his ears. This was the most extraordinary application he had ever heard.

'If I understand you correctly, Mrs Druce,' he said, 'you are requesting me to grant you a faculty for the exhumation of your father-in-law's coffin, which was buried in consecrated ground at Highgate Cemetery. And the reason for this peculiar request is that you say he did not die thirty-four years ago in December 1864, as everyone believes, and indeed, was represented by his funeral at that time. Your assertion is that the funeral in 1864 was a charade, and that in fact your father-in-law carried on living in secret, under an assumed identity.'

The woman who stood before him continued to look ahead unwaveringly. 'Yes, my Lord,' she replied. 'That is exactly what I seek.'

There was a collective catching of breath from the clutch of lawyers, journalists and curious onlookers crowded into the pews of the Wellington Chapel of St Paul's Cathedral. From the tall, stained-glass chapel windows lately designed by the illustrious Victorian craftsman, Charles Eamer Kempe, a thin shaft of sunlight hit the large font of Carrara marble somewhat incongruously installed in the centre of the room. Now known as the Chapel of St Michael and St George, the Wellington Chapel was at this time used for sittings of the consistory or church court. An application such as Mrs Druce's would normally have been heard in private in chambers, but given the gravity of the allegations, Chancellor Tristram had ordered it to be heard in open court.

There was a long pause. Chancellor Tristram was at a loss. A diminutive and portly figure, he had always looked younger than his true age, even in his big wig and splendid scarlet robe. But despite his youthful looks, he was one of the most senior judges of the ancient church courts. He was also the last surviving member of the old civil courts or 'Doctors' Commons', which had been reviled by Charles Dickens earlier in the century, and abolished in the 1890s. He was, in addition, a leading practitioner in the Chancery court that had recently taken over from the church courts in contentious matters relating to wills. Chancellor Tristram was a dry and seasoned lawyer, tough as the riding boots which he often forgot to take off when he got off his horse to take the train to London every day. He was known for his encyclopaedic knowledge of the law and hard-headed approach to legal argument. Encounters with eccentricity — if not downright madness — were a not uncommon feature of his professional life. There had been, for example, the 1867 case of a disputed will, *Smith and Others* v. *Tebbit and Others*, involving the will of a certain Mrs Thwaytes. Mrs Thwaytes — who had been left the then immense fortune of

£500,000 – had been convinced that she was the third person of the Holy Trinity and that her medical attendant, Dr Simm-Smith, was the Almighty, with whom she held frequent conversations by question and answer. She believed that Our Lord's Second Coming and the Last Judgment would take place in her drawing room at Hyde Park Gardens, which she had decorated accordingly in white and gold. In her will, she left small sums to her relatives, and the residual estate to Dr Simm-Smith. Chancellor Tristram had represented Mrs Thwaytes' relations in court. He had contended that the will was not duly executed, that the deceased was not of sound mind, memory and understanding when she made it, and that it was procured by the undue influence of Dr Simm-Smith and others. He won, and the will was set aside.

In contrast to Mrs Thwaytes, the woman who now stood before Chancellor Tristram on this blustery March morning of 1898 appeared to be of entirely sound mind. Anna Maria Druce was a pale woman on the 'wrong' side of forty, with a slightly receding chin and hooked nose. She bore trace of having once been very handsome. Her plain outfit – unadorned jacket with leg o'mutton sleeves and a straw boater perched on her head, hair screwed tightly in a simple bun – signalled genteel poverty, the all too common sight of a female member of the late-Victorian middle classes fallen on hard times. Despite this, Anna Maria had a mesmeric presence that seemed to hold all who heard her in thrall. Never had the chancellor come across a litigant so determined, so sure of her facts, and so well versed in labyrinthine court procedures. Mrs Druce knew every case in support of the ancient ecclesiastical jurisdiction for the granting of permission – known in technical legal jargon as a 'faculty' – for the exhumation of a corpse. She knew of the church court's presumption against granting such permission, based on the sound premise that a dead body should stay where it had been laid to rest. She also knew the exceptional circumstances when such permission might be granted. She knew that the government had muddied the waters forty years before by introducing the Burial Act 1857, which in certain circumstances required the home secretary's permission before an exhumation could be carried out. She could cite every exhumation case in the book, including the many upon which Chancellor Tristram himself had sat as ecclesiastical judge. He found it difficult to believe that this woman was mad.

And yet Anna Maria Druce's case was, quite simply, extraordinary. Her father-in-law had been the late Thomas Charles Druce, a successful Victorian businessman who in the 1850s had owned and run a highly profitable London department store, known as the Baker Street Bazaar. T. C. Druce had occupied a spacious residence called Holcombe House in Mill Hill, then part of Hendon.* He had lived with a woman known as 'Annie May' for several years before finally marrying her in 1851, by which time she had given birth to three children out of wedlock. This was a highly unusual situation for a Victorian middle-class couple, and was kept secret from the children, who believed that at the time of their births their parents were married. The couple's eldest son was Herbert Druce, born in

---

* Mill Hill used to be a part of the ancient civil parish of Hendon, within the historic county boundaries of Middlesex. Mill Hill as part of the Municipal Borough of Hendon was merged into the London Borough of Barnet, Greater London, in 1965.

1846. He was followed by a son, Sidney, and a daughter, Florence. The first child born after T. C. Druce's marriage in 1851 – and therefore the first legitimate issue – was Walter Thomas Druce, Anna Maria's husband. T. C. Druce died in 1864 – or at least, so everybody thought. However, Anna Maria's contention was that her father-in-law was still very much alive at that date, and that his 'death' and burial in 1864 were faked.

The background to these remarkable claims was not set out in Anna Maria's affidavit, but Chancellor Tristram knew of it from the gathering tide of newspaper reports and gossip that was already beginning to grip the late-Victorian public. According to these reports, Mrs Druce's astounding contention – and the underlying reason for her application for the exhumation of her father-in-law's grave – was that the man everybody in Baker Street knew as the businessman Thomas Charles Druce was, in fact, the late William John Cavendish-Scott-Bentinck, the 5th Duke of Portland. At that time, the Cavendish-Bentincks were one of the richest families in the country. Their official seat – that of the Dukes of Portland – was the vast and ancient Nottinghamshire estate of Welbeck Abbey. However, another branch of the family had inherited huge swathes of central London in the newly gracious districts of Harley Street and Marylebone. This was evidenced by the myriad streets and squares in their name: Great Portland Street, Portland Place, Cavendish Square, Great Titchfield Street, Bolsover Street. When the notoriously eccentric 5th Duke of Portland had died – apparently childless – in 1879, his cousin William had inherited the dukedom as the 6th Duke. But if the 5th Duke of Portland had indeed masqueraded under a double life as T. C. Druce of the

Baker Street Bazaar, he would not have died childless. In fact, he would have had a legal heir – Walter Thomas Druce, the first legitimate son of T. C. Druce, and the husband of Anna Maria. Walter Thomas was now dead; but Anna Maria's son Sidney was alive and well, and living in Australia. And it was for her son's benefit that Anna Maria sought the faculty to open her father-in-law's grave.

FAMILY TREE OF T. C. DRUCE

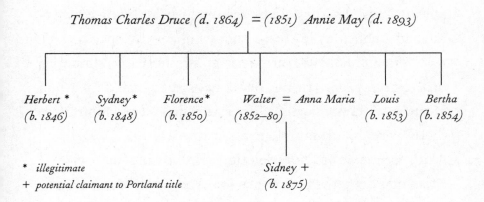

According to Anna Maria's story, T. C. Druce's coffin had been filled with lead to mimic the weight of a dead body. The duke, who had tired of his complicated double life, had apparently simply decided to 'bury' his alter ego and return to his former life. This was, therefore, the reason for the application for a faculty to open the Druce family vault in the Highgate cemetery: for according to Anna Maria's case, were the grave to be opened, it would be found to be empty. And if it was, Mrs Druce would be a step closer to proving that her son was heir to the Portland millions.

Chancellor Tristram was perplexed. Much of the press reporting of Anna Maria's story was patent nonsense. It was claimed, for example, that 'Annie May' – the woman T. C. Druce had married in 1851 – was the illegitimate daughter of the 5th Earl of Berkeley. Frederick Augustus Berkeley, the 5th Earl, had shocked society at the end of the eighteenth century by fathering a number of illegitimate children with Mary Cole, the daughter of a local butcher, and subsequently marrying her. But Chancellor Tristram would have known that Annie May could not possibly have been an illegitimate daughter of the Berkeleys. Any such offspring, after all, would have been at least fifty-five years old by the time of T. C. Druce's marriage to Annie May in 1851: a highly unlikely prospect.

On the other hand, turning from the more lurid fantasies of the newspapers to the real legal issues raised by Anna Maria's affidavit, Chancellor Tristram had to admit that there were disturbing elements to the case. T. C. Druce's death certificate had not been signed by any medical officer – a fact that bothered the chancellor. And Anna Maria alleged that, when her husband Walter was interred in the Druce family vault in the cemetery at Highgate in 1880, the coffin beside his – that of T. C. Druce – had completely collapsed, giving the impression that it would likely have been empty. And then, there had always been whisperings about the extreme eccentricity of the 5th Duke of Portland. It was well known that the 'burrowing duke' had constructed an enormous maze of underground tunnels beneath his estate at Welbeck Abbey. A famous recluse, he had turned his back on the world. Was it not plausible that such a man might have led a secret life?

Mrs Druce claimed, moreover, to have seen her father-in-law alive after his alleged death and burial in 1864. Some years after the supposed funeral, she said, she had been driving with her husband in a carriage in Castle Hill, Maidenhead, when she spotted the elder Druce in the street, accompanied by another man. She had immediately stopped the carriage and asked them who they were. The man accompanying the person Anna Maria believed to be T. C. Druce said that he was a warden at a private Richmond mental asylum, where his companion had been admitted as a patient, under the name of Dr Harmer.

Could T. C. Druce/the duke have masqueraded as a lunatic named Dr Harmer after his supposed death in 1864, until his 'real' death in 1879? To assert as much seemed nothing less than preposterous. And yet Mrs Druce was not the only person to identify T. C. Druce and the asylum patient Dr Harmer as one and the same man. The identification was supported in court by Dr Forbes Winslow, a celebrity lunacy practitioner and a person for whom Chancellor Tristram would have had the greatest respect. Winslow's father, Dr Forbes Benignus Winslow, had been a key witness in the famous 1843 trial of Daniel M'Naghten, a lunatic suffering from a persecution complex who had shot and killed the then prime minister's secretary Edward Drummond, mistaking him for the prime minister himself, Sir Robert Peel. The elder Winslow's intervention had led to M'Naghten's trial for murder being called to a halt, and the establishment of the famous legal rules for insanity pleas in murder trials, the M'Naghten Rules. On the death of his father, Forbes Winslow junior had taken over his successful lunacy practice, and had been involved in a number of sensational cases. They included the campaign to release the American housewife Florence Maybrick, convicted in 1889 of poisoning her husband, James Maybrick, with arsenic.

A rotund gentleman with large chops and a bushy beard, Dr Lyttleton Stewart Forbes Winslow cut an impressive figure when he appeared before Chancellor Tristram as a witness. This eminent Victorian had enjoyed a decidedly unusual upbringing, his illustrious father being of the view that lunatics should be cared for in the surroundings of a family home. Young Forbes Winslow had therefore grown up with the shrieks and groans of the insane as a normal child might have been rocked to sleep by his mother's lullabies. The child who had been raised in a lunatic asylum dedicated his life to understanding the madness that had surrounded him, and by the 1890s was one of the most controversial and prominent lunacy experts of the day. He was in no doubt, he told Chancellor Tristram, that the photograph of T. C. Druce that was shown to him in court was that of his former patient, Dr Harmer. Dr Harmer, he stated, was under his care until his death about twenty years earlier, first at his asylum in Richmond, then at Sussex House in Hammersmith. He had given his profession as that of a homeopath.

Dr Tristram remained some time in perplexed consideration of the issue. Faculties for the exhumation of bodies – for whatever reason, whether to retrieve valuables that had inadvertently been buried, make room for another body, or move a body to another grave – were granted every week in the church courts of Victorian England. The chancellor himself had granted more of them than he cared to remember. On the other hand, the actual plunder and desecration of the crowded graveyards of England's towns and cities was a cause of much contemporary disquiet. Rumours abounded of bodies being dug up for their hair, teeth and fat to provide the wigs, dentures and wax candles demanded by the wealthy. And there were tales of the so-called 'Resurrection Men', grave robbers who unearthed human remains for the dissecting tables of the scientists. Increasingly, the vaults of the wealthy were being protected by iron bars to keep out the grave robbers. Indeed, it was partly in response to such scandals that the Burial Act 1857 had been introduced, requiring a licence from the home secretary for disinterment of a body except in such cases where the body was to be disinterred and reinterred in consecrated ground. But Chancellor Tristram was absolutely certain that this was not a case where a licence from the home secretary would be required: after all, Highgate Cemetery *was* consecrated ground. After considerable reflection, he considered that Anna Maria Druce did have a legitimate interest in the disinterment, and had made out a case for it being carried out. He therefore granted the application for a faculty to exhume the coffin of T. C. Druce in Highgate Cemetery, to ascertain whether it did indeed contain a body. The faculty was to take effect in fifteen days, in the absence of objection from any interested party.

Anna Maria was jubilant. After all, she was one small step closer to proving that her son was heir to the Portland millions. As she left the west entrance of St Paul's Cathedral to join the crowds in Ludgate Circus, a swarm of journalists gathered round her. The Druce–Portland affair – as the case was called – had already provided a field day for the penny press, the nascent tabloids of a new, media-hungry era. The British public – and indeed, the wider English-speaking world, for the case had been reported in newspapers as far afield as Newfoundland and New Zealand – was intrigued at the prospect of this diminutive woman single-handedly taking on one of the mightiest aristocratic families in England. Overnight, Anna Maria had become a celebrity, her case discussed in inns, parlours and private gentlemen's clubs around the country.

Beyond the consistory court, however, legal machinery manipulated by other interested parties was beginning to grind into action. A few miles to the east of St Paul's, at the far end of the great thoroughfare of Cheapside, urgent discussions were taking place at the offices of Messrs Freshfield & Williams of New Bank Buildings, solicitors to the businessmen of Threadneedle Street since 1743. The distinguished clients of Freshfields included no less an institution than the Bank of England. The discussions centred on Anna Maria Druce and the faculty that had been granted by Chancellor Tristram to take effect, subject to any objection from an interested party, in fifteen days' time.

Two days after the hearing at St Paul's Cathedral, a clerk left the doors of Freshfields and hurried down Cheapside. He hailed a horse-drawn cab, instructing it to make haste to the chambers of 12 King's Bench Walk, Temple. In his hand, he bore a letter addressed to Chancellor Thomas Hutchinson Tristram.

Highgate Cemetery

March 1898

Good friend, for Jesus' sake forebeare
To digg the dust enclosed heare;
Bleste be the man that spares thes stones,
And curst be he that moves my bones.

Epitaph of William Shakespeare

M r Bois, the superintendent of Highgate Cemetery, looked out of the window of the cemetery lodge and sighed. The pale, gaunt figure in widow's weeds, fluttering anxiously up and down the paths of the cemetery in the chilly December light, flitting in and out of the rows of mossy tombstones and crumbling sepulchres, was by now a familiar sight. The stir Mrs Druce caused by her – virtually daily – visits to the cemetery was most unwelcome. She persisted in her demand that Mr Bois open the grave of her father-in-law, Thomas Charles Druce. This was despite him explaining to her countless times that, as far as he was concerned, he could not do so without the home secretary's permission. Then there was the day she assaulted two of the undertakers who had been trying to dig up an old grave to make way for a new one, her absurd claim being that they had been attempting to dig a secret passage to the Druce family vault, in order to tamper with the remains buried there. She had even brought a mining engineer with her, to certify whether this was the case. And then, only a few days ago, a journalist from a national newspaper had come nosing around, asking for information about the funeral and burial of Mr Druce, thirty-four years back in December 1864. Mr Bois had given the man short shrift. While he himself had not been at Highgate Cemetery in 1864 – his tenure there had started two years later – the records clearly showed that Mr Druce had been buried at the cemetery in the family vault, on 31 December 1864. The respectable firm of undertakers Messrs Glazier and Son of Tottenham Court Road had carried out the arrangements. The vault at Highgate had cost £61, the shell of the coffin was lead, and the outer case of elm. The whole proceedings had been highly elaborate, with two four-horse coaches, heavily feathered and plumed, and twelve men involved in the affair.

'Depend upon it,' Mr Bois had told the journalist firmly, 'I shall open the grave, and at the bottom, in the coffin concerned, I will find bones.'

And yet, there were aspects of the case that caused Mr Bois to have some doubts. For instance, the owners of the vault had placed a stone slab over the bottom coffin – that of T. C. Druce – after the funeral of his widow Annie May, in 1893. Rumour had it that this was to conceal the true state of the coffin, which had collapsed at the funeral of his son Walter in 1880. Mr Bois could think of no other plausible explanation for this action. The case certainly intrigued him, and he had admitted as much to the reporter: 'I shall be immensely curious about opening that grave. It is a unique case in my thirty-two years' experience among the tombs of Highgate.'

None the less, the digging up of graves at Highgate

– officially or unofficially – was nothing new in those days. At a time when people often died young and the rituals of mourning were a national pastime, it was not uncommon for a bereaved husband or lover – his ardour cooled with the passage of time – to petition to recover jewels or other tokens of affection buried with his loved one. Mr Bois himself had known of several such cases. There had been, for example, the hushed exhumation by the poet and artist Mr Dante Gabriel Rossetti of the remains of his late wife, Elizabeth Siddal, in 1869, just three years after Mr Bois had started work at Highgate. Mr Rossetti, grief-stricken at the death of Elizabeth, had buried the manuscript of his poems alongside her in the Rossetti family vault. Seven years later, he regretted his impulsive action. In that case, the relevant government minister, Mr Henry A. Bruce, was remarkably amenable to granting a licence for the exhumation, having apparently overseen the commission of an altarpiece by Mr Rossetti for Llandaff Cathedral. On the evening of 5 October 1869, workmen removed the slab over the grave, dug down in the narrow space to the coffin, prised open the lid and lifted out the notebook of poems. Lid, earth and slab were then replaced, and the workmen tipped with beer money. The whole operation was conducted in the strictest secrecy and overseen by an acquaintance of Mr Rossetti's, a dubious art dealer by the name of Charles Howell, who had been instrumental in persuading Rossetti to dig up the body. Howell later spread fanciful nonsense about Mrs Rossetti's corpse, claiming that her hair still glowed red and luxuriant with posthumous growth.

In the present case, however, the home secretary – Sir Matthew White Ridley – was stubbornly refusing to grant a licence for the exhumation of Mr Druce's coffin. And here was another thing that could not fail to have struck Mr Bois, with his weighty experience of burials and exhumations. In the late Victorian period, licences for digging up graves were not uncommon. Why was this particular application meeting with so much resistance? Who was determined to stop the Druce vault being opened, and why?

Had Mr Bois been able to contemplate the tombstones of the other Victorian grandees that lined the wooded walks of Highgate with the benefit of hindsight, he might have come to the conclusion that, if Mr Thomas Charles Druce had indeed led a double life as the 5th Duke of Portland, he was in good company with many others there laid to rest. In the same west side of the cemetery as the Druce vault – barely a stone's throw away – lay the tomb of Catherine Dickens, the long-suffering wife of the late author and pillar of the Victorian literary establishment, Charles Dickens (whose remains, of course, repose in Westminster Abbey). Philanthropist, performer and patriarch, Dickens seemed the embodiment of the Victorian domestic virtues of family, hearth and home. But in fact, he had a secret mistress for much of his married life. She was the actress Ellen Lawless Ternan, twenty-seven years his junior (the same age as his youngest daughter), whom he housed in a succession of properties conveniently near him. While close friends and acquaintances were well aware of 'Nelly's' existence (Dickens was to fall out permanently with the novelist Thackeray when he mentioned her name in public, outside the Garrick Club), virtually all correspondence relating to her was destroyed by Dickens himself and by zealous relatives after his death. Dickens' relationship with Ellen was only made known to a wider audience in a revelatory biography by the author Claire Tomalin in the 1990s. It is now believed that the 'official' account of Dickens' death in 1870 was a fabrication: that he did not, in fact, die having dinner with his sister-in-law Georgina at his home in Gads Hill, as the world was led to believe at the time, but rather in the house nearby, in which he had installed Nelly.

And then there was Dickens' lifelong friend and fellow novelist Wilkie Collins, credited with the invention of detective fiction in his mystery novel *The Moonstone* (1868). A bachelor throughout his life, Collins, like the 5th Duke of Portland, preferred the company of those socially below him. A master of the double existence, he had two mistresses – Caroline Graves, a widow from a humble family, and Martha Rudd, also a working-class girl, with whom he had several children. When in the company of Martha he assumed the name William Dawson, and she and his children by her took the last name of Dawson themselves. Lodging very close to the Duke of Portland's London residence with his 'official' mistress Caroline Graves, Collins' separate household headed by Martha Rudd was installed at the top of the very same road. As a result, Collins was able to switch identities between 'Collins' the dilettante writer and 'Dawson' the family man, with the same ease that he changed his frock coat for his overcoat, according to the weather.

Victorian celebrities who had led less than straightforward private lives were represented equally well on the eastern side of the cemetery. For here were to be found the graves of the female novelist George Eliot (in real life Mary Ann Evans, author of *Middlemarch*). She was laid to rest next to her lover, the philosopher and critic George Henry Lewes. The couple lived together in Richmond, despite the fact that when he met George Eliot, Lewes was already married to another woman, Agnes Jervis, with whom he had agreed to have an 'open relationship'. In fact, Agnes had children by both Lewes and other men, several of whom were falsely registered on their birth certificates as Lewes' children. Also living in Richmond, although not buried at Highgate, was the Victorian sensation novelist Mary Elizabeth Braddon – author of the bestselling novel *Lady Audley's Secret* (1862). Her partner, the periodical publisher John Maxwell, was already married with five children when he met Mary, his wife conveniently locked up in an Irish asylum. Mary acted as stepmother to Maxwell's children until his wife died in 1874, finally enabling the couple to marry. She had six children by him, several born before they were married.

Nor were double lives limited to bohemian members of the Victorian literary establishment. Members of the solid middle class also indulged in alternative existences. On 22 November 1875, a respected businessman who had owned a brush-making firm stood trial at the Old Bailey. Henry Wainwright, aged thirty-eight, was married with four children, kept a house at the eminently respectable Tredegar Square, and was a pillar of the local church. However, he had also maintained a second establishment in the East End where he went by the name of Percy King, with his mistress Harriet, who was known as 'Mrs King', and their children. When his business failed and he ran short of cash, Wainwright downgraded Harriet to a less salubrious abode. Understandably unhappy about the new arrangements, she threatened to reveal all to

Wainwright's wife. Wainwright lured her to his warehouse at Whitechapel, shot her in the head, 'inexpertly' chopped her body into ten pieces, and buried them in lime under the warehouse floor. When he subsequently went bankrupt, he attempted to remove the remains in parcels, fearing they would be discovered by the new occupier of the warehouse. He got one of his former employees to help him remove the parcels. Unfortunately for Wainwright, the man – who was later to claim that a supernatural voice urged him to 'Open that parcel!' – looked into one of the boxes, and discovered a human hand. Wainwright was followed to a pub in Borough, where he was arrested and charged with murder, along with his brother as an accomplice. Having made a full confession, he was hanged in December 1875.

From the famous to the infamous, real-life cases showed that it was by no means unheard of for eminent and even ordinary Victorians, faced by the restrictive social and moral conventions of the time, to adopt double lives. Victorian literature, too, was saturated with motifs of duplicity and deception. As Dr Jekyll explains at the end of Robert Louis Stevenson's late Victorian novella *Strange Case of Dr Jekyll and Mr Hyde* (1886), when in the character of Dr Jekyll he was cursed with a 'certain impatient gaiety of disposition, such as has made the happiness of many, but such as I found it hard to reconcile with my imperious desire to carry my head high, and wear a more than commonly grave countenance before the public'. Hence it came about that the pressures of living an irreproachably 'moral' life led Dr Jekyll to develop another persona – Mr Hyde – to indulge in the immoral, sensuous, shocking and, ultimately, murderous fantasies that social convention obliged him to conceal from the world. In short, he 'stood committed to a profound duplicity of life'. A sensation on publication, *Strange Case of Dr Jekyll and Mr Hyde* reached an even wider audience when it was adapted as a stage play in 1887, originally in the United States, but subsequently touring Britain in the 1890s, with the great actor Richard Mansfield performing the two title roles.

Hot on the heels of *Jekyll and Hyde* in 1895, only three years before Mrs Druce filed her astonishing claim, a new play, *The Importance of Being Earnest,* was successfully produced in the West End. In a razor-sharp satire of the age's obsession with adopting a high moral tone, or 'earnestness', the play portrayed two young men who each took on another 'persona' in order to have free rein to indulge in their fantasies and more wayward leanings, away from the prying eyes of society. Thus Jack, the guardian of the young ward Cecily, claims to have a fun-loving younger brother by the name of Earnest in town. As he says:

> when one is placed in the position of guardian, one has to adopt a very high moral tone on all subjects. It's one's duty to do so. And a high moral tone can hardly be said to conduce very much to either one's health or one's happiness.

Jack is therefore 'Earnest in town and Jack in the country'. Similarly, Jack's friend Algernon invents an ailing invalid of a friend called 'Bunbury' – a pretext which enables him to escape from town, to a freer life in the country, when he chooses. *The Importance of Being Earnest* ran for just under a year, until it was suddenly cancelled, owing to the newly surfacing scandal surrounding the homosexual double life of its author, Oscar Wilde. The battle between Wilde and the Marquess of Queensberry – the father of Wilde's lover, Lord Alfred Douglas or 'Bosie' – led to a notorious libel trial, which Wilde lost. This was followed by his conviction for sodomy and gross indecency, and his subsequent social disgrace and incarceration in Reading Gaol.

Secrets, lies, aliases and double identities: all were integral to, and enmeshed within, the very fabric of late Victorian society. In the circumstances, if the 5th Duke of Portland had led a double life, would there have been anything exceptional in that? Would he not simply have been following in the footsteps of dozens of other ostensibly 'respectable' members of the Victorian establishment?

Baker Street and Cavendish Square

1860s

Je est un autre.

ARTHUR RIMBAUD

Nobody knew much about the past of Thomas Charles Druce of Baker Street, for he kept himself to himself. He first appeared in town in 1830 – turning up, as if from nowhere, to work as a salesman for old Mr Munns, an Oxford Street upholsterer and furniture dealer. By the end of 1832 he had left Munns for the Baker Street Bazaar.

'Bazaars' did not mean the same thing to Victorians as they mean to us today. A 'bazaar' was not a colourful local market, but rather an early precursor of the department store – one of the vast and spectacular shopping centres which were then springing up around the capital. First came the Soho Bazaar, specializing in ladies' fashion and millinery, and occupying several houses in the north-west corner of Soho Square. The impressive queue of splendid carriages drawing up at the bazaar's doors at the height of the 'season' was proof of its prestige. The Pantheon Bazaar was newer and flashier. Formerly a place of eighteenth-century public entertainment – whose site is now occupied by Marks and Spencer's 'Oxford

Street Pantheon' branch — it was, in Victorian times, a shopping complex. Converted from an old Oxford Street theatre that had fallen on hard times, its entrance, by way of a statue-adorned vestibule, gave way to a picture gallery on the first floor (the pictures being, by general acknowledgment, of rather indifferent merit), flanked by a bird-filled conservatory of hothouse plants and a shop selling children's toys, knick-knacks, trinkets, photograph albums and other ephemera. The combination of toys and trinkets with the presence of wildlife inevitably acted as a magnet for London's young ladies, governesses and their charges, leading to the bazaar also being frequented by a certain type of dissolute *flâneur* or lounger — that is, a London gentleman at least as interested in the bazaar's clients as in its wares. Then there was the bazaar known as the Pantechnicon: a splendid establishment in Belgravia that sold larger items of furniture and horse-drawn vehicles, stocking everything from the dress carriage to the light gig.

The Baker Street Bazaar was a direct rival of the Pantechnicon. Originally a market for horses, this bazaar had, by the 1830s, become a forum for a hotchpotch variety of goods: everything from carriages, harnesses and horse-furniture to stoves and 'furnishing ironmongery' could be acquired there. It was also the initial home of Madame Tussaud's waxworks, before it relocated to Marylebone Road in 1883.

Once at the Baker Street Bazaar, the humble furniture salesman of obscure origins rose through the ranks with astonishing swiftness. By the 1850s Thomas Charles Druce was a partner in the business, earning a small fortune. But he was a man of abstemious habits. He travelled unostentatiously, driving to and from his office in a discreet brougham. He dined just once a day, at midday, on a plain meal of fish or chicken (the sight of red meat was abhorrent to him). He did not smoke, and had an aversion to wine. His dress, however, was distinctive. He typically wore a high hat and old-fashioned collar, and had a particular fondness for wigs, which he had fitted by the fashionable London wig-makers, Truefitt & Co. of Bond Street. Sometimes he wore a rose or flower in his buttonhole. Sporting an impressively large, bushy beard and sideburns, with a sallow complexion and a slightly jaundiced appearance, T. C. Druce cut a formidable figure as he strode about his business in the bustling precincts of Baker Street. An immensely hard worker, he imposed the same demands on his staff as he did on himself: he was stern and overbearing towards his employees, and brooked no contradiction or argument. He had a habit of turning up when least expected, entering the shop via one of the underground passages that ran from the mews at the rear, and surprising his unsuspecting employees. 'The old man', one of his sons was later to remark, 'had an eye that could see right through you.' Around his office, which was separate from the shop, there were red curtains. If these were open, the shop staff knew they might approach him. If they were drawn, no one could do so, however urgent the reason.

At some point in the 1840s, Druce took up with a beautiful young girl called Annie May, over thirty years his junior. It was whispered that the couple did not marry for many years, despite Annie bearing him several children. The rumours were enough for the Druces to be ostracized by polite society. This may have been exactly what old T. C. Druce wanted, for he never showed much inclination for genteel company. Much, in fact, was said about Thomas Charles Druce, but virtually nothing was known about him. His response to questions on the subject of his antecedents was always the same: that he had neither father nor mother, and that he was 'sprung from the clouds'. A relative was later to say of him that 'Mr Druce never divulged anything with regard to his parentage or friends and kept the subject a profound secret'. In all matters he was incredibly reticent, refusing to deal with all but his regular business acquaintances. He changed house frequently: every two years or so, the family was forced to relocate, criss-crossing London in a series of moves which appeared to defy any logical pattern. It seemed, indeed, as though T. C. Druce were on the run from something... Or someone.

Thomas Charles Druce's last home – to which he moved in 1861 – was a majestic mansion called Holcombe House, situated in Mill Hill, Hendon. Mill Hill at that time was still in the country, but it had, from the eighteenth century, become a favoured abode for the rich and fashionable seeking a spacious retreat within easy reach of London. An imposing, three-storeyed mansion of grey stone enclosed by a high wall with iron gates, Holcombe House had been built in 1775 for a former Lord Mayor of London. The house was surrounded by beautiful lawns, gravelled paths and flowerbeds, and boasted five hothouses and a conservatory. The interior of the house was equally impressive. The hall had a sweeping balustrade and marble floor. The dining room was furnished in crimson velvet, with walls to match, and had a thick Turkish carpet on the floor. Next to the well-appointed kitchen were a scullery and butler's pantry. The bedrooms of Mr and Mrs Druce were located on the second floor. On the third floor, where the children slept, were a night nursery, a day nursery, bathroom, pantry and five bedrooms. In the grounds of the mansion were stables and coachmen's quarters, and the outdoor staff included three gardeners, two coachmen, a groom, a cowherd and a lampman. There was no butler in the house, on account of Mrs Druce being 'very nervous'. There was a governess for the children, a nurse, a parlourmaid, housemaid, schoolroom maid, kitchen maid and cook. This was, without doubt, the residence of a man of means.

It was in his bedroom on the second floor of Holcombe House that Thomas Charles Druce supposedly drew his last breath. It was December 1864, and he was – according to the official story – seventy-one years old. The wishes he had expressed for his funeral were simple. There was to be no fuss or show, and the funeral expenses were not to exceed £20. In the event, the ceremony was actually rather grand: twelve men and two four-horse coaches, heavily feathered and plumed, were hired for the occasion. The workers at Mr Druce's Baker Street offices were bitter about the whole business, for the lavishness of the event contrasted so greatly with the meanness he had shown to them. 'Not even so much as a pair of gloves to commemorate the event,' grumbled Mr Redgell, a former shop worker, to a journalist from the *Daily Express* many years later. But Druce's employees were more frightened than resentful. For there was persistent talk that the old man's ghost still paced the warren of underground passageways beneath the shop in Baker Street. In fact, rumour had it that old Mrs Pledger, the shop forewoman, had gone out of her mind in fright from seeing the figure of her erstwhile

master loom up among the packing boxes, just as he used to do
in life. She died soon after the event, and her last words were
said to have been: 'I see him now, the dead man!' Yes, there
was a great deal of queerness surrounding Thomas Druce.
The old man had carried many secrets to his grave in 1864.
That is, if he *had* gone to his grave in that year…

As Thomas Charles Druce sat behind the scarlet curtains of
his Baker Street office, another reclusive individual paced,
imprisoned, in the vault-like gloom of his London home,
barely a mile away. Harcourt House was the London residence
of the 5th Duke of Portland. An eighteenth-century town-
house occupying almost the entire west side of Cavendish
Square, it did not benefit from its privileged position in one
of London's most prestigious locations. Rather, it confronted
the square with a vast and forbidding expanse of wall, punctured by heavy wrought-iron gates topped with sharp spikes.
Behind the walls was a stucco-fronted, cavernous house,
barely more welcoming than the gates. Originally designed
for Lord Bingley in the 1720s, Harcourt House had become a
London landmark known for its dismal grandeur and exces-
sive privacy. Thackeray used it as the model for Lord Steyne's
dreary mansion, Gaunt House, in *Vanity Fair*:

> All I have ever seen of it is the vast wall in front, with the
> rustic columns at the great gate, through which an old porter
> peers sometimes with a fat and gloomy red face – and over
> the wall the garret and bedroom windows, and the chim-
> neys, out of which there seldom comes any smoke now. For

the present Lord Steyne lives at Naples, preferring the view of the Bay and Capri and Vesuvius to the dreary aspect of the wall in Gaunt Square.

The writer E. Beresford Chancellor was one of the few people allowed to visit Harcourt House. He wrote of the house in his 1908 book, *The Private Palaces of London Past and Present*:

> ...nothing could have exceeded the dreariness of its interior, except perhaps the gloom which sat perpetually on its outward walls. The very size of its rooms, and the remains of their former magnificence, with their elaborately carved and moulded cornices; their ceilings painted 'en grisaille' and their fine old chimneypieces, added to the sense of desolation which seemed to have irrevocably settled on the whole place.

As if the towering surrounding walls and spiked entrance gates were not enough, the 5th Duke had tall iron and glass screens built round the garden of Harcourt House to shield him from the curious eyes of his neighbours. The screens were a massive 80 feet high by 200 feet long, and presented an extraordinary sight. The duke's fear of public appearances was such that he took most of his exercise within his private garden, which had a large, circular path running round it for precisely this purpose. Little else existed in the garden save for a few stunted trees and some blackened grass that pushed up in miserable patches around the path. The basement of the house was taken up almost entirely by a huge bathroom containing various baths, in which the duke spent a great deal of time trying out vapour treatments for his mysterious skin disease. A trapdoor from this bathroom led directly up to his bedroom above.

Although he was always shy, in his youth the 5th Duke of Portland had not been the eccentric recluse that he was to become in later years. Known to his friends and family as Lord John, he joined the army in 1818 to serve a relatively undistinguished career, becoming lieutenant and captain in the Grenadier Guards in 1830. On the death of his elder brother in 1824, he succeeded him as heir-apparent to the dukedom, taking the title of Marquess of Titchfield. He also – reluctantly – replaced his brother as Tory MP for King's Lynn. On the day he was elected, he did not even attend the hustings: his uncle, Lord William Bentinck, filled his place. Sir William Folkes (who lost to the marquess by 177 to 89 votes) remarked, somewhat caustically:

> To the present Marquess I feel not the slightest hostility. He is, however, a perfect stranger to you; you have never seen him – perhaps you never will see him; and I must say that had it not been for that most useful work 'The Peerage' I should never have known that such a person existed.

In the event, the marquess served as MP for only two years, gladly giving up the seat to his uncle Lord William, having little taste for active politics. He even delegated the writing of his farewell speech to his father, the 4th Duke.

Timid and endlessly plagued by mysterious ailments, Lord John never matched up to his brilliant younger brother. On the face of it, Lord George seemed a much better embodiment of the Cavendish-Bentinck tradition of political and public service, begun by the original Hans-Willem Bentinck, and epitomized by the 3rd Duke of Portland, who had twice been prime minister of Great Britain. The old 4th Duke was not slow to express his impatience at the shortcomings of his heir as compared to his younger son, and rumour had it that relations between the marquess and his father were less than cordial. It was an odd circumstance that, when the old duke died in 1854, Lord John was absent from the funeral. A contemporary newspaper report stated simply that 'the present Duke of Portland was prevented by illness from attending'. Nor was the new heir to the dukedom a favourite of his mother: the old duchess never forgave Lord John for surviving her favourite eldest son, and the marquess was noticeably absent from her funeral as well.

As far as the female sex was concerned, there was only one woman whose name was publicly linked to the 5th Duke. This was the opera singer Adelaide Kemble, with whom the duke fell in love when he was Marquess of Titchfield. Adelaide was the strikingly handsome younger daughter of the actor Charles Kemble. Her aunt, Sarah Siddons, was the most famous stage actress of the age. So intense were the marquess' feelings that he would haunt the Opera House at Covent Garden when Adelaide was performing, sending her gifts and passionate letters. He commissioned the fashionable society portraitist, John Hayter, to reproduce Adelaide's likeness from every angle, lending the artist his private box at the Opera House to enable him the better to study his subject. Unfortunately, the marquess' passion for the stately diva was unreturned. When he did, finally, pluck up the courage to offer her his hand, he was rejected. This was probably for the very good reason that Adelaide was, at that point, engaged to another man: she married the businessman Edward John Sartoris in 1843, whereupon she retired from her brief, but brilliant, stage career. Called to Cavendish Square by urgent dispatch one windy evening, the portraitist Hayter found the marquess icily alone in the gloom of the drawing room at Harcourt House. Every one of the dozens of portraits of Adelaide that hung in the room had been turned to face the wall. 'Take them, Hayter,' said the marquess, with a grandly desolate sweep of the arm. The artist duly took away the offending paintings, which remained with him long after the 5th Duke's death and until his own, whereupon they reverted to Welbeck Abbey. There they hang to this day, a melancholy testimony to the 5th Duke's unrequited passion.

After the Adelaide affair, the 5th Duke seemed – at least, to the outside world – to take no further interest in women. This led to a certain amount of speculation. 'None of the three Bentinck brothers was married, and none of them was likely to marry,' wrote Lady Londonderry, a family friend, without further comment. It was rumoured that there was some mysterious physical or psychological reason why the 5th Duke could not marry or have children. In recent years, it has been mooted that he was a repressed homosexual.

In the winter of 1851–2, the duke was involved in a serious accident, in which the wheel of a horse-drawn cab actually passed over his head, injuring him severely. From that moment on, he could no longer bear to sit on a horse or listen to music. Already fragile in health, he became a veritable hypochondriac. In the view of his closest friends, this was the point at which his eccentricity started to increase.

Whether because of his rejection by Adelaide Kemble, the strange circumstances of his younger brother's sudden death, the physical or psychological consequences of his carriage accident or some other unknown cause, the marquess began progressively to withdraw into his own, private phantasmagoria of shadows. Until 1864, he was most often to be found at Harcourt House rather than Welbeck Abbey. (The fact that the duke resided mainly in London until 1864, the year of T. C. Druce's supposed death, was cited in support of the double-identity theory.) A tall, spare figure, a good five feet nine inches in height,* his Grace was notorious for his sallow complexion, said to be a side-effect of his skin complaint.

That the 5th Duke suffered from some form of skin disease is certain, but the precise nature of the ailment remains a mystery. References to the duke's 'unhealthy pallor' are numerous, and he appears from his behaviour – including his preference for darkened rooms, blinded carriages and underground tunnels – to have been extremely chary of daylight. There was speculation in the newspapers that he suffered from smallpox, and his wig-maker believed that he had a form of eczema. In one of his letters the duke referred to an 'intense irritation of the skin', incurable by medication, relief from which could only be obtained by bathing in scalding then cold water, bleeding with a lancet, or sleeping between wet sheets. One of his valets, Henry Powell, recollected that the eruptions – which took place very frequently, especially in the springtime – caused the duke great inconvenience. At such

---

* The average height of the Victorian male was about five feet six inches.

times, 'he could not bear to have his clothes on, and would wear loose flannel trousers and a jacket'.

Long averse to red meat, the duke in later years took to dining on chicken alone – in the morning and evening only, and never at lunchtime. This was, of course, exactly the reverse of Druce, who ate only at lunchtime (and also disliked red meat), and it therefore became another argument to support the idea that the two men were one and the same person. Like Druce, the 5th Duke was abstemious in the extreme: he was a non-smoker, and had a marked dislike of alcohol, save for the occasional glass of champagne. His dress, always eccentric, became increasingly peculiar. Already famed for his tall silk hat and stiff, upturned collars, he took to carrying around with him the umbrella for which he became notorious. He started to tie his trousers up around his ankles in the fashion of a navvy, no doubt inspired by the habit of the workmen toiling in the mud at Welbeck Abbey.

All of the 5th Duke's clothes were supplied by Messrs Batt & Co. of Lower Seymour Street, Portman Square. He was the best customer they ever had. Years later, the son of the firm, Mr Charles Batt, recalled how the duke always bought his clothes in sets: three sets of overcoats and frock coats, twelve pairs of trousers, thirty night-caps, and sixty pieces of under-linen at a time. The peculiarity of the sets of coats was that the second had to be a trifle larger than the first, and the third a trifle larger than the second. This enabled the duke to put on and take off extra coats, according to the weather. If it froze, the duke would wear all six coats at once – the overcoats on top of the frock coats. They were distinguished by tabs of different colours for each set of coats (green for the first set, blue for the second and red for the third). Within each set, they were identified by the number of tabs (one tab for the first coat, two for the second and three for the third). In his *Reminiscences of the Turf*, the trainer and jockey William Day recalled of the 5th Duke:

> He once came to Danesbury in the height of summer, dressed in a long, heavy sable fur coat, that nearly touched the ground when he stood erect – a garment I should have thought more calculated to resist the inclemency of a Siberian winter than the overpowering heat of a midsummer day.

The duke's trousers were always made of the same grey fabric, of different thicknesses for summer and winter. Once, he returned twelve pairs of trousers because they weighed an ounce and a half more than those of the year before. After this, Messrs Batt & Co. bought a pair of scales, and made the clothes to weight, as well as measure. His under-linen was made of silk, embroidered with the ducal coronet, the initials 'S.P.' (for 'Scott-Portland'), the number of the set, and the year of delivery. Occasionally, sets with other, unexplained initials were ordered – as when the duke asked for a new 'L.S.' set to be delivered with the 'coronet' set, to weigh in at 3 ounces heavier than the previous set.

The 5th Duke was also very fond of wigs: bouffant creations that made his long, lean face more cadaverous still. Thomas Keetley, his coachman, recalled that one day he was riding with him in the park at Welbeck during the fawning season when a fawn suddenly sprang out of the bracken and frightened the duke's pony, which bolted off under a tree. A branch knocked off both the duke's hat and wig – revealing that his Grace was quite bald underneath. The duke's chosen wig-maker was none other than Messrs Truefitt & Co. of Bond Street, who also numbered T. C. Druce among their clients. The foreman of the firm had a vivid recollection of his first wig-fitting visit to Harcourt House in the 1850s. On arriving at the forbidding front door of the duke's London residence at eight o'clock in the morning, the wig-maker spied an ancient butler peering at him through the glass. After a tremendous amount of unbolting of rusty locks, the door was opened, and he was escorted upstairs to a room honeycombed with pigeonholes. Each pigeonhole contained a wig – no fewer than five or six hundred of them in all. In the half-lit chamber sat the duke, face muffled, waiting to be fitted. Every six months or so, the wig-maker would be summoned. The ritual was always the same: an appointment at eight o'clock sharp in the morning, the same ancient butler, the same journey to the wig-lined room, and the duke waiting alone in the darkened room. There was never any conversation, save for instructions relating to the fitting of the wig.

The extreme fastidiousness manifested by the 5th Duke in his dress was reflected in his personal habits. His Grace's servants were frequently called upon on Sundays to help him arrange and rearrange his books, of which he had a vast number. He would file great quantities of newspapers, carefully marked and arranged in bundles. His papers were always ironed before they were handed to him. If the 5th Duke wanted money – whether silver or coppers – every coin had to be carefully washed before he would touch it. (Cab drivers frequently thought the sparkling coppers too good to be true.) Perhaps with the memory of his terrible accident all too fresh in his mind, his Grace would refuse to step into a new carriage until the carriage-maker had taken a turn in it first, to demonstrate that it was safe.

After 1864, the duke spent more and more time at Welbeck Abbey. It was at this time that he embarked on an extraordinarily ambitious programme of building works: new lodges, workmen's dwellings, a new riding school, a glass-covered exercise ground (known as 'the Gallop', over a quarter of a mile long), stables, dairies, workshops, a church, museum and picture gallery – to say nothing of the labyrinth of passages underground, in which his Grace might be found wandering at any hour of day or night. The duke, in fact, appeared to be withdrawing gradually from all human contact.

Communication with staff was conducted via written notes placed in heavy brass letter boxes outside the ducal suite – the very boxes which were later to be noted by the sharp-eyed, six-year-old Ottoline, on her first visit to Welbeck. When the duke wished to converse with a servant, he would place a note in the letter box and ring his bell. In the room he usually occupied was a large trapdoor, set in the floor. If his Grace wanted the suite to be cleaned, he would place a memorandum to this effect in his letter box, pull the bell and disappear through the trapdoor, until the work was completed. The duke's bedroom, moreover, was most curiously arranged: the bed was large, square and shut in with doors, so that when they were closed, it was impossible to tell if the bed were occupied or not. As his own valet conceded, 'He might have been in the house for weeks at a time without my being aware of it. I only knew he was there by getting written orders, either to provide his meals or other attentions.'

Whether the 5th Duke faked his death as T. C. Druce in 1864 or not, there is no doubt that he left Welbeck Abbey for the last time on Sunday, 1 September 1878. For a year he lay ailing at Harcourt House, and finally died there on 6 December 1879. On his own instructions, the 5th Duke's funeral was an understated affair. He had asked in his will that the burial expenses 'be as small as possible consistently with decency', that the funeral take place early in the morning, and that the usual attendance of family be dispensed with. Accordingly, he was buried in Kensal Green cemetery, with minimal ceremony.

Withdrawn from the world in his secret ducal suite and underground passages, shut up in his darkened carriage, possessed of a multitude of wigs, tall hats and muffling collars, the movements of the 5th Duke had been a mystery even to his closest aides. If he had chosen, like so many of his neighbours, to adopt a secret identity, would anyone have been any the wiser?

In any event, a certain determined lady from Marylebone had been doing some digging of her own.

The Streets of London

Summer 1898

When Adam delved and Eve span,
Who was then the gentleman?

Sermon by JOHN BALL,
a leader of the fourteenth-century Peasants' Revolt

August 1898, in the south of England, was sunny, warm and unusually dry. In the long, sultry afternoons that blended imperceptibly into twilight, there was one subject alone that – more than the Dreyfus affair or the Fashoda incident – animated the conversation of bowler-hatted commuters in the packed carriages of suburban trains; one subject that was sure to spark off a lively discussion over the dinner table; one subject that was eagerly debated over cigars in the overstuffed armchairs of private members' clubs. That subject was, naturally, the Druce case. Everybody agreed that it was quite the best 'rummy go' since the Tichborne case, over twenty years before.

The Tichborne case had been the legal *cause célèbre* of the 1870s. The baronetcy dated from 1601, when Sir Benjamin Tichborne was knighted by Elizabeth I. His descendants inherited great wealth, together with the position of one of the leading titled families in England. In 1854, Roger Tichborne, heir to the baronetcy, disappeared in a shipwreck off the coast of South America. He was widely accepted to have drowned, the insurance was paid, and his will proved. The only person who refused to accept his death was his mother, the Dowager Lady Tichborne. Clinging to the belief that her son was still alive, Lady Tichborne advertised extensively in newspapers the world over for anybody with information to come forward. A butcher calling himself Thomas Castro, from Wagga Wagga, Australia, duly presented himself in 1866, claiming to be the missing heir.

Despite his unrefined manners and coarse appearance, Lady Tichborne embraced the claimant as her son. She gave him an allowance of £1000 a year, accepted his illiterate wife as her daughter-in-law, and handed over to him the letters and diaries of her missing son. He gained an enormous following, with hundreds of people signing a petition for his claim to be recognized. Other Tichborne relatives, however, were convinced that the would-be claimant to the Tichborne title was one Arthur Orton from Wapping, who had sailed for Chile in the early 1850s and ended up in Australia. At a civil trial that lasted from 1871 to 1872, over a hundred people swore that Castro was indeed the missing baronet. However, a very strong point against him was the absence of certain tattoo marks borne by the original Roger Tichborne. In the event, he lost the civil case and was subsequently tried for perjury in 1873, found guilty, and sentenced to seven years' imprisonment.

For a time, the man from Wagga Wagga was a popular hero. When, in 1875, Parliament unanimously rejected a motion by his counsel, Dr Kenealy, to refer the case to a Royal Commission, there were threats of a riot in London, and the military had to be held in readiness. He was finally released in 1884, by which time the fickle public had lost interest in him. He died, destitute and in oblivion in 1898 – the year Mrs Druce first brought her claim before Chancellor Tristram. The Tichborne mystery was a legal and factual puzzle that was never resolved. Everybody had a theory as to the truth of the matter. Chancellor Tristram himself had been one of the lawyers involved in the case, and had his own views on the affair. His suspicion, he told his colleagues, was that the claimant was an illegitimate brother of the lost baronet.

The Druce–Portland affair differed from the Tichborne case in many respects, but they did both tap into issues of pressing concern to the late Victorian public: social anxiety about an increasing class fluidity, coupled with resentment at a society which, still rigidly organized according to class divisions, refused to grant due recognition to those who had climbed the ladder on merit. In the eighteenth century, there had been little doubt as to who could claim the status of a 'gentleman'. The term defined a specific class of people, essentially the landed gentry, about whose membership there was little dispute. During the course of the nineteenth century, that situation was to be revolutionized. The increasing impact of industrialization, the advent of 'new money' in the form of fortunes coming from far-flung regions previously considered off the social map – the industrial north, the countries of the New World – all made the definition of the term 'gentleman' increasingly open to debate. 'New money' was making wealthy men of businessmen as opposed to the traditional, landowning classes. A new, more flexible definition of the word 'gentleman' was therefore required. In Dickens' novel *Great Expectations* (1861), set in the late Georgian period, the hero Pip, an orphan who inherits a fortune from a secret benefactor, starts life aspiring to be a 'gentleman' in the wrong sense: not someone to be distinguished for his chivalry, self-sacrifice and heroic conduct, but rather a swell or a dandy, idling away his time on gambling and drinking with the rowdy group of young men who form the fast set of 'The Finches of the Grove'. This is the image of the 'gentleman' represented by Regency dandies, the most prominent of which was 'Beau' Brummel. Generally, they were middle-class men trying to ape aristocratic manners, like the dissolute chancer Dazzle in Boucicault's comedy of 1841, *London Assurance*:

> Nature made me a gentleman... I live on the best that can be procured for credit, I never spend my own money when I can oblige a friend, I'm always thick on the winning horse, I'm an epidemic on the trade of a tailor. For further particulars, inquire of any sitting magistrate.

Of course, Pip's dandified idea of a 'gentleman' is proved to be both shallow and anachronistic. No longer able to rely on his benefactor and source of wealth – the deported convict Abel Magwitch – he learns that he has to rise up the social ladder by his own efforts and hard work, not the deceptive chimera of inherited riches. In this sense, he comes close – by the end of the novel – to a very different and much more forward-looking definition of a 'gentleman', that of Samuel Smiles in his bestselling 1859 manual, *Self-Help*:

> A well-balanced and well-stored mind, a life full of useful purpose, whatever the position occupied in it may be, is of

far greater importance than average worldly respectability...
Riches and rank have no necessary connexion with genuine
gentlemanly qualities. The poor man may be a true gentleman
– in spirit and in daily life, he may be honest, truthful, upright,
polite, temperate, courageous, self-respecting and self-sup-
porting – that is, be a true gentleman. The poor man with a rich
spirit is altogether superior to the rich man with a poor spirit.

Cases of disputed identity such as the Tichborne trial or
the Druce–Portland affair raised intriguing – and disturbing
– questions for the late Victorian and Edwardian public. Did
low-class pretenders to upper-class titles like the Tichborne
claimant and Mrs Druce represent a liberating upheaval in the
social order – a brave new world in which a butcher could
just as well be a lord? Or were they idle, get-rich-quick fan-
tasists seeking to avoid the modern, meritocratic challenge
of ascending the social ladder through hard graft by harking
back to an outmoded world of titles and inherited wealth?

In the case of the Druce affair, the complexity of the issues
that it raised was more than matched by the compelling factual
riddle at its heart. Was Thomas Charles Druce *really* the duke?
Everybody had their opinion on the matter, divided between
those who were convinced that the 5th Duke of Portland did
indeed lead a double life, and those who were firmly persuaded
that the whole affair was the most scandalous fraud. Indeed,
the great beauty and mystery of the Druce case lay precisely
in the fact that every statement met with an objection, and
every objection with an explanation. Thus the discussions
circled round and round the contents of the Druce vault,
always ending where they began. Just what *was* in that grave?

On one point, however, one and all were united: that it was mighty strange that old Druce's eldest son, Herbert Druce — who, although illegitimate, had inherited the Baker Street business through his father's will, as the 'official' heir — was being so obstructive about his sister-in-law's application to have the vault opened. For since Mrs Druce's initial triumph in March before Chancellor Tristram, Herbert Druce, through his solicitors Freshfields, had cast every obstacle in Mrs Druce's way. First, they had applied to the Queen's Bench Division for a judgment that Chancellor Tristram had no jurisdiction to order the disinterment, without the permission of the Home Office. Then, when the Court of Appeal rejected that application, they contested Chancellor Tristram's order directly in front of him. In order to try to find a way out of the impasse, the chancellor had suggested — during a crowded hearing at St Paul's in July, packed with smartly dressed ladies — that Mrs Druce apply for an order to have the grave opened from the president of the probate court. This was because, alongside her application to the church court for a faculty to disinter the coffin, Mrs Druce had also commenced proceedings in the civil courts to have T. C. Druce's will set aside on the grounds that he did not die. The application to the probate court should, Chancellor Tristram suggested, be for 'letters of request' addressed from the president back to himself, asking him to make the order for exhumation of the grave. In effect, the legal issue of disinterment was being batted between the church and secular courts, with the shadow of the home secretary and the (as yet unresolved) issue of a Home Office licence looming ominously in the background.

Sir Francis Jeune, the president of the probate court, duly

heard Mrs Druce's application for letters of request. In the course of the hearing, he was most impressed by a witness presented to him in support of her case. This witness was a respectable elderly lady called Mrs Hamilton. She appeared in court dressed entirely in black, with a deep veil. Mrs Hamilton testified that she had seen Thomas Charles Druce on two occasions after his alleged 'death' in 1864. The letters of request were therefore duly issued by Sir Francis to Chancellor Tristram, asking for the faculty to be granted. The civil judge evidently shared the chancellor's view that the simplest way to settle the matter was simply to open the grave, to see if T. C. Druce's body was there. He stated as much in a letter to Sir Kenelm Digby, under-secretary of state to the Home Office. Herbert Druce promptly appealed against the judge's order. His appeal was roundly rejected.

Why was Herbert Druce so vehemently opposed to the exhumation of his father's body? A stout man of fifty-two with a hooked nose and copious beard, Herbert bore an uncanny physical resemblance to his father. Like him, he appeared to be the embodiment of late Victorian respectability. He had been groomed by T. C. Druce to take over the prosperous family business in Baker Street, and he ran it with capable hands. When he was not poring over the firm's accounts in the Baker Street office, he would retire to the luxurious villa that he occupied with his wife and family in Circus Road in the affluent London suburb of St John's Wood. But all was not as it seemed in Herbert's life, and his placid exterior concealed a tumult of deeply felt emotion.

Until a decade before, Herbert had been in complete and blissful ignorance of his illegitimacy, which had only surfaced as a result of the actions of his meddlesome sister-in-law, Anna Maria. The fact that he – along with his two younger siblings – had been born a bastard had been revealed during a most uncomfortable meeting with his mother, Annie May, and the Druce family solicitor, Edwin Freshfield.

Edwin, a senior partner of the law firm Freshfields, had been alerted to the fact of Herbert Druce's illegitimacy by the unlikely source of the tax authorities. This was because Anna Maria Druce, believing (incorrectly) that Herbert could not inherit under his father's will because of his illegitimacy, had informed the tax authorities of this fact. The Inland Revenue concluded that as the named beneficiary of his father's estate, Herbert *could* inherit, but that because the first three children were illegitimate, the wrong amount of estate duty had been paid. Edwin Freshfield was therefore left with the unpleasant task of confronting Annie May – in the presence of Herbert – over the fact that she had not been married to T. C. Druce at the time of the birth of these children. Many years after the meeting, Edwin still cringed at the recollection, as he recorded in a later memorandum to the Home Office:

The writer of this memorandum had the first interview with Mrs Annie Druce when the claim [by the tax authorities] was made, and also had the task of informing Mr Herbert Druce of the true state of the case [i.e. his illegitimacy]. The interview was a very painful one. Mrs Annie Druce stated that she had been married but it ended with her being taken, as was not unnatural, very ill. When she had in part recovered she absolutely declined to give any further information and declared herself ready to pay whatever was claimed by the

Authorities at Somerset House. The writer saw the Authorities, heard the whole story from them, and obtained a discharge from the executors on payment of duty amounting to
£3,200 on 16th May 1884.

Disconcerting as the meeting had been for Edwin, it was
even worse for Herbert. In one moment, all his comfortable,
middle-class illusions about himself had collapsed in a heap.
The remote figure of his father – always something of a
mystery to him – was now becoming, increasingly, a source
of embarrassment. He dreaded the unearthing of some other
secret, were the grave to be opened. As an illegitimate son
of T. C. Druce, Herbert had nothing to gain if it were to be
shown that his father was the 5th Duke of Portland. Since he
was born out of wedlock, he would be automatically barred
from inheriting any title. Conversely, he had everything to
lose if the grave were empty: for if T. C. Druce did indeed
'fake' his death in 1864 in order to return to his life as
the 5th Duke of Portland, his will – the instrument which
bequeathed the Baker Street business to Herbert – would be
set aside. It was vital, for Herbert's interests, that there *was*
a body in that grave; and given the secrets in his father's life,
he was not minded to take a chance on the fact by having it
opened.

For the popular press, on the other hand, Herbert's stub-
born refusal to accede to his sister-in-law's request, marshal-
ling instead the mighty muscle of the top ranks of the legal
profession against her, suggested at best a marked lack of
chivalry, and at worst, that he had something to hide. As one
contemporary newspaper remarked:

Public interest is now fully aroused in the mystery of the Highgate vault; and the growing opinion is that exhumation, and nothing but exhumation, can afford a solution of the strange case. The remark heard on every hand is: 'If Mrs Druce be a deluded lady, why not have this straightway proved by opening the grave and the coffin therein?'

In the meantime, the occupants of Welbeck Abbey maintained a dignified silence. The 6th Duke of Portland gave not the slightest outward hint that the Cavendish-Bentincks were remotely ruffled at the prospect of being ousted from their ancestral seat by the descendants of a furniture salesman. Indeed, the Duke had no overt reason to comment, as no case had as yet been brought directly against him or the Portland estates. To date, the only proceedings currently on the court lists were Mrs Druce's application for a faculty for exhumation of the vault in the church court, and her separate proceedings in the civil court to set aside the probate granted on T. C. Druce's will. Each of these proceedings was being fought with dogged insistence by Herbert Druce. The case so far was therefore (at least, in public) an internecine conflict between rival branches of the Druce family, who either did or did not want T. C. Druce's grave to be opened.

Behind the scenes, however, the man who two decades before had anxiously surveyed the ruined splendour of Welbeck as a pale and nervous twenty-two-year-old, was anything but complacent. After all, William the 6th Duke had never even met his eccentric predecessor. No official photographs existed of the mysterious and elusive 5th Duke of Portland. Nobody knew how the 'burrowing duke' had passed the bulk of his time, hidden from view in his underground labyrinth · at Welbeck, or shut off from the world behind high walls at Harcourt House.

For all his lofty public indifference, the 6th Duke was, in private, deeply anxious. So much so that he instructed a leading firm of private investigators to hunt down every piece of information that could conceivably shed light on the 5th Duke's movements, along with those of T. C. Druce.* Furthermore, the 6th Duke's solicitors actively co-operated and assisted Freshfields. Many and frequent were the letters that passed between the Berners Street offices of Baileys, Shaw & Gillett, the duke's legal advisors, and those of Herbert Druce's solicitors in Bank Street (the parties even fell out, on occasion, over who was to pay the investigators' bills). Documents were exchanged, evidence assessed, anonymous agents were sent to shadow Mrs Druce's every move. Above all, a common strategy evolved: that of using Herbert Druce as a 'front' to obstruct the proceedings as much as possible, in order for both parties to gather evidence to build a case. Surely it could not be so difficult to prove that the 5th Duke and T. C. Druce were in different places at the same time? Or to track down a birth certificate for T. C. Druce? Either of these would wipe out, in one fell swoop, the claim that they were one and the same person. Swarms of agents combed through parish records, interviewing hundreds of Druces the length and breadth of the country,

---

* The fact that the duke's representatives had taken such a step was not known until decades after the events.

in an attempt to uncover one or other of these vital pieces of evidence. They searched in vain.*

By the beginning of August 1898 the long vacation had arrived,† and the grey-haired lawyers of Lincoln's Inn, Gray's Inn and the Temple hurried to pack their bags and file in a great exodus to the elegant squares of Brighton, or the fashionable resorts of the Lake District. Bundles of documents and pleadings lay stranded on deserted desks; mounds of post accumulated dust in neglected pigeonholes; rats gambolled under the silent floorboards of the winding passageways of the Royal Courts of Justice. Grass sprouted between the chinks of the paving stones in Lincoln's Inn, to be chewed thoughtfully by idle ticket porters, taking refuge from the sun in the shadow of empty porches. There was just one duty judge left in town for emergencies. Even he came only once a week to town to sit in chambers, clean-shaven and unrecognizable, having dispensed with full-bottomed wig, scarlet robes and white wand in favour of a summer suit and dapper white hat, a strip of plaster on his sun-blistered nose.

And so, for the present, on a dusty desk of an empty court, the application to exhume T. C. Druce's body stagnated. But the press sensation ran on throughout the whole summer of 1898. In fact, it seemed that neither the newspapers nor the

---

* No birth or baptismal certificate for T. C. Druce has ever been found.
† The law terms were (and still are) Hilary, Easter, Trinity and Michaelmas. The long vacation (when London was the most empty) extended from 10 August to 24 October.

public could get enough of the Druce affair. Enterprising individuals offered excursions to the Druce vault in Highgate, which was swift becoming the most-visited sepulchre in England. Four miles to the south, heads turned in unison as horse-drawn omnibuses clattered past the entrance of the Baker Street Bazaar. The bazaar itself heaved with curious sightseers, hopeful of spotting the ghost of the unburied ducal tradesman stalking among the goods that had replaced the stock he left behind him, four-and-thirty years before. At a spiritualistic séance, a young woman fell into a trance and, when recovered, breathlessly related how she had 'seen' the Druce coffin, with nothing in it. 'Mrs Druce', announced the *Daily Mail*, 'is now the most interesting woman in England. She occupies more space in the newspapers than is claimed by the Queen of England.' In August the same newspaper announced a forthcoming 'novelty for *Daily Mail* readers' – no less than the imminent publication, day by day, of a serial story entitled *The Double Duke*, allegedly 'founded on fact' (although what facts was never stated). The serial was to be 'quite the most interesting romance ever published in the *Daily Mail*.' Where, wondered many a spectator of the media circus, did fact end and fiction begin?

Anna Maria Druce herself revelled in the attention. With the gracious condescension of a dowager duchess-in-waiting, she granted interviews to the newspapermen clamouring at her door. Anna Maria's official story about her origins was suitably genteel. 'I myself was a Miss Butler,' she informed the gathered pressmen with haughty conviction. 'My father being agent for Lord Pembroke, the latter acted for a time as my guardian. It was through going to the same school as my husband's sister that I first met him.' She had given 'land steward' as her father's profession on her marriage certificate in 1872. In truth, however, Anna Maria was the daughter of a humble Irish paperhanger, a workman who scraped a living hanging rich wallpapers in the houses of the wealthy and fashionable. She had met her husband Walter – the third son of T. C. Druce – when employed as governess to the Druce household. A tendency towards socially aggrandizing fantasies about their origins was not uncommon in women of modest background, who had ascended the Victorian social ladder. Wilkie Collins' 'official' mistress Caroline Graves, for example, used to describe herself as the daughter of a gentleman called Courtenay, when she was in fact the daughter of a carpenter by the name of John Compton.

Given the lowliness of her origins, the fact that Anna Maria managed to reach the rank of governess was testimony to her determination. By the 1860s, however, it was becoming increasingly common for women from the working classes to enter this genteel profession, formerly the preserve of distressed gentlewomen. The increase in social mobility over the course of the century meant that the faded middle-class ladies, who had previously made up the ranks of the governess profession, slowly became infiltrated by a new, cannier, more upwardly mobile type. Contemporary observers, like Lady Elizabeth Eastlake, were scandalized. 'Farmers and tradespeople are now educating their daughters for governesses as a mode of advancing them a step in life,' she observed sniffily in 1848. As a result, 'a number of underbred young women have crept into the profession who have brought down the value of salaries, and interfered with the rights of those whose birth and misfortune leave them no other refuge'.

The canny, low-born adventuress Becky Sharpe, the devious and unscrupulous anti-heroine of William Thackeray's mid-century novel *Vanity Fair*, is an example of exactly the type to which Lade Eastlake was referring. Employed as a governess by a country baronet, Becky manages to carry off the son of the house, before abandoning him for greater prizes down the line. And then there is Lydia Gwilt, the scheming governess featured in Wilkie Collins' 1866 novel *Armadale* – a fortune-hunter and, even worse, a murderess. Not to mention the devious Lucy Graham, the doll-like blonde in Mary Elizabeth Braddon's *Lady Audley's Secret* (1862). Far from conforming to the Victorian female domestic ideal of the 'angel in the house', Lucy, a former governess, turns out to be a criminal who has attempted murder, committed bigamy and abandoned her child. The admittedly very different heroine of Charlotte Brontë's novel *Jane Eyre* (1847) is also a governess, who breaks convention by marrying the master of the house.

The obsession of the nineteenth century with the figure of the 'governess' matched its preoccupation with that of the 'gentleman'. In fact, virtually every self-respecting Victorian novel had to have one in its cast of female characters, usually of the scheming sort. This was another reflection of the intense social anxieties of the age, of which the 'governess', like the 'gentleman', became a potent symbol. For whether she was a distressed member of the gentry or social upstart, the governess also reflected a new social fluidity, at once both dynamic and destabilizing. She was a reminder that, in this brave new world, one could go up – but also down – the social ladder with startling rapidity. 'Reader, I married him,' Jane Eyre triumphantly asserts – words that would have filled the average Victorian mistress of the house with dread for the safety of her son.

Whether Annie May, the widow of T. C. Druce, had any such misgivings when Anna Maria arrived as a governess in the Druce household in the early 1870s, has not been recorded. By then, old T. C. Druce had been dead about ten years. After her husband's death, Annie May had moved from the palatial house in Mill Hill to a rather more discreetly grand address at 43 Belsize Square. There she was slightly more socially adventurous than in the days when her reclusive husband was alive, venturing forth in a carriage and pair and regularly spending the season in Brighton. Of the six Druce children, only three remained in the house – Florence, Walter and Bertha. Anna Maria was taken on as a governess to the fifteen-year-old Bertha.

With her pale complexion, black hair and forceful personality, the new governess was more than a match for the rather insipid Walter, four years her junior. A passionate romance followed, ending in the governess' dismissal. Walter followed Anna Maria until a succession of pleadings and reproaches by a family friend persuaded him to leave her and return to the family in Belsize Square. Anna Maria, however, held the final and fatal trump card. Late in 1872, the former governess paid a visit to the former mistress in Belsize Park. What was discussed at that meeting, neither the elder Mrs Druce nor Anna Maria ever divulged. What is known, however, is that a marriage was arranged swiftly afterwards. On 9 December 1872, in the wettest year on record in England, Anna Maria Butler married Walter Thomas Druce at the parish church of St John in Upper Holloway, amidst strong winds and heavy rain. She was twenty-four years old; he was just twenty, and therefore under the then legal age of majority. Eight months later, on 7 August 1873, their eldest daughter, Florence, was born.*

Walter Druce did not know much about old T. C. Druce – he was, after all, a mere twelve years old when his father died – but he did keep saying that there was a certain mystery about him, some family secret that he did not fully comprehend. After all, why had T. C. Druce waited so long before he finally married Annie May?

Given the unpromising start to their relationship, the marriage between the high-spirited ex-governess and weak-willed draper's son was never going to be easy. For a while, the couple made an attempt at farming in Staffordshire. Florence was followed by four other children: Marguerite in 1874, Sidney George in 1876, Charles Walter in 1877, and finally Nina Bertha in 1878. The couple lived extravagantly, eating into the capital left to Walter in his father's will. But by 1880 Walter's health was deteriorating, and after a number of business failures, the family returned to London. In November of that year, Walter died from typhoid. He was buried in the family vault at Highgate, beside the coffin of his father.

Walter's will – proved at below £1500 – was hardly sufficient to sustain a family. Worse, relations with old Mrs Druce

---

* Florence Druce's birth date was usually given in census and other official documents as 'about 1874', instead of the actual year of 1873, and her age was generally stated as a year younger than she really was. This disguised the fact that she was born only eight months after the marriage of her parents, as shown on her birth certificate.

– never the most cordial – broke down in a series of bitter arguments, reaching a peak when Anna Maria quarrelled with the family over the administration of T. C. Druce's will. In the end, the money ran out, and Anna Maria and her young family were left with no choice but to enter that most bleak of Victorian institutions: the workhouse.

In February 1884 – a month of coldly bright dawns and colder drizzle – Anna Maria entered the forbidding gates of the institution on Northumberland Street officially known as the 'Marylebone Workhouse', and unofficially as 'the Spike'. At the time when Anna Maria arrived, the Marylebone Workhouse had moved on from earlier in the century, when its most hated and feared Master, Richard Ryan, was dismissed for beating female inmates senseless. Nevertheless, it remained the largest workhouse in London and a grim and chilling place.

The procedure for the reception and incarceration of workhouse inmates barely varied from institution to institution. On arrival at the workhouse gates, Anna Maria would have been placed in a reception room, disrobed and thoroughly scrubbed to get rid of germs. Her clothes would have been taken away and ticketed, and then she herself would have been dressed in the standard female workhouse uniform – a gown in a print known as the 'workhouse stripe', covered by a white shift, bonnet and shawl. She and the children would have been separated. Meals were served in a hall at wooden trestle tables, the men and women separated in long, silent rows that permitted no conversation. Admonitions from the scriptures frowned down in scarlet-lettered anger from the blue walls in the gaslight, with such exhortations to reflection and self-improvement as, 'GOD IS GOOD', 'GOD IS TRUE' or, perhaps the most open to question in the eyes of the inmates, 'GOD IS MERCIFUL'. Regularly on the hour came the clang of the workhouse bell, tolling out the course of the day's activities, from rising and the daily roll-call at 6 a.m. to lights out at 8 p.m., when the inmates would gossip and whisper tales in their communal dormitories of their lives 'outside', in the gaps between the heavy footfalls of the patrolling night attendant.

If Anna Maria's lot was wretched at this point in time, so too was that of the rest of Walter's family. Florence, the eldest daughter, was put out to work as a general servant with a family in Willesden. Sidney and Walter, the two sons, were apprenticed as sailors; Walter stayed on the training ship HMS *Exmouth*, while Sidney decamped for Australia in 1895. Marguerite, an invalid, stayed with Anna Maria, while Nina, the youngest, was sent to board at the Field Lane Industrial School in Hampstead, a missionary establishment where well-meaning evangelicals attempted to instil Christian virtues in the unruly street urchins committed to their care. Not long after his transfer to HMS *Exmouth*, Anna Maria's younger son, Walter, fell sick and was moved to the Workhouse Infirmary at Rackham Street in Ladbroke Grove. He died there in 1891, at the age of fourteen. Despite Anna Maria's pleading, the recalcitrant old Mrs Druce could not be persuaded to give her grandson a decent burial. The Druce vault at Highgate remained firmly shut, and the child was buried in a pauper's grave. Anna Maria never forgave the slight: 'Yes, yes, it's a vile conspiracy against me and mine!' she would cry to the assembled pressmen, shaking her fist and swearing to have the dead child Walter reinterred in his rightful place. 'That will be exhumation number two, but, if necessary, I will exhume and exhume until I get my rights!'

By August 1898, however, dark memories of the workhouse seemed to belong to the distant past. Anna Maria was now the toast of London, indeed the entire country. Journalists fought over her for exclusive interviews; she was on the guest list of every fashionable hostess in town. Old Mrs Druce was finally out of the way, dead and buried in 1893. Herbert Druce had been exposed as illegitimate in the pages of the popular press, every man on the street aware of the fact that the old man of Baker Street had produced several offspring before he finally made an honest woman of his mistress. Most importantly, as far as Anna Maria was concerned, Herbert was now considered a bounder, who refused to allow a simple step to be taken – the inspection of his father's grave – that would speedily clear up the whole affair.

Recently, Mrs Druce had even been approached by City financiers proposing to issue bonds to the public to fund her case. It was a most attractive proposition, given that Mrs Marler, the landlady of her lodgings in Tavistock Square, was at that moment hammering on her door for nine months' unpaid rent. Mrs Marler had, unsportingly, refused to accept a future invitation to Welbeck Abbey in lieu of ready money. Mrs Druce's lawyers had shaken their heads at the idea of auctioning shares in the outcome of her case, warning that if she did proceed with such a plan, they would be unable to continue to represent her interests. But Anna Maria did not care for the warnings of old men. Her opponents were evidently alarmed, and that was what mattered. In the past few months she had been approached by the legal representatives of both the Duke of Portland and Herbert Druce, with offers to settle the case for upwards of £60,000, which she had refused.* Six judges had already decided in favour of her application to open the grave, and three courts had ruled for her.† How could she fail to win?

Mrs Druce could not, of course, possibly have guessed at the ominous wind that was even then gathering across the sea, and which was about to swallow her into a whirlpool from which there was little, if any, hope of escape.

---

* Enormous sums for the day, worth over £6 million in today's money.
† It is a remarkable fact that Mrs Druce, making allegations which on the face of them appeared to be highly improbable, managed to convince every judge before whom she found herself that she had a *prima facie* case.

SCENE SIX

Featherstone Buildings

December 1898

If a scandal of more than usual piquancy occurs
in high life, or a crime of extraordinary horror
figures among our *causes célèbres*, the sensationist
is immediately at hand to weave the incident into a
thrilling tale.

Quarterly Review, 1863

T he man from the *Star* shuddered and retreated further
into his muffled greatcoat against the damp December chill that permeated the crooked streets. Even
though it was early morning, a smoky veil already hung over
the house tops, a dense and heavy yellow fog that condensed
in oily drops on the windowpanes. The *Star* man recalled with
grim amusement how, like Esther in *Bleak House*, on setting
foot for the first time in London, he had asked the driver of
the stagecoach whether there 'was a great fire anywhere?'
'Oh no, sir,' had come the sniggering reply. 'This is a London Particular. A fog, yer know.' London fogs – also known
as 'pea soupers' – were made up of a thick greenish-yellow
or black smog that hung like an almost permanent veil over
the City skyline. They were caused by a combination of soot
and sulphur dioxide released from the burning of millions of
coal fires, together with the mist and fog of the Thames Valley. The *Star* man smiled to himself at the recollection of his

youthful innocence. His confusion over the London fog had occurred when he was but a youngster, newly arrived in the capital from a sleepy village. Now of course, although still young in years, he was a wise old hack in terms of worldly experience, expertly steering his course through the winding alleys with no heed to the thick swirls of the pea souper that wreathed around him.

Even at this early hour, Fleet Street was abuzz with activity. Indeed, in those days, it was a street that never slept. All around the *Star* man, crammed into every available building, were newspaper offices: the *Daily News* in Bouverie Street, the *Daily Telegraph* in Peterborough Court, his own newspaper, the *Star*, in Stonecutter Street. Towering over Shoe Lane was the stately pile of the *Standard*, while the *Morning Advertiser* confronted the *Daily Chronicle* on opposite sides of the thoroughfare. Further away, aloof from the rabble, *The Times* stood in gloomy isolation under the shadow of St Paul's Cathedral, like a mournful reminder of a bygone age: the only morning newspaper whose offices were not within the immediate precincts of Fleet Street. The entire area was dotted with newspaper offices, and it was impossible to turn left or right without being confronted by a publication of some kind: religious, comic, sporting and society newspapers; papers of every conceivable political persuasion and platform – conservative, radical, liberal, historical or just plain heretical. Every garret, cellar and attic room, it seemed, was occupied by some pale-faced correspondent, busily wiring telegrams to his editor in Chicago or Cork in the dim light of a gas jet, racing against the deadline of the approaching dawn.

The roots of the Fleet Street frenzy of the 1890s dated back earlier than the *Star* man could remember. In all probability it had started with the abolition of stamp duty on newspapers in 1855, the doing away with the old 'tax on knowledge'. For from that moment onwards, the established sixpenny papers – led by the venerable *Times* – had been subject to fierce assault from a battery of new publications, costing a mere penny or even halfpenny apiece. The *Daily News*, the *Daily Telegraph*, *Pall Mall Gazette*, *Sun*, *Daily Chronicle*, *Star* – such papers represented but a handful of the quarrelling upstarts that had sprung up over the past twenty years, and which now jostled for space on Fleet Street. These were a new generation of newspapers for a new generation of readers: young folk, the first in their families to read and write, brought to the gates of learning in the Board Schools established by Forster's Education Act.* This new and eager readership of clerks, tea boys and housemaids – often clubbing together to share a battered penny paper between them – preferred thrills to politics, inclining more towards devouring the gory details of the Whitechapel Murders than mulling over the knotty issues of Irish Home Rule. Savvy, sensation-seeking and worldly wise, they sought a savvy, sensational, worldly wise kind of journalism; and the new newspapers provided them with the diet for which they hungered. In America, the pages of the 'yellow press' owned by media magnates such as Randolph

---

* The Elementary Education Act of 1870, commonly known as Forster's Education Act after the Liberal MP, William Forster, who drafted it, set forth the principle of universal elementary education for children aged five to twelve years old through the establishment of so-called Board Schools.

Hearst were full of stories of crimes, adventures and family sagas. They also employed new reporting techniques, such as interviews and investigative journalism. Inspired by this, the British newspapers in the 1880s followed suit. From the popular freaks of the penny fairs – bearded ladies, dwarves and Joseph Merrick the Elephant Man – to the lurid waxworks of the newly established Madame Tussaud's with its notorious Chamber of Horrors, the Victorians delighted in everything that was grim, ghoulish and grotesque. Their newspapers did not disappoint them.

Of course, as the *Star* man himself would have acknowledged, had he put his mind to it as he padded down the street, it had all started off very admirably indeed, with a laudable and messianic zeal to educate and entertain the masses. As the great founder of the *Star* himself, the Irish Nationalist MP Thomas Power O'Connor, had declared on the front page of the newspaper's first issue: 'The rich, the privileged, the prosperous need no guardian or advocate; the poor, the weak, the beaten require the work and word of every humane man and woman to stand between them and the world.'

One of the leaders of the new journalism had been the great W. T. Stead, editor of the *Pall Mall Gazette*. Convinced of journalism's mission to educate and entertain, this visionary Nonconformist from the north-east had shocked the late Victorian public in 1885 with his series of articles, 'The Maiden Tribute of Modern Babylon', a controversial exposé of child prostitution. A tour de force of early investigative journalism, 'The Maiden Tribute' revealed, in all-too-graphic detail, the luring and abduction of underage girls to London brothels. The 'infernal narrative', in Stead's own words, shocked its middle-class readership with a hellish vision of a criminal underworld, unscrupulous procuresses, drugs and padded chambers where well-heeled paedophiles could delight in the torture and cries of an 'immature child'. The serialized newspaper report was a sensation: in London, crowds laid siege to the *Pall Mall Gazette* offices for reprints. With attention-grabbing headlines such as 'The Violation of Virgins' and 'Strapping Girls Down', 'The Maiden Tribute' threw London into a state of panic. It also led to the passing of the Criminal Law Amendment Act, which raised the age of consent for girls from thirteen to sixteen, thus fulfilling the New Journalism's sense of moral purpose. Stead's zealotry acquired him as many enemies as it did friends, and he would later find himself jailed for using illegal methods in the course of his investigation. Undeterred, he spent his time 'inside' writing an essay on 'Government by Journalism'.

Heady with idealism and reforming zeal as those early years of the New Journalism had been, the *Star* man knew all too well that things had changed since then. An ominous new publication had appeared on Fleet Street a couple of years back in 1896, undercutting the penny papers with even more sensational headlines for the ludicrous price of a halfpenny. This was the vastly popular *Daily Mail*, founded by the audacious Mr Harmsworth. The prime minister, Lord Salisbury, had described the latest offspring of Fleet Street with the greatest contempt, as 'written by office boys for office boys'. But the paper of the office boys was now selling better than the journals of the establishment. As more and more newspapers entered the fray, the original mission to educate the masses gave way to a grubby circulation war, where everybody scrambled to print the latest, headline-grabbing shocker.

In this respect, the *Star* was no better than other newspapers, as the *Star* man well knew. The paper had been involved in many a cut-throat battle to drive up circulation figures, not least over the Whitechapel Murders or 'Jack the Ripper' case, ten years back. Indeed, the *Star* owed Jack the Ripper a favour. As the drama of the murder spree that was unfolding in London's East End in 1888 was reported in ghastly detail over successive editions of the then newly established paper, its circulation went up to 232,000 – a record – as the public became convinced there was a dangerous serial killer on the loose. There were even murmurs in Fleet Street that several of the letters taunting the police, supposedly sent by the killer, were in fact hoaxes written by *Star* men to 'keep up the business'. Not that our *Star* man knew anything – officially – about such hoaxes, of course. What he did know was that the Ripper was the best 'rummy go' of the 1880s, and that the Druce case showed very promising signs of being the new runner of the 1890s.

As he wound his way from the bustling pavements of Fleet Street to the more sedate thoroughfares of Holborn, the *Star* man reflected on how all the papers were now fighting over the Druce affair. The *Daily Mail* (which, by its own account, was the first newspaper to have published an interview with Mrs Druce) was currently at loggerheads with the *News of the World* over the accuracy of plans that the *News of the World* had published of tunnels that supposedly existed under the Baker Street Bazaar. The *Mail* claimed that the plans were inaccurate, while the *News of the World* countered that they were based on documents from the Land Registry. Not to be outdone, the *Mail* had proceeded to publish samples of the duke's and T. C. Druce's handwriting, along with an analysis by the handwriting expert George Inglis, which suggested that there were strange parallels between the two hands. It had also published two portraits of Druce and the duke, along with a commentary by 'one skilled in the science of the head', who concluded that 'not only have the general expression and shape of the head and features been found strikingly similar, but the chin, mouth, and the eyes are seen to be almost identical'.

This was the era of the birth of forensic science, when pseudosciences such as phrenology and physiognomy jostled for space in the criminologist's armoury, along with new and groundbreaking techniques such as fingerprinting. It was the age when the modern detective was born, whole murder cases turning on the ingenious resolution of puzzles involving such apparently mundane objects as a lock of hair or a missing button. In the Druce affair, everybody – journalists, housewives, butlers and laundry maids – had turned into super sleuths, bent on unravelling the mystery of the Highgate vault. Newspaper editors were deluged with suggestions from members of the public as to what might hold the key to the affair. John Hughes of the Analytical Laboratory in Mark Lane pointed out in a letter to the Editor of the *Daily Mail* that, even if Mr Druce's remains had decomposed in the phosphate of lime in which his body had been wrapped, the presence of mineral constituents, commonly known as 'bone earth', would determine the fact of previous mortal remains. A member of the Downlay Golf Club pointed out that there were some illustrious precedents for the exhumation of human bodies. After all, the bodies of Edward the Confessor, Edward I and

Henry IV had all been disinterred for purposes ranging from the purloining of a royal ring (that of Edward the Confessor) to ascertaining whether – as in the Druce case – there was a body there at all. The latter exhumation was that of Henry IV, whose coffin was opened up in 1832 to establish whether his body had been buried in Canterbury Cathedral or thrown in the Thames, as had been alleged in certain quarters.

When all was said and done, the *Star* man was of the opinion that the Druce case was actually even better business than the Ripper affair. For while the Ripper had been inconsiderate enough to vanish without trace after his last purported murder in 1888, the Druce case just kept on running and running, turning up new twists and turns in its tortuous path through the courts. First, there had been the granting of the faculty by Chancellor Tristram in March, followed by a series of appeals and every possible attempt to prevent the opening of the grave by Herbert Druce. Then – just when it seemed that Herbert's resources were exhausted and Mrs Druce was calling in the men with spades to start digging – there was the surprise declaration by the home secretary, a matter of days ago in early December, ordering the London Cemetery Company to desist from permitting the disinterment without his permission, and that of Herbert Druce as the rightful owner of the grave. Quite what or who had persuaded the home secretary to take this belated course of action was, in the *Star* man's mind, open to question. Was it not whispered that the present Duke of Portland himself was acting, shadow-like, behind the scenes? Nor had the home secretary's intervention in the proceedings put an end to the sensational revelations. Oh no, far from it. Even now, rumours were circulating in Fleet Street that were quite the most astounding developments to date in this extraordinary affair. Oh yes, old T. C. Druce had kept a skeleton in his closet, all right. It was just not the skeleton that everybody had expected. Now, there was a new twist to rattle the bones of an old story.

At this juncture, the *Star* man was interrupted in his thoughts by his abrupt arrival at his destination, the front door of which loomed suddenly through the mist. Featherstone Buildings gave every appearance of being a once genteel, but now faded Georgian terrace in Holborn, soot-faced as most London buildings were in those days.* There, sure enough, freshly painted on the door of no. 5, was Mrs Druce's name beneath the firm of 'Driver and Driver' on the ground floor. When he knocked at the door of Mrs Druce's new office – for such this was – it was opened by an old, shifty-looking man who introduced himself as Mr Beaumont of Driver and Driver.

'Mrs Druce is not in,' said the old man. 'She's living at a secret address nearby, for fear of being pestered to death. But she will be here presently. Would you care to wait inside?'

'Much obliged,' replied the *Star* man. Once inside, the old man divulged that he was acting as Mrs Druce's agent for the selling of bonds in the Druce–Portland case.

'Ah, yes,' replied the *Star* man. 'Mr Plumbly of Queen Victoria Street was her old agent, was he not?' In fact, as the *Star* man well knew – like all of Fleet Street – Mrs Druce

---

* Featherstone Buildings in Holborn was a charming Georgian terrace that was hit by a 250kg bomb in the London Blitz and completely destroyed. It now houses the rather less lovely Mid City Place.

had, on the Wednesday last, stormed out of the offices of Mr Plumbly in high dudgeon. Quite what the reason was for her falling out with him was unclear. What was only too apparent, on the other hand, was that she was losing many of her old friends as fast as she was making new enemies. In truth, Mrs Druce's most recent behaviour showed the distinct possibility that her mind was becoming unhinged. Her solicitors, Messrs McArthur & Co., along with her former barrister, Arnold Statham, had both warned her as long ago as August that they would have no choice other than to step down from her case, if she were to float bonds on the market in order to raise funds. Ignoring their advice, she had proceeded to do so, and thus lost their support. At least in Mr Plumbly, however, Mrs Druce had had a vaguely reputable agent to deal with her case. Driver and Driver, a.k.a. Beaumont, however, was another matter. It was immediately apparent to the *Star* man that he was a distinctly shady type, rather like the other queer folk that Mrs Druce had been seen with recently. She had, for instance, been spotted with a dubious pair of company promoters – the brothers known as Thomas and Henry Marlow, who operated on the fringes of the City underworld. Mrs Druce had also been spotted with the notoriously sharp young journalist John Sheridan, who had been plugging her case incessantly in his column in the newspaper *Society*. Sheridan in particular would have been known to the *Star* man as a journalist living on his wits, and on the very edge of legitimacy. He had been given the column on *Society* because the editor of the paper apparently thought highly of him for divulging certain information about the Dreyfus affair, but the *Star* man was sceptical as to how he could have laid hands on such information, or whether there was any truth in it. Whatever the Marlow brothers, Sheridan and these other queer folk were up to with Mrs Druce, it was certainly with the purpose of making money out of it.

'Bonds selling well?' asked the *Star* man innocuously.

'Like hot cakes, sir,' replied Driver and Driver. 'Applications coming in from all over the country. Yesterday, I was unable to leave my office because of all the personal callers.'

'Right,' replied the *Star* man, glancing around the deserted office.

'In fact, I've an even better case for yer,' said Driver and Driver hopefully. 'It beats Mrs Druce's into fists. A case of a poor woman from the Potteries, who was swindled out of her husband's wealth. A case with forgery, suicide, murder and a gas explosion in it!'

The *Star* man was about to reply, when Mrs Druce entered the room with a female companion. She was breathless with excitement.

'I don't care *that* for McArthur's,' she cried, snapping her fingers. 'I have retained a great firm of parliamentary lawyers – people, mind you, that want £10,000 put down on the table before they will move, you can say that!'

The *Star* man ventured to ask how much Mrs Druce intended to raise by the bonds. 'I am Mrs Druce of Baker Street,' the lady replied hotly. 'And I am going to take up my proper position. I am going to ride in a carriage. I don't care for their Duchess of Portland. I'll let them see. I've got three witnesses now who saw the lead put into the coffin!' Hardly pausing to take breath, she went on: 'Lord Salisbury has promised to take £500 of my bonds, and everybody at his club is on my side – the Prince of Wales is, too!'

The *Star* man was, to say the least, somewhat taken aback by the assertion. So too were Driver and Driver, and Mrs Druce's lady companion, who tried to calm the overexcited lady as she swept out the office in pursuit of Lord Salisbury at his Club. When she had departed, the old man opined that Lord Salisbury's investment in the Druce bonds should perhaps be taken with a pinch of salt. He would believe it himself, when he 'saw the cheque'. But people were certainly queuing for the bonds; why, only the other day, an earl had sat in the very chair upon which the *Star* man was perched.

The *Star* man nodded sagely as he bade his goodbyes. Poor Mrs Druce, as everybody knew, had been overtaken by events. Her bonds would not be exchanging hands any time soon for notes, gold, silver or even… dare one whisper it… copper. The story had left her behind and, as had become characteristic of this affair, the newest events were the most sensational yet. Oh yes, the Druce case was quite the best 'rummy go' in town…

The New London Law Courts

Three years later

Standing on a seat at the side of the hall, the better to peer into the curtained sanctuary, is a mad little old woman in a squeezed bonnet, who is always in court, from its sitting to its rising, and always expecting some incomprehensible judgment to be given in her favour. Some say she really is, or was, a party to a suit; but no one knows for certain, because no one cares. She carries some small litter in a reticule which she calls her documents: principally consisting of paper matches and dry lavender.

CHARLES DICKENS
Bleak House

On the morning of Tuesday, 3 December 1901, a queue of expectant members of the public wound its way along the pavement before the cast-iron gates of the new Law Courts on the Strand. It was a damp, foggy morning, mild for the season, as had been the whole winter so far. As usual for the time of year in London, a damp drizzle saturated with soot and the carburetted hydrogen of coal smoke smothered the streets in a blanket as suffocating as any to be found on the Essex Marshes. The weak sunlight did little to mellow the hard edges of Portland stone that defined the outline of the new civil court buildings, which rose with Gothic foreboding on the junction of Fleet Street and the Strand.

The buildings were an extravagant affair, flourishing with turrets, pinnacles and pilasters. Her late Majesty the Queen herself – for Victoria had died in January that year – had opened the courtrooms nineteen years earlier, in December 1882. Then, cheering crowds had thronged the pavements of the Strand, and the great entrance hall – an imposing hundred and forty feet high – had been filled to the brim with a bobbing mass of big wigs and scarlet robes. The queen had ascended the daïs and made a speech expressing her satisfaction at the admirable work performed by the architect of the works, the late Mr George Edmund Street, Esq. She had expressed her hope that 'the uniting together of the various branches of judicature in this Supreme Court will conduce to the more efficient and speedy discharge of justice to my subjects, upon which the chief security of the rights to my Crown, and the liberties of my people, depend'.

Peering into the semi-darkness of the same entrance hall in December 1901, an observer might question whether Her Late Majesty's hopes had been fulfilled. The courtrooms had a peculiar odour unique to them: a Law Court Particular, different from the London Particular that swirled outside the gates. For one contemporary visitor, it was a sort of 'amalgamated effluvium' produced by the 'reek of stuff gowns, dog-eared papers, mouldy parchment, horse-hair wigs, imperfectly washed spectators, police constables and witnesses', with a bracing whiff of ammonia from the dung and mud on the pavement in the Strand outside. To this must be added, on days when a sensational trial such as this one was in progress, the warm scent of Pears soap and the heady waft of Houbigant perfume emitted by fashionable ladies, who flocked like brightly coloured birds to listen, with breathless attention, to the scandalous unfolding of a salacious case.

Victorian ladies were fascinated by court cases, particularly those that centred on women, whether the trial involved a murder, divorce or a dispute over a title. The *Pall Mall Gazette* noted this grisly interest, mockingly observing of the female spectators at the trial of a murderess that: 'Hour after hour did these ghoulish women, armed with opera glasses, sherry flasks and sandwich boxes, hang with eager curiosity upon every movement and look of their miserable sister.'

The reason for the large crowd that assembled before the Law Courts on this particular day was that it was the start of the long-anticipated hearing of *Druce* v. *Young*. This was the case to set aside the probate on T. C. Druce's will that had been started by Anna Maria Druce in the civil court, back in 1898. After three long years of protracted legal wrangling, the case was finally up for trial. Anna Maria's contention was that, as T. C. Druce had not died in 1864, the probate granted on his will was invalid, and should therefore be discounted. The principal defendant in the case was the accountant Alexander Young, an old friend of T. C. Druce and one of the executors of his will. Anna Maria's application to the church court before Chancellor Tristram for a faculty to open the Druce vault had stalled, halted by the home secretary as long ago as December 1898, as the *Star* man had observed. Anna Maria had hoped that, by issuing these alternative civil proceedings, she might secure the exhumation by a different route.

As the crowds milled round the court building, hoping

for entry, the gates were guarded by a burly policeman with truncheon at the ready. Members of the public lucky enough to gain entry would have been confronted with a pale-faced attendant, lurking in a forest of coats and umbrellas. They would then have followed the passageway that led to the courts of the probate, divorce and admiralty division, leading to a winding staircase that ended with a long, thin corridor linking the warren of panelled courtrooms. Here they would have been confronted by a tide of human flotsam and jetsam: grey-wigged and black-gowned barristers flapping and bobbing amidst a wave of copy clerks, process-servers, solicitors, wealthy merchants and shabby litigants in person. The doors of the courtroom, thrown open at 10 a.m., would have revealed a dark and ill-ventilated, panelled room where seats were arranged, amphitheatre-like, in ascending tiers, from the carved rows in front dedicated to the newly renamed King's Counsel, to the narrow benches for the clerks at the back.

On this first day of the hearing of *Druce* v. *Young*, an impressive array of bigwigs and stuffed gowns assembled in the rows of seats on the defendant's side of the courtroom. They were attended by bustling clerks carrying bundles of papers tied with red tape and green ferret, the shiny string used to tie bundles of legal documents. Behind the bearded King's Counsel, junior barristers whispered to each other and passed notes. Behind them sat the sleek, well-groomed lawyers of the firm of Freshfields, presided over by the venerable senior partner, Edwin Freshfield. One of the canniest solicitors of his generation, Edwin had taken over the helm of the family firm of solicitors, and was personally in charge of the Druce case on behalf of Alexander Young and Herbert

Druce. With his silvery locks and elegant morning dress, a huge pelisse lined with the costliest Russian sable thrown over his shoulders, he called to mind a rich Venetian merchant in an old Renaissance portrait, more than a City lawyer. Beside the men-at-law sat Herbert Druce, pale and drawn. As the eldest son of T. C. Druce he was not an actual defendant in the proceedings, although in practice he stood accused of lying because he had certified his father's death. He had the fearful look on his face of someone who dreaded the revelation of some new and sordid secret about his family's past.

In all this hurly burly, one part of the packed courtroom appeared strangely deserted. This was the row of pews on the plaintiff's side of the court. They were completely empty, save for the figure of one diminutive lady clutching a pile of yellowing papers. It was now getting on for four years since Anna Maria Druce had first brought her application for the Druce vault to be opened before Chancellor Tristram in the London Consistory Court. But she had aged at least two decades in that time. Previously energetic and forceful, she now seemed old and ill. She had been hounded from pillar to post, application after application refused or appealed. After her request for a faculty to open the Druce vault had been called to a halt, she had been forced to pursue the case in the civil court. Now, with the full civil case finally coming up for hearing, she had lost both her barrister and solicitor. Her bond issue had failed, and she was entirely without funds. Dr Forbes Winslow, having testified so convincingly before Chancellor Tristram that the photograph of T. C. Druce shown to the court was that of a man in his asylum known as Dr Harmer, had hastily revised his view, after the wife of someone alleged to be the real Dr Harmer had announced herself to the newspapers, loudly protesting his separate identity. Mrs Druce's key witness, Mrs Hamilton – the mysterious old lady who had testified to seeing T. C. Druce after his supposed death, and who had made such an impression on the president of the probate division, Sir Francis Jeune – had unaccountably withdrawn from the case. The truth of the matter, although nobody knew it at the time, was that Mrs Hamilton had backed out of the case, owing to pressure exerted by the 6th Duke of Portland's private investigators.

Anna Maria had called no witnesses. While she had appeared to be in complete possession of her faculties when she originally brought her case in the spring of 1898, she was certainly no longer in possession of them now. Opposing her, Herbert Druce had marshalled a formidable array of the leading lights of the Edwardian Bar: the former attorney general and future law lord Sir Robert Reid KC, and the future judge Mr Bargrave Deane, KC. They were more than a match for a frail and mentally unstable woman.

The fashionable ladies and journalists in the courtroom, however, were not interested in Mrs Druce, except perhaps to titter at her mad and dishevelled appearance. Everybody knew her case to be dead long ago. Instead, all eyes were riveted on two mysterious, anonymous-looking lawyers who sat demurely on the middle benches. For they represented a person who had newly arrived on the scene. This person was, it was said, an 'Intervener' or third party that had recently joined the case. He was no other than a new claimant to the Portland millions, who apparently had a prior title to Mrs Druce's son Sidney. For the story that had been gradually unfolding in the newspapers over the past two years had alternately shocked and enthralled the public of the English-speaking world. The old man of Baker Street, it was whispered, had led more than one double life; and the latest of his secrets to be revealed had almost certainly killed off Anna Maria Druce's claim.

'Silence in court!'

The command of the court usher caused a hush to fall on the palpitating mass of humanity. In came the officers of the court in splendid array, followed by the learned judge in black robes, upon whose entrance everybody rose and bowed their heads. The judge, looking decidedly displeased at the crowded state of his courtroom, bowed curtly to the ranks of the assembled Bar and took his seat.

Mr Justice Barnes was one of the most respected judges of the probate, divorce and admiralty division of the High Court. In just four years' time, on the retirement of Sir Francis Jeune, he was to be made its president; and he was to be elevated to the peerage, as the 1st Baron Gorell, in 1909. Judge Barnes was one of the breed of lawyers who prefer the purity of legal principle to facts. An Admiralty practitioner of astuteness and skill, he detested criminal work – saying 'there was no law in it' – and explained his unrivalled mastery of shipping law by the remark that there was 'a great sameness and simplicity about it'. No doubt he suffered from the fact that, in his day, the abstract purity of Admiralty work was thrown in with the sordid and fact-heavy fields of probate and divorce; thus compelling this admirer of the sublime charms of bills of lading, when elevated to the bench, to have his mind taxed with the shabby and pitiable human motives of greed, envy, lust and violence. A man of great reserve, Barnes once confessed to his own son that he did not believe in great intimacy with anybody, thinking it 'tended to loss of individuality'. With its sheer and unexpurgated messiness, accusations of fraud and illegitimacy, hysterical females, unopened graves and sensational newspaper revelations, the Druce case was exactly the kind that gave Mr Justice Barnes nightmares. He could only pray that it would be thrown out of his court as soon as possible.

The hearing started badly for Mrs Druce, with an argument over who should pay the fees of the Special Jury, which she herself had wished to try the case.

'Madam, you cannot have a Special Jury unless you can show that you are able to pay for it,' explained the judge impatiently.

'My Lord! Do you think I am not worth twelve guineas? I am worth £300,000 a year!' exclaimed Mrs Druce, to a chorus of titters from the ladies in the public gallery.

'Are you willing to take your chance?' demanded the judge of the jurymen, to more laughter. After a general coughing and shuffling of feet, the jury intimated that they were not willing to take a risk on Mrs Druce paying their fees. Heated discussion ensued, resolved only when Sir Robert Reid, KC, acting for Alexander Young, undertook to guarantee the jury's fees, whereupon the hearing proceeded.

At this point, one of the mysterious lawyers in the middle seats stood up abruptly. Frederick Andrew Inderwick, KC, probate and divorce lawyer, antiquarian and former Liberal MP, was about to lob a hand grenade into the heart of the Druce–Portland case. His astonishing revelation was that T. C. Druce had been married thirty-five years before he met Annie May, to a young woman called Elizabeth Crickmer.

Like John Maxwell, the lover of the novelist Mary Elizabeth Braddon, Druce had still been married to his first wife
when he set up house with Annie May in the 1840s. Thus the
secret of T. C. Druce's late marriage to Annie May, and the
birth of several children to them out of wedlock, was at last
publicly revealed. Old T. C. Druce could not have married
Annie May earlier than he did because he was – unknown
to most of the world, including his own children by his
second wife – married already. In fact, the reason Druce
finally made an honest woman of Annie May in 1851, was
because that was when his first wife died. Like Braddon's
lover, John Maxwell, Druce was at last free to marry again.
And it was this stunning revelation which finally scuppered
Mrs Druce's claim: for there had been children, including
several sons, from the previous marriage of T. C. Druce to
the lady known as Elizabeth Crickmer. If the contention
that T. C. Druce was in fact the 5th Duke of Portland were
correct, then the descendants of these sons would have a
prior claim to that of Mrs Druce's son to the Portland millions; and indeed, it was one of them that Mr Inderwick
represented. This new pretender to the dukedom was, Mr
Inderwick stated, on his way to England that very day from
Australia, to stake his claim. He had applied for the trial
of the matter to be adjourned to enable him to prepare his
case, but as his application had been refused by the judge,
Mr Inderwick was instructed merely to take a note of the
proceedings, with the object of challenging any judgment
that might be given.

The appearance of the lawyer for the Intervener put Mrs
Druce into a great state of agitation.

'He is not the plaintiff!' she exclaimed. 'It is my right to begin my own case, surely!'

'I think,' replied the judge dryly, 'as far as I can gather, he means to relieve you of any trouble.' (Laughter in court.)

'Where is your pedigree, sir? I want to see it, to have it sworn before a commissioner for oaths, and verified now, this moment! You have no case at all!' cried Mrs Druce furiously, at the Intervener's representative. 'You are wasting the time of the court! I think I have had enough of this gentleman!'

Complain as she might, however, it was to no avail. The gentlemen representing the Intervener remained in court, assiduously taking notes. And as Anna Maria as plaintiff had called no witnesses, it was Sir Robert Reid, KC – on behalf of the defendant, Alexander Young – who proceeded to open the case, and call the defendant's witnesses.

There was much that was powerful in the evidence called by the defendant on that day, leaning towards proving that T. C. Druce did indeed die, and was buried, in December 1864. First in the witness box came William Arthur Tootell, Assistant Registrar of Births, Marriages and Deaths for the district of Edgware. His evidence was that, until 1875, it was not obligatory for a death certificate to be signed by a doctor. Before that date, he said, death certificates were frequently not attested by any medical man. Nobody, however, was called to give an adequate explanation as to why the ownership of the Druce vault in Highgate – originally registered in the name of Mrs Druce's son, Sidney – had abruptly, and with no explanation, been subsequently transferred into the name of Herbert Druce, after the litigation started.

Next came the Druce's family nurse Catherine Bayly, a

middle-aged lady who had served the family all her life. She gave grim and graphic evidence as to the nature and circumstances of T. C. Druce's death, supported by the testimony of his medical attendants, Doctors Shaw and Blasson, and his son, Herbert Druce. T. C. Druce, it was said, had died after a protracted illness, as a result of abscesses in the anal region, causing a gradual putrefaction of the lower body (the judge cut short the oral evidence at this point, and seemed much discomfited by the graphic detail of the medical evidence). Catherine Bayly had seen T. C. Druce's body wrapped in chlorate of lime, then an enclosing shell, followed by an encasing of lead and, finally, a coffin of oak. The body had lain in state in the Druce family home at Mill Hill until the funeral, and Nurse Bayly had been ordered by the mistress of the house, Annie May, to lock the door to the room where the body lay to prevent anybody from entering.

The family accountant Alexander Young, executor of T. C. Druce's will and defendant to the proceedings, subsequently gave evidence. He revealed that – and here there was another collective intake of breath – in addition to T. C. Druce's will of March 1860, a codicil had been signed in November 1864, just a month before his death. By the terms of this codicil, T. C. Druce left a bequest of £1000 'to my son George Druce by my former marriage, now in Australia'. The money had been duly sent to the attorneys of this son in Australia, and a receipt had been received. The circumstances of the signing of the codicil were, to say the least, unusual: concluded a mere month before T. C. Druce's alleged death, it had been witnessed by old Druce's solicitor Henry Walker, now dead, and a lady named Miss Bruce, said to have been a governess in the

Druce household at the time. None of the other children of
T. C. Druce's first marriage had been mentioned in the codicil, other than the son George – even though it was said that
there was a daughter of the first marriage, Fanny, of whom old
T. C. Druce had been exceptionally fond.

Mrs Druce's cross-examination technique during the trial
was eccentric. When the nurse Catherine Bayly testified to
locking up the coffin of T. C. Druce on the instructions of
Annie May, Anna Maria exclaimed:

'Why did you lock up the room – to keep out the devil?
What was in there – a corpse? A skeleton? What was in this
wonderful Bluebeard's chamber – an effigy, ha! ha! A wax figure, ha! ha! A face, or what?'

When the great-nephew of T. C. Druce's solicitor, the late
Henry Walker, who had witnessed the original will, gave evidence as to his great-uncle's signature, Mrs Druce's questions
were no less bizarre:

'Do you know that Mr Walker did not die? Do you know
that he is living there at this very moment?'

'I know perfectly well he is not,' came the reply.

'A second case of burying a skeleton or something – the
same family,' muttered Mrs Druce. 'The same Highgate Cemetery, and the same people doing it.' Then her face brightened.
'If we open the Druce vault, we may open Mr Walker's vault.
Do you see any objection to opening Henry Walker's vault?'

'No, I see no objection,' replied the great-nephew blandly,
to a roar of laughter in court.

'And if I bring some of the Duke of Portland's servants to
prove that that man stoked the fires at Welbeck, I suppose you
have no objection then to showing us what is inside the vault,

have you?' Mrs Druce rambled on. She was, it appeared, raving.

'Do not answer that question!' the increasingly furious judge commanded the witness.

It was when Mrs Druce announced that she had a letter from T. C. Druce and waved a newspaper before the court, however, that Mr Justice Barnes decided he had had enough.

'Is there any reason at all for your going into a lot of rubbish that has nothing to do with the case?' he demanded. 'Unless you keep more in order, I must stop you. Put that newspaper down, it has nothing to do with the case at all!'

'Is that Druce's writing?' Mrs Druce squinted at the yellowing newspaper print.

'It cannot be his writing, it is a newspaper!' roared the judge.

But Mrs Druce was not to be deterred. 'The original letter is to be had!' she declared defiantly. (In fact, in all probability, Mrs Druce was here holding up the sample of T. C. Druce's handwriting mentioned earlier, which was published in the *Daily Mail*.)

The second day of the hearing went as badly for Mrs Druce as the first. As she had not called any witnesses, she was examined by the judge and cross-examined by Sir Robert Reid, KC, raving, for the most part, about the undead Henry Walker and the necessity to dig up multiple graves at Highgate.

By the end of the proceedings, Mr Justice Barnes had no hesitation as to how he was to direct the jury in his summing up.

'Members of the jury,' he said, with even more than his customary terseness, 'I do not suppose there is the slightest difficulty in your returning your verdict, and making an end of a matter that ought never to have been brought into court.'

Accordingly, the official verdict of the jury was that the will dated 28 March 1860, and codicil dated 14 November 1864, of T. C. Druce were duly signed and valid, and that T. C. Druce did, in fact, die in December 1864.

And there, perhaps, the case might have ended. Powerful evidence had been produced that T. C. Druce had died and was buried in December 1864. The issue of whether he had led a double life as the 5th Duke of Portland, on the other hand, had not been tried, being strictly irrelevant to the proceedings to set aside probate on the will. Those proceedings had been narrowly confined to the issue of whether T. C. Druce did, or did not, die in 1864. Moreover, while the evidence called by the defendant as to the circumstances of the death of T. C. Druce was indeed powerful, there were awkward questions that had not been satisfactorily answered, mainly because Mrs Druce had lacked a legal representative properly to argue her case.

For instance, who precisely was the governess Miss Bruce, shadowy witness to the deathbed codicil? Why had the nursemaid Catherine Bayly been given keys to the room in which the coffin of T. C. Druce lay, with strict instructions to allow nobody to enter? Why had the ownership of the vault in Highgate been transferred by the London Cemetery Company from Anna Maria's son Sidney to Herbert Druce, abruptly and with no explanation? These were all questions relevant to the circumstances of the will, codicil and alleged death of T. C. Druce, as well as to the issue of the validity of the probate granted on the will.

No doubt, such questions would have been put to the court, had Mrs Druce been in a position to do so herself, or through her counsel. Alas, the poor lady was now bereft not merely of counsel, but of her wits. After a few spats with the courts over minor issues in the next few years, the woman whose extraordinary request to the Ecclesiastical Court had set the entire Druce–Portland case in motion, disappeared completely from view. The official story was that she had been committed to a lunatic asylum. However, it was rumoured that she had been bought off by somebody – the duke or Herbert Druce – and was living in opulence at a secret address. Whatever the truth of the matter, old Mrs Druce was not to be heard of again (at least, not officially). The Druce vault at Highgate retained its secret, and for those determined to oppose its opening, a new – and rather more menacing – challenger to the Portland millions had now thrown his hat into the ring.

Act Two

RESURRECTION

Shams and delusions are esteemed for soundest myths,
while reality is fabulous.

HENRY DAVID THOREAU, *Walden*

G. H. Druce watches the proceedings in Clerkenwell Police Court
(the *Penny Illustrated Paper*, 30 November 1907)

Bury St Edmunds

October 1816

There is no limit, in England, to what a bad husband
may do – as long as he sticks to his wife.

WILKIE COLLINS
Man and Wife

Eighteen-sixteen, in the western hemisphere, was the
year without a summer. Never, in human memory,
had winter stretched its chilly grasp so far into the
year. In both Europe and America the August sun glowed like
a dull red spark in a flinty sky, and summer winds blew with
icy keenness. In New Hampshire, an amateur meteorologist
reported foot-long icicles at midday, and summer ice covered
the surface of lakes and rivers as far south as Pennsylvania.
Newly shorn sheep perished in the cold, and birds fell dead
from the sky. In Ireland, the summer rain pelted down non-
stop for eight weeks, destroying the potato harvest and creat-
ing widespread famine. Throughout Britain also, crops failed,
riots broke out and village uprisings caused members of the
prosperous middle classes to tremble in their beds.

The true causes of the catastrophic global summer temperature abnormalities of 1816 were not fully understood
at the time. They are now, however, believed to have been
the result of low solar activity combined with a number of

volcanic events, culminating in the massive eruption in April 1815 of Mount Tambora in the Dutch East Indies. Average global summer temperatures decreased dramatically as a result, causing the crop failures and severe food shortages described above. However, the catastrophe did have some positive, although accidental, cultural effects. The 'incessant rainfall' of the 'wet, uncongenial summer' of 1816 prompted Mary Shelley and her friends to stay indoors and invent ghost stories during their July holiday in Switzerland, resulting in the birth of the classic gothic novel *Frankenstein*. And the unusually spectacular sunsets of the period, caused by high levels of volcanic ash in the atmosphere, are said to have inspired the artist J. M. W. Turner.

Deep in the heartland of the usually rich and fertile fields of eastern England, the weather in the provincial town of Bury St Edmunds did not escape the year's meteorological malaise. Bury was famed as a magnet for the gentry, and boasted more titled families than almost any other settlement in England. However, even this prosperous and bustling market town, with its ivy-clad Georgian façades, witnessed unwelcome unrest during the course of the year. On 8 May, a large, menacing crowd assembled on the ancient market square. A week later, local farmer Robert Gooday's barns on Southgate Street were destroyed by the mob. And at about the same time, a great number of people assembled in the Butter Market at eight o'clock in the evening to demand that the town hosier, Mr Wales of Abbeygate Street, give up his spinning machines. Things being 'very tumultuous', the magistrates ordered the suppression of the riots, after which the situation quietened down, at least in Bury. But agrarian riots continued elsewhere in Suffolk throughout the year, notably in the nearby village of Brandon, where over a thousand armed men attacked a butcher's shop, demanding 'bread or blood'.

In the autumn – by which time the situation had settled down somewhat and the weather improved – an uneasy quiet reigned over the town. Farmers got on with gathering the harvest as best they could, and Bury's famous St Matthew's Fair went ahead in late September, although in more subdued fashion than usual. It was hardly an auspicious year in which to be married, however: a fact that could not have failed to strike the mind of the Reverend William Stocking, rector at the village of Tuddenham and reader at St James' Church in Bury, as he surveyed the small group of young people assembled before him in the picturesque churchyard one chilly October morning. Reverend Stocking was a seasoned veteran of hastily arranged matches. However, even he could not help but be moved by the little group that clustered round him in the blustering wind. They were so very young. Even the most credulous bystander would hardly believe that the bridegroom was the twenty-one years of age required for a marriage licence to be granted, still less the bride. The Reverend Stocking wondered if they were of age – especially the bride-elect, who was one of the most beautiful young women he had ever seen.

Despite his doubts, he thought it best to let things well alone. A devout follower of the Church of England, Stocking nevertheless bore the imprint of the Nonconformism for which Bury was famous. A number of Bury families had been founders of the pioneering New World colony of Massachusetts Bay, and the town's ancient grammar school – attended by the reverend's own son – had provided some of the leading

Puritan thinkers of the English University of Cambridge. A man's conscience, in Stocking's view, must ultimately be a matter between himself and God.

So it was that on Saturday, 19 October 1816, Thomas Charles Druce, linen draper, married Elizabeth Crickmer, spinster, at St James' Church, Bury St Edmunds. There was no crowd of well-wishers in attendance. The ceremony was witnessed only by the bride's youthful brother and sister, William and Mary Crickmer, and an older couple, family friends Samuel and Sarah Hurst. The kindly rector must have wondered what could have prompted such secrecy.

The truth of the matter, had he known it, would have doubtless turned Stocking's hair an even lighter shade of grey than it was already. Elizabeth Crickmer was not only beautiful, but rich. She came from a prosperous family of the nearby town of Bungay, and it was rumoured that she had a fortune of no less than £7000. Elizabeth had met the young Thomas Charles Druce when she was a pupil at an exclusive girls' boarding school in Bury. Full of charm and apparently of good breeding, the dashing young man claimed to be a linen draper from Bury (although no draper of that name was ever recorded in the town, nor was any draper's shop registered in his name). A whirlwind romance followed, culminating in the couple's elopement – a fact confirmed many years later by Elizabeth's grandson, Charles Hollamby Druce: 'The old man [Druce] took her [Elizabeth] away from school,' he stated. 'She ran away from school to get married.'

The school attended by Elizabeth at Bury has not been identified with certainty. The most likely establishment seems to have been an exclusive girls' boarding school at the edge of town on Southgate Street, run by a Miss Cooke. It is believed to have been the inspiration for the school in Charles Dickens' *The Pickwick Papers*, which was also in Bury St Edmunds, thinly disguised in the novel as 'Westgate School'. Miss Cooke's school – with its red-brick walls and crumbling, mellow walled garden – is almost exactly replicated in the school described in Dickens' novel. There is also an uncanny parallel in the elopement story: for Mr Pickwick's mission in scaling the old school wall is to rescue a rich and beautiful heiress, a boarder at the school, from the clutches of the villainous Alfred Jingle, masquerading as the aristocratic Fitz-Marshall. When Dickens visited Bury in the 1830s, the Druce case was in the distant future. However, the rumours of a long-ago elopement from Miss Cooke's school might well have still been in circulation.

How did the mysterious, non-practising linen draper and the rich, beautiful heiress fare in their wedded life? On the surface, all seemed to be well at first. The couple lived in an impressive house on Great Market, one of the principal streets of Bury, rented out for the then considerable sum of £18 a year. They enjoyed every luxury that their privileged station in life could afford, including that of having their full-size portraits painted by the resident town portraitist. Four children were born to the couple in rapid – some suspected rather *too* rapid – succession: Henry Thomas in 1817, Charles Crickmer in 1818, George in 1819 and an only daughter, Frances Elizabeth ('Fanny'), in 1821. The name of T. C. Druce was noticeably absent, however, from the roll-call of public functionaries of the town. Indeed, Thomas Druce seems to have exhibited in his early years the same secrecy that would be characteristic of his later life in Baker Street. Contrary to the normal practice of wealthy townsfolk, the only public office he appears to have held in the borough of Bury was that of an overseer of the poor.

Beneath the surface, however, the life of this superficially privileged couple was not quite all it seemed. For Elizabeth found out her husband's fatal weakness very quickly after their wedding. Thomas Charles Druce was, quite simply, an inveterate womanizer. His infidelities, which continued throughout his two marriages, were to become legendary. One published newspaper account in 1898 – corroborated by the 6th Duke of Portland's private detectives – claimed that he had got a young woman 'in the family way', and that the girl in question was subsequently admitted to a nunnery that took in fallen women. A former polisher at Druce & Co., a Mr Charles Benjafield, stated to Freshfields that his brother-in-law Mr Payne, also employed at the Baker Street Bazaar, was in fact an illegitimate son of T. C. Druce by a woman called Ann Payne. Payne, Benjafield said, had a sister older than him, also said to be a child of T. C. Druce. It seemed that no woman was safe from T. C. Druce's advances, no relationship or tie of the blood too sacrosanct for him not to try his luck. Elizabeth discovered this all too soon to her cost, when her husband – very early in their marriage – is said to have broken a taboo as powerful as it was ancient. It was this act that probably doomed their marriage almost from the start, although its true nature and extent were not revealed until much later. There was nothing, however, that Elizabeth could do about it at the time. She was trapped.

At some point in the early 1820s, when the couple were

still living in Bury, Thomas Charles Druce vanished without trace. What unknown troubles or temptations prompted his sudden disappearance are not known. What is known, however, is that the town records are wiped clean of all mention of him. Instead, we find Elizabeth struggling on with her little family on her own. Since she could no longer afford to live in the fine house in Great Market, from the summer of 1822 she rented a cottage in a much shabbier quarter of the city, Lower Baxter Street. This was barely large enough to accommodate all four of her children, the eldest of whom were sent out to earn what they could, to keep the family from the streets. Elizabeth's son George was later to recall that from the time he could run about, he had to hold horses' heads in the market place and gather turnip tops and odd sweepings of vegetables for the family dinner. Fanny, the only daughter, was sent to Yarmouth to live with her cousins, the Burtons, for Mary Crickmer (Elizabeth's sister who had witnessed her marriage in 1816) was now married to a prosperous Yarmouth lawyer, Samuel Burton.

It seems that Elizabeth was so poor that, on several occasions in the 1820s, she was forced to apply to the Poor Law Officers of Bury to be excused from paying rates. The applications were generally granted, her unfortunate story being well known in the town. Local worthies did their best to help her by turning a blind eye to repeated financial defaults. The kindly Charles Blomfield, a churchwarden, alderman and Justice of the Peace, regularly excused Elizabeth from the poor rate rental for her home of 6 shillings. Likewise, the Reverend William Stocking – who doubtless remembered his misgivings on her wedding day – kept a kindly watch over her.

In all this time, there was no sign of the husband who had taken Elizabeth's dowry and deserted her, and even if there were, there was little that Elizabeth could do to improve her position. In those days, a woman's property automatically devolved on her husband when she married. As a result, it was a common occurrence for abandoned wives like Elizabeth to be left destitute. It was not until 1882, with the passing of the Married Women's Property Act, that wives were granted the right to own property independently of their husbands. That was sixty years too late for Elizabeth Crickmer.

It was during this time that Elizabeth seems to have sought solace in the arms of a local gamekeeper. The details of the liaison, including the identity of the man concerned, have been lost, but what is certain is that Elizabeth gave birth to a fifth child after she was estranged from T. C. Druce: William, born in October 1827. It was George Druce's son, George Hollamby Druce, who first claimed that William Druce was illegitimate. However, it also seems to have been taken for granted by contemporary lawyers that William was not T. C. Druce's son: a Freshfields note, for example, states that 'William is illegitimate'.

For some years, Elizabeth continued to battle on. But in 1829, disaster struck when the benevolent Reverend Stocking, her staunch ally, died. The unwelcome event was at once reflected in Elizabeth's change of circumstances. Immediately, she moved to a cottage in a poorer area of the town, Eastgate Street. Then, after only a few months, she moved again, to an even cheaper cottage in the same street. In neither of these places was she able to pay the rent. Finally, it seems that she wisely decided to throw herself on the mercy of her relations. In or about 1830 she left Bury for London, where her brother Charles – a prosperous wine merchant – had a home in Kennington.

Quite what thoughts ran through Thomas Druce's head when, some time in 1835, his wife at last caught up with him at the Baker Street Bazaar, are difficult to imagine. For years, he had carefully avoided being traced, even as he grew rich on the profits of the business he had founded with the fortune he had acquired from her. He had changed address with baffling frequency, keeping the mystery of his past life secret. Yet somehow, Elizabeth managed to track him down. Finally, Thomas Druce was compelled to recognize the family that he had abandoned. Reluctantly, he agreed to support Elizabeth on the modest allowance of 12 shillings a week. He then turned his attention to the children. Henry Thomas, the eldest son, had already gone to sea, where his ship, the *Nimble*, was subsequently lost in a wreck off Petershead. Charles Crickmer, the second son, was set up by his father in a modest business as a tailor. George, the third son, then at sea with the Revenue cruiser the *Prince of Wales*, was recalled ashore by his father, and sent to school after being shown round the Baker Street Bazaar. William, the youngest, then only eight – a Druce for form's sake only – stayed on with his mother, and was eventually apprenticed to a master mariner in Yarmouth.

Most of all, however, Thomas Druce wished to keep the only child of Elizabeth's for whom he felt genuine affection – his beloved daughter Fanny – to himself. Unlike the other children, who were given minimal assistance, Fanny was sent to an expensive boarding school to receive a lady's education – first to Rosewood Ladies' School run by a Mrs Gibbons in Kew Foot Lane, Richmond, and subsequently to a private governess, Mrs Whitwell, at the Claverley Park estate in Tunbridge Wells. 'I hope and trust', T. C. Druce wrote to Fanny anxiously when she was at school, 'that you will exert yourself to advance in your reading, writing and cyphering in particular. Indeed, I cannot express to you the great anxiety I feel for your improvement, therefore let that, combined with the great advantage and pleasure of a cultivated mind, induce you to the most energetic perseverance in your studies.'

Once her education was completed in 1842, Fanny was sent to live in seclusion in London, with a lady by the name of Eliza Tremaine, whom her father claimed was the widow of an army officer. While there is evidence that T. C. Druce assigned the lease of a house at 71 Edgware Road to Mrs Tremaine in 1850, there is no trace in contemporary army records of an officer with that surname. It is probable that 'Mrs Tremaine' came from less genteel origins than T. C. Druce claimed, and that she was a mistress kept by him. She seems, in fact, to have been one of several women apparently 'maintained' by T.C. Druce, and introduced to his children as 'aunts'. T. C. Druce's son, George, was later to recall that Annie May – before she married his father – was introduced to him in this way. Once again, Thomas Druce seemed to show a devotion to Fanny matched only by his carelessness to the other Crickmer-Druce children. He was a frequent visitor to the house in which she lived with Mrs Tremaine, signing his many letters to her as 'your affectionate father'.

T. C. Druce's possessive and tyrannical love for his

daughter seems to have excluded all others, including her own mother. Fanny had barely arrived at boarding school in 1836 when her father told her that Elizabeth had died in Bury St Edmunds. However, nothing could have been further from the truth; in fact, Elizabeth lived on quietly in Yarmouth and then London for the next fifteen years, collecting her weekly allowance from her husband at her brother's house in Kennington. But Fanny meekly accepted her father's word, at least in public; indeed, throughout her life, she stayed loyal to the 'official' version of her mother's death in Bury in 1836. However, informed by her brother Charles that her mother was still living, Fanny continued to see Elizabeth in secret. She would visit her at Charles' house, bringing for her mother's use her own cast-off clothes – for Elizabeth, on an income of 12 shillings a week, could hardly afford to dress like a lady. She was, however, an expert needlewoman, making best-quality white shirts for a firm in Southwark; and she tried to maintain whatever contact she could with her children, saving copies of old newspapers for her son George, her 'sailor boy', which she used to give him when he returned from a voyage, to read when he went back to sea.

Contemporaries recalled Elizabeth Crickmer as tall, finely built and good-looking, with dark eyes. By most accounts, she was handsome even in middle age. In later years she turned to drink, haunting the street corner outside the Baker Street Bazaar and deeply embarrassing her estranged husband – now a prosperous pillar of Victorian society – with her drunken and dishevelled appearances. The Baker Street salesman Joseph Lawledge recalled how, one evening in about 1849, he went outside with a colleague to lock up at the Baker Street Bazaar and saw the first Mrs Druce 'hanging about outside'. In Lawledge's view, 'she appeared to be intoxicated'. When Elizabeth did, finally, really die in October 1851 at the premature age of fifty-six, she was buried quietly in Norwood Cemetery.

Seeing little to tie them to a homeland where they had encountered mainly hardship and exclusion, two of the Crickmer sons, George and William, took outbound ships to Australia, eager to find their fortunes in the excitement of the gold rush. Charles Crickmer was to follow them in 1878. Fanny lived on quietly with Mrs Tremaine in Edgware Road and subsequently St John's Wood, marrying after her 'aunt's' death a butcher by the name of John Izard. For the proud and possessive father, the encroachment of another man in his daughter's life was not to be tolerated, and while Thomas Druce did continue to see his daughter after her marriage, the bond between them was broken. Fanny would not receive a penny in her father's will.

At some point in the 1840s – some twenty years after deserting Elizabeth – Thomas Charles Druce met and set up house with the woman who was to become his second wife, Annie May. Annie was initially described on census forms as Druce's 'housekeeper', but relations between them were clearly of a more intimate nature, evidenced by the birth of three children before the couple's marriage, barely a month after Elizabeth's death in October 1851.

Nothing could be more marked than the difference in treatment of the children of the first and second wives. For while the children of Elizabeth (with the exception of Fanny) were largely left to fend for themselves, the children of Annie were brought up in pampered luxury, with private tutors, pet ponies, holidays in Brighton and a country home. Never would Thomas Charles Druce allow the children or associates of the first wife into the presence of the children of the second.

Elizabeth's nephew, John Crickmer, the son of brother Charles, used to go to the Baker Street Bazaar to collect his aunt's allowance on her behalf. Many years later, he recalled that T. C. Druce never spoke to him about the family of his second wife, that he was never introduced to any of them, and that he was not even allowed into the Baker Street office when they were present. He attributed this reticence to Druce being 'too much of a gentleman' to enter into conversation about his second 'wife', when the representative of his first was present. But it could also have been to maintain the ruse – which Thomas Druce seems to have tried to keep up – that Elizabeth was dead. This was the story he had told Fanny, and which the children of the second marriage appear to have believed also, since they did not know that their parents had lived together outside wedlock in the 1840s, until Herbert was told this by Edwin Freshfield.

In December 1864, Fanny received the following letter from Mr Edney, a manager at the Baker Street Bazaar:

68 Baker Street,
December 30th, 1864

My Dear Madam —
Your poor dear departed father will be buried at Highgate
Cemetery tomorrow, Saturday, at half-past one o'clock.
Will you, if convenient, call here one day next week, and
oblige.

Yours faithfully,
W. Edney

Fanny had already been informed that her father was ill,
with ulcerated legs. She had not been told the truth that it
was in fact anal ulcers from which T. C. Druce was suffering, presumably to protect the delicacy of Victorian sensi-
bilities. Fanny tried to come to pay respects to her father's
body at Holcombe House, but found that she was locked out
of the room in which it was laid out, Nurse Bayly holding
the keys. On the morning of the funeral she and her brother
Charles Crickmer walked to Highgate Cemetery, no carriage
in the funeral cortège having been provided for them. Charles
Crickmer was present at the official reading of his father's
will, at which it was revealed that the wife and children of the
second marriage were the sole beneficiaries of T. C. Druce's
estate. The only one of the Crickmer children to receive a
legacy was the second son, George, who had emigrated to
Australia, and who was bequeathed £1000 in the codicil to the

will. Here was another mystery. Why had Charles Crickmer, the eldest surviving son of the first marriage, been passed over in favour of his younger brother George?

At last, however, Elizabeth Crickmer's children could breathe a sigh of relief. They had finally been freed from the shadow of their tyrannical father. There was also a strange irony in the fact that both Elizabeth and Thomas Charles Druce could be said to have died false deaths. While the question of whether or not T. C. Druce faked his own death was to be debated in subsequent years, there is no doubt that he *did* fake the death of his first wife. But despite all Thomas Druce's efforts to bury his first wife and family, he failed to do so. And the shadow of the Crickmer-Druces – the outcast, wronged branch of the Druce clan – was to haunt their favoured cousins for many decades to come. Even though vengeance did not come until some forty years later, and from a most unexpected quarter.

The new century, in fact, had many surprises in store.

On Board RMS Oroya

May 1903

'Ah, you would not believe me; the world never
believes — let it pass — 'tis no matter. The secret
of my birth—'

'The secret of your birth! Do you mean to say—'

'Gentlemen,' says the young man, very solemn, 'I
will reveal it to you, for I feel I may have confidence
in you. By rights I am a duke!'

MARK TWAIN
Adventures of Huckleberry Finn

The two men stood silently on deck in the wind, gaz-
ing intently ahead as the shadowy outline of the
London docks took on concrete form, looming ever
closer as the steamship ploughed towards the approaching
shoreline. Each was wrapped in his own thoughts. The first
man thickset and swarthy, with close-set eyes, darkly tanned
face, and a rough handlebar moustache; the second lighter
in build, more refined-looking, with heavy eyes and pursed
lips, sporting merely a trace of hair on the upper lip.

The land drew nearer, as RMS *Oroya* forged ahead. Soon,
bustling figures could be discerned on the wharfs and jet-
ties, accompanied by the boom of ships about to leave and
the scream of whirling gulls. The stocky, swarthy man gave a

sharp intake of breath, his knuckles clutching the ship's railing so tightly that their sun-parched skin seemed on the verge of tearing. For George Hollamby, this day – 6 May 1903 – was one for which he had waited so long that he could hardly believe it was actually happening. At last, for the first time – at forty-eight years old – he was seeing the land of his forefathers, the distant country that had shadowed him throughout his life like a riddle, a question that haunted his past and hung tantalizingly over his future. It held the key to the destiny of which he had so often dreamed, and which had, for so long, eluded his grasp. For George Hollamby had come to claim his inheritance, as the grandson and rightful heir of Thomas Charles Druce. The rightful heir of the 5th Duke of Portland.

Not that George Hollamby had found it easy to adopt his new, ducal mantle. He still flinched when his friends called him 'Your Grace'. The son of George Druce, the 'sailor boy' – for whom Elizabeth Crickmer used to save newspapers for his return from the high seas – George Hollamby had been born in a mining camp at Campbell's Creek, Victoria, at the height of the Australian gold rush of the 1850s. It was here that his father, George, had arrived in 1851, after the death of his mother, Elizabeth Crickmer. At Campbell's Creek, George had met the daughter of another settler family – Mary Hollamby – and set up home as a farmer and prospector.

The Australian gold rush had gripped the country in a wild frenzy during the second half of the nineteenth century, in the wake of the earlier Californian gold rush. It had been started by an Australian pioneer of the American diggings. Edward Hammond Hargraves, an unsuccessful prospector in the American rush for gold, had spotted the uncanny resemblance

between the landscape of California and his Australian homeland. Returning to Australia with the burning conviction that
there was gold to be had in New South Wales, he made the
long trek from Sydney across the Blue Mountains, to a trib-
utary of the Macquarie river. There – in his own words – he
felt himself 'surrounded by gold'. Sure enough, effluvial gold
was discovered at Ophir, the spot at which he came to a halt.
His words, on raising the first nugget to the sun, proved an
illuminating insight into the hopes and dreams of the average
Australian settler of the time. 'This,' he exclaimed to his puzzled guide, 'is a memorable day in the history of New South
Wales. I shall be a baronet, you will be knighted, and my old
horse will be stuffed, put into a glass-case, and sent to the British Museum!'

Hargraves' discovery of gold in the mountains of New
South Wales in 1851 launched a deluge of fortune seekers onto
the Australian continent, such as had never been seen before.
Overnight, it seemed that the image of Australia was transformed. Previously a grim convict colony, it now became a
land of opportunity, where all those who were outcast, down-
at-heel or purely adventurous, could try their luck. Inevitably, the days when the tin-sieve-shaking prospector, with
his rough tent and billycan, could stumble on a fortune, were
short-lived. In a matter of a decade, the big mining companies had taken over. Some made it rich, some did not. George
Druce was one of the many unlucky ones, scraping together
a living on a farm in the shadow of the gold fields of Mount
Alexander. George Hollamby's earliest memories were of
growing up in a makeshift slab hut, a child of the diggings.
All this, however, was soon to change irrevocably.

In 1865 – when young George Hollamby was about ten years old – his father received a letter from a man called Alexander Young, acting executor to the late Thomas Charles Druce of the Baker Street Bazaar. The letter stated that George Druce had received a legacy of £1000. George Hollamby's father set off immediately for Melbourne, a distance of some two hundred miles from Campbell's Creek. When he returned, to the great excitement of all at his unexpected enrichment, he made the momentous decision to leave the diggings and purchase a business in Melbourne.

For those brought up in towns and cities, it would be impossible to imagine the delight and wonder of the child George Hollamby when he saw the bustling city of Melbourne for the first time. As he was later to recall, even a two-storey house was amazing, and the noise and clatter of the city was terrifying to a child who had been brought up in the silence of the bush. Gradually, however, he became accustomed to town life. His father had bought a market-gardening business, which was prosperous at first: in the early days, cauliflowers would bring as much as 12 shillings a dozen. But hard times were to follow, and with the failure of his father's business, George Hollamby found himself apprenticed to a fireproof-safe maker in the city. It was a miserable experience. Subjected to a terrifying and painful 'tarring' by his fellow-apprentices – that is, being doused in hot tar and rolled in feathers – George soon made his escape. Finding nothing much else coming his way, he made up his mind to head for adventure – out in the Australian bush.

When George Hollamby announced his intention to his parents, his father presented him with a new billycan, a loaf of bread, some tea, sugar and 3 shillings, saying: 'There you are now, you can be off.' He then added, as an afterthought, 'And you can take the dog with you.' His mother fetched a blanket and rolled it round a change of clothing. 'That', George Hollamby was later to remark, 'was the start in life she gave me.' And so, the following morning, whistling as heartily as any seasoned swagman with his dog at his heel and his billy-can over his shoulder, George Hollamby sallied forth into the dark and inscrutable forests of Victoria.

George Hollamby spent the next three years wandering in the Australian bush. He moved from makeshift camp to camp, picking up whatever work he could – gold prospecting, clearing bush, working as a casual labourer on remote farms. Finally, he settled as a 'selector' – or pioneer farmer – clearing scrubland in a corner of the remote area known as Gippsland. This was the wild, dark forest known as the Tableland of Neerim, populated by some of the tallest trees on earth: the mountain ashes of Victoria, many of them more than 300 feet high, through whose tangled canopy the sun shone with a sickly, watery green light. There were no natives in this district, but their former presence was revealed by the exotic names of the locations and the ancient stone axes and other implements that littered the forest floor. George Hollamby's home was a small hut, to make space for which he himself had made a clearing in the thick scrub. The mail came by packhorse once a week, and his nearest neighbour – another selector – was a mile away. They would meet on Sundays and at night, when one would pay the other a visit, striking out across the beaten track with gun on shoulder. Their only entertainment was what they made themselves – poems, bush ballads and the occasional moonlit possum or wallaby hunt.

For many years, George Hollamby remained living in his slab hut by the billabong, one of the countless lone swagmen of the Australian bush. However, the time arrived when the urge came upon him to leave the wandering life and settle down. Thus, in his thirties, he found a job as a carpenter in Melbourne, married a local girl and set up home with his new family. Settled in the northern suburb of Brighton, a soon-to-be – but not as yet – fashionable beach haunt of the smart Melbourne set, he devoted the daytime to his humble trade. By night, he pored over charts and equations, immersing himself in his abiding passion: the construction of machines – specifically a contraption that would resolve the problem of perpetual motion. And so, perhaps, he might have remained – a somewhat eccentric former swagman in the heart of a bustling New World city – had not something extraordinary happened.

It was late 1898. George Hollamby was sitting at home, poring over one of his mechanical contraptions as usual, when his younger brother Charles burst into the room.

'George, you are the Duke of Portland!' he cried, in a fever of excitement. He proceeded to show his astonished elder brother an article in a Melbourne newspaper. The piece was about an English widow called Anna Maria Druce, who was then claiming in the London courts that her father-in-law, the Baker Street businessman Thomas Charles Druce, had lived a double life, and had, in reality, been the 5th Duke of Portland. On this basis, Anna Maria claimed that her deceased husband Walter, as T. C. Druce's first legitimate son, had been the rightful heir to the vast Portland estate, which had therefore devolved on their son, Sidney, upon her husband's death. What the article did not mention – but which George Hollamby and his brother well knew – was that Anna Maria's husband was *not* the first legitimate son of T. C. Druce. Druce had, as we know, been married before, and there had been several sons from his first marriage, including George Hollamby's father, George Druce, who was now dead. As George Hollamby gazed at the glaring newspaper headline, he realized that here, at last, was the key to the mystery of his grandfather's life – the mystery to which his father George had referred so many times, but which had constantly eluded his comprehension. His grandfather was not Thomas Charles Druce, but the 5th Duke of Portland.

From then on, George Hollamby was a man with a mission. He was going to redress the double wrong done to the Crickmer-Druce family – the dual inheritance of which they had been deprived. True, his family had been denied a decent share in the fortune of T. C. Druce, the businessman. But what did that matter if George Hollamby could lay a claim to the title of Duke of Portland?

When it came to raising funds for his cause in Melbourne business circles, George Hollamby found a receptive audience. New Worlders claiming Old World titles were all the rage at the turn of the century. There had been, for a start, the celebrated Tichborne case, in which a butcher from Wagga Wagga had laid claim to the ancient Tichborne baronetcy, and had been accepted by the missing heir's own mother. The theme had also surfaced in America, where it had been treated extensively by the satirical writer Mark Twain. Twain's classic

1884 novel *Adventures of Huckleberry Finn* featured two other-wise unnamed con artists calling themselves 'the Duke' and 'the King', who became entangled in many of Huck's adventures. The middle-aged 'Duke' claimed to be the missing Duke of Bridgewater (which he frequently mispronounced as 'Bilgewater'), while the elderly 'King' claimed to be the long-lost Dauphin of France. Twain had attended a hearing during the Tichborne perjury trial and had met the claimant at an event in London, concluding that he 'thought him a rather fine and stately figure'. Twain had, moreover, a personal interest in the case. His own distant cousin, Jesse M. Leathers, an insurance broker, had sought his advice on a potential claim to the earldom of Durham. Twain's reply to his cousin's query is instructive:

Hartford, October 5, 1875

Dear Sir:

I have heard cousin James Lampton speak of his Earldom a good while ago, but I have never felt much interest in the matter, I not being heir to the title. But if I were heir to the title & thought I had a reasonable chance to win it I would not cast away my right without at least making enough of a struggle to satisfy my self-respect.

You ask me what I think of the chances of the American heirs. I answer frankly that I think them inconceivably slender. The present earl of Durham has been in undisputed possession thirty-five years; his father, the first earl, held possession forty-three years. Seventy-eight years' peaceable possession is a pretty solid wall to buck against before a court composed of the House of Lords of England—backed, as it seems to be, by a limitless bank account. It cost the Tichborne claimant upwards of $400,000 to get as far as he did with his claim. Unless the American Lamptons can begin their fight with a still greater sum, I think it would be hardly worth while for them to go into the contest at all. If the title & estates were in abeyance for lack of an heir you might stand some chance, but as things now are I cannot doubt that the present Viscount of Lampton (lucky youth!), son of the reigning Earl, will succeed to the honors & the money, all in due time. That lad was born lucky, anyhow—for he was a twin & beat his brother into the world only five minutes—& a wonderfully valuable five minutes it was, too, as that other twin feels every day of his life, I suspect.

No, indeed. The present possessors are too well fortified. They have h jeld their lands in peace for over six hundred years; the blood of Edward III. & Edward IV. flows in their veins; they are up in the bluest-blooded aristocracy of England. The court that would try the case is made up, in a large measure, of their own relatives; they have plenty of money to fight with. Tackle them? It would be too much like taking Gibraltar with blank cartridges.

I heartily wish you might succeed, but I feel sure that you cannot.

Truly yours.
Mark Twain.

Twain was to take up the 'lost title' theme again in 1892, in his humorous novel *The American Claimant*. This features the dreamy and eccentric Colonel Mulberry Sellers of Washington, a dabbler in many trades who is convinced that he is the long-lost and rightful heir to the earldom of Rossmore, and therefore entitled to the fictional Warwickshire pile, Cholmondelay Castle. Colonel Mulberry's white picket-fenced suburban house in Washington is emblazoned with the Rossmore coat of arms, and he fires off claim after claim to the English usurper of his title from his 'library', which is also his 'drawing room', 'picture-gallery' and 'workshop'. The walls are covered in portraits of 'dead Americans of distinction', which have been relabelled as former Earls of Rossmore. Like George Hollamby, the colonel is an engineer of some talent: he makes marvellous mechanical toys, which, if patented, would make money, as a friend points out. 'Money – yes; pin money: a couple of hundred thousand, perhaps. Not more,' is the colonel's dismissive response. It could just as well have been George Hollamby speaking. What after all is a few hundred thousand dollars, compared to the Portland millions? The prospect of an ancient title and fortune fulfilled the ultimate New World settler's fantasy. For it carried with it not only the promise of riches, but also the priceless asset of *belonging* – of being not only a member of a hierarchy from which so many in the New World had been expelled or excluded – but at its very pinnacle. What better vengeance to take for such expulsion or rejection than to return in triumph to claim a title?

Twain's writing, like that of his contemporary Charles Dickens, contained an implicit warning about such dreams. The message of Colonel Mulberry's wasted talents seemed to suggest that the success of the New World lay in skills and hard graft, rather than inherited riches. But stronger men than George Hollamby would have failed to resist such a seductive prospect as now offered itself to him.

As George Hollamby's knuckles flexed white from gripping the ship's railings, his companion and fellow passenger on the steamship *Oroya* frowned, deep in thought. Thomas Kennedy Vernon Coburn, solicitor and barrister of the Supreme Court of Victoria, presented as great a contrast with his fellow passenger as chalk from cheese. Still in his late thirties, he was some ten years younger than George Hollamby. And yet, in his self-confidence and sophistication, he far outshone his travelling companion. This sometimes had awkward results: on being introduced to the pair as the new parties to the Druce case, most observers tended to assume that the pretender to the Portland dukedom was the suave and polished Coburn, rather than the rough-and-ready George Hollamby.

Coburn had been inclined to give the carpenter from Brighton short shrift, when he first appeared in his Melbourne office asking for his help. In fact, he could barely hear out his fanciful tale of double lives and dukedoms. But when, some weeks later, George Hollamby returned to Coburn's office, claiming to have received a confidential offer of £50,000 to settle the case from the leading Melbourne law firm of Blake & Riggal, acting on behalf of an undisclosed person, Coburn changed his mind. The sum of £50,000 was, quite simply, enormous (equivalent to £5.1 million in today's money). Although it was never openly admitted, it was generally understood that Blake & Riggal were acting on behalf of the 6th Duke of Portland. If this was indeed the case, the fact that the duke was prepared to make such a substantial offer to settle the matter showed just how desperate he was to be rid of it. Clearly, the 6th Duke of Portland was taking George Hollamby's claim seriously. All of which meant that Thomas Coburn began to take the case very seriously indeed.

The more Coburn looked into the Druce case, the more excited he became. There was, he was sure, something in it. The only solution was to travel to England, and stake a claim. Coburn therefore threw his energy into raising funds from his powerful Melbourne business colleagues. Soon, he had collected sufficient money to buy tickets for the pair to set sail for England to investigate further. Coburn's obsession with the Druce case was such that he had even christened his two-month-old son, whom he had left behind in Melbourne with the rest of his family, Alan *Thomas Druce* Coburn. Perhaps, on the other hand, he had not a great deal to lose. The reality was that Coburn had already been bankrupted on several occasions. Hanging around the courthouse of Dandenong, in the suburbs of Melbourne, in the hope of picking up a brief, was hardly the greatest of vocations.

At home, Coburn was viewed with a certain amount of scepticism. 'His career has been rather a chequered one,' observed the Melbourne finance agent, J. Howden. 'He is very clever and smooth-spoken, but is regarded with suspicion here, and is considered unreliable.' But Thomas Kennedy Vernon Coburn was not one to harbour self-doubts. He was certain that he had been made for a grander fate than to frequent provincial Australian courthouses. In his eyes, the ticket he had purchased on the Orient Line to London was, without a doubt, the route to greater glories.

A great hustle and bustle arose as the *Oroya* finally hit the London docks. George Hollamby and Coburn were immediately caught up in the tide of excited passengers who swarmed onto the deck, weeping and waving to relatives fluttering white handkerchiefs on the quayside. Stevedores rolled out crates and cargo, and the ship's horn sounded imminent disembarkation with a long, low boom. Coburn stepped forward eagerly. George Hollamby, however, held back. A lurking fear gnawed at the back of his mind. There was something that he had buried, a secret that he ought to have told his financial backers, but had not divulged to them. He knew that it would come back to haunt him.

SCENE TEN

An Office on London Wall

March 1907

> But what a strangely mysterious land is Australia.
> Rightly has she been called 'the land of the dawning,'
> since she is yet enfolded in the mists of early morning,
> and her future destiny looms vague and gigantic...
> dwelling in a solitude that is akin to desolation, with
> no knightly legend or tender sentiment of romantic
> story to soothe or charm the ear.

> VENI COOPER-MATHIESON,
> *A Marriage of Souls: A Metaphysical Novel*

The woman hesitated before the heavy black door with its bulbous brass knocker protruding like the knuckle of a fist. She could just glimpse, through the glass door panes, an entrance hall with a staircase that opened in a majestic curve onto a dark expanse of plush blue carpet, the polished handrail set imposingly on a dark green, heavily wrought cast-iron balustrade. She glanced nervously at the slip of paper she clutched in her hand: 65 London Wall. Yes, this was the correct address. Taking a deep breath, she entered the gloom of the vestibule, where a shadow was just visible behind a polished mahogany reception desk.

'Good morning. I have an appointment at the offices of Mr George Hollamby Druce.' The woman's voice was soft but steady, with an Antipodean lilt.

'Second floor,' came the mechanical reply.

The woman commenced the slow climb up the sweeping staircase. She was perhaps forty-odd years old, pale, with aquiline features that defined her as handsome rather than pretty. At the second floor, she paused, then pushed open the heavy door on the landing. Two men awaited her.

'Mrs Gibson, I presume?' The taller and more confident-looking of the two men stepped forward, proffering his hand. 'Thomas Vernon Coburn.' Then, turning to his companion, he said – pronouncing the words slowly, as if to mark with due emphasis the solemnity of the moment – 'This, Madam, is George Hollamby Druce. Otherwise known as his Grace, the Duke of Portland.'

'Good morning, Sir... I mean, Your Grace.' The woman paused, somewhat confused. She was unsure of the etiquette required of a ducal introduction. Was one expected to curtsey? Fortunately for her, however, his Grace appeared to be as uncomfortable with ceremony as she was herself. A craggy man with rough-hewn features, a handlebar moustache and the gnarled hands of a labourer, the would-be duke appeared ill at ease in his imposing surroundings. This was in marked contrast to his more poised companion, who looked entirely at home.

Thomas Coburn – for it was he who did most of the talking – explained that he and his client were much obliged to Mrs Gibson for coming to see them. Her husband Earlam Gibson, an esteemed friend and legal colleague of theirs, had mentioned that his wife was a stenographer by profession, and owned a typewriter. This was a happy chance, as they were looking for an amanuensis to type out and send correspondence on behalf of G. H. Druce, Ltd, the company which he and George Hollamby had set up in 1905 as a vehicle for raising funds to prepare and pursue the Druce claim in court.* Would she be willing to work in their office, for around 30 shillings to £2 a week?

Amanda Gibson had been expecting this. Her husband, Earlam, was a New Zealand lawyer down on his luck, who had arrived in England from Australia in 1906 and had tried – unsuccessfully – to make it at the London Bar. He had recently visited George Hollamby and Thomas Coburn after seeing them advertise for a lawyer in the newspapers, in the hope of getting a job. Although they had turned him down with the explanation that they needed an English and not a New Zealand lawyer, they had expressed an interest in offering a job to his wife. Not that Amanda Malvina Thorley-Gibson was exactly thrilled at the prospect of a post as a secretary. Her real aspirations were much loftier. She wanted to become a writer and leader of the New Thought movement in Australia, as famous as Mary Baker Eddy, founder of the Christian Science movement in America. The New Thought movement, which swept the world in the early twentieth century, questioned the old faiths. It contained the beginnings of a novel belief system: the cult of secular spiritualism, of seeking success through personal fulfilment, the triumph of mind over matter. Amanda Gibson had already written a book outlining

* G. H. Druce, Ltd, was incorporated with a capital of £11,000, divided into 10,000 shares of £1 each and 20,000 shares of one shilling, all held by George Hollamby himself except for statutory nominees. He soon began to sell the shares to raise funds, and by 1907 had sold over 10,000.

her beliefs. It was called *A Marriage of Souls: A Metaphysical Novel*. She had brought the manuscript to England with her, in the hope of finding a publisher. Unfortunately for Amanda, however, her attempts at launching her literary career in England had so far proved as fruitless as her husband's attempts to conquer the London Bar. So there seemed little choice but to accept the post as amanuensis for the Druce office.*

Despite her reluctance to take the job, Amanda was intrigued by the Druce case. The newspapers in Australia had filled their columns with the story of the aristocratic bushman from the Antipodes. More importantly, a central tenet of her own beliefs – in common with many leaders of the New Thought movement – was that the New World would one day rescue the Old World from its corrupt and decadent ways. George Hollamby seemed rather an attractive candidate for a prospective Second Messiah: red-blooded and rugged, from the depths of the Australian bush, he presented a marked contrast to the effete and degenerate aristocracy of the Old World.

On 25 March 1907, therefore, Amanda Gibson began work as an amanuensis for the Druce claimants at 65 London Wall.

---

* Although she did not know it when she took on the job as secretary for G. H. Druce, Ltd, Amanda was to find fame (and notoriety) in the future as the spiritual healer, writer, guru and self-publicist extraordinaire, Sister Veni Cooper-Mathieson. Throughout the 1930s and 1940s she was to set up a number of churches in Australia along Christian Science lines. She was also to publish numerous books on positive thinking that were, in essence, early predecessors to the modern self-help manual. Her 1906 'metaphysical novel', *A Marriage of Souls*, was finally published in Perth in 1914, and is believed to be the first novel published in Western Australia.

These were hectic times. Not a day went by without the sending out of a press release, reporting on the most recent developments in the Druce affair. Every day, journalists besieged the company's doors for the latest news of the case. G. H. Druce, Ltd, had been formed with the assistance of John Crickmer, Elizabeth Crickmer's nephew, son of her brother Charles. John had gone as a boy to the Baker Street Bazaar, to collect his Aunt Elizabeth's weekly allowance from T. C. Druce. Now, he was a respected City stockbroker. George Hollamby had assigned to G. H. Druce, Ltd, all his rights in the outcome of the case, so that subscribing shareholders would receive a stake in the winnings if his claim to the dukedom was successful. Coburn and George Hollamby had already raised funds for their initial trip to England in 1903 in this way, by establishing similar fund-raising enterprises in Australia. G. H. Druce, Ltd, was followed by the incorporation in 1907 of the Druce-Portland Company and the New Druce-Portland Company. These, like their predecessor, were formed to promote and fund the claims of George Hollamby to the Portland dukedom.

From the beginning of her employment, the hard-pressed Amanda had much to occupy her time. Letters poured in daily to the offices of G. H. Druce, Ltd, from all over the world: general inquiries, would-be subscribers requesting prospectuses or shares, existing shareholders seeking news about when the case was due to come to court. There was also a constant stream of visitors to the office. Members of the company's committee were the most frequent in attendance. There was a lawyer called Mr Fearnley, who was the company secretary and an old acquaintance of George Druce's from a solicitor's office in Melbourne; a sharp-looking English solicitor called Edmund Kimber, the leading evidence-gatherer, who always seemed to be in a terrible hurry; and an Australian mining engineer named Francis Coles, an old acquaintance of Coburn's from Melbourne, and one of the principal fund-raisers for the company in the City. Everybody, naturally, respectfully addressed George Druce as 'his Grace'. Francis Coles and a grave-faced businessman in his fifties by the name of Alfred Suart were the initial – and principal – investors in the company. Coles and Suart had made an advance to Druce and Coburn in exchange for a £500,000 bond,* redeemable within six months of Druce coming into the Portland millions. When G. H. Druce, Ltd, was formed, they exchanged the bond for shares in the company.

Francis Coles was an indefatigable advocate for the Druce case. He organized a petition to the Home Office to have the grave opened, collecting hundreds of signatures. He even had the audacity to offer shares in the company to the Duke of Portland himself, arguing that the duke would be wise to hedge himself against defeat in the case against him. (The duke's solicitors, somewhat unsportingly, declined the share offer.)

Alfred Suart, the second principal investor in G. H. Druce, Ltd, along with Coles, was a wealthy merchant and ship-owner, a pioneer in the oil industry and a major City figure. Amanda recalled how Suart had at first been highly sceptical of the Druce claim, demanding that his solicitor attend a meeting with Druce and Coburn to form a view as to the credibility of

* Worth over £50 million in today's money.

the case. The solicitor's opinion was that it must be proved, beyond all doubt, that the claim of George Hollamby to the dukedom was not scuppered by any prior claim. And here lay George Hollamby's guilty secret, which had haunted him on the day of his first landing in England, back in 1903.

In setting forth his case to investors in Australia and the City of London, George Hollamby had been less than candid about the existence of a possible rival to his claimed title. From the very beginning, he had implied that his deceased father George was the *eldest* son of T. C. Druce. When he had intervened in Mrs Druce's action before the probate court as long ago as 1900, for example, George Hollamby's application to the court had described his father as 'the eldest son of Thomas Charles Druce by his marriage with Elizabeth Crickmer, his first wife'. And yet Elizabeth Crickmer had borne two sons *before* George Hollamby's father, George: Henry Thomas and Charles Crickmer. The eldest son, Henry Thomas, had died in a shipwreck as a boy. However, the second son, Charles Crickmer (who, like George, had emigrated to Australia), had married and had a son, Charles George; and Charles George himself had had a son, Charles Edgar. Although Charles Crickmer and Charles George were now dead, Charles Edgar was alive and living in Sydney. On the face of it, as a surviving direct lineal descendant of Charles Crickmer Druce, Charles Edgar would take precedence over George Hollamby in the matter of inheriting a title. And yet, both Charles Crickmer's and Charles Edgar's names had been excluded from prospectuses issued by George Hollamby and Thomas Coburn, when they made their fund-raising applications to City investors.

George Hollamby's misgivings about his having withheld the information about Charles Crickmer's and Charles Edgar's existence were well founded. When, after prolonged cross-questioning by the lawyers, he finally admitted that his father George had not been T. C. Druce's eldest son, City investors were furious. Many stormed away in disgust. John Crickmer's own firm of stockbrokers, who had at first agreed to invest in the case, now refused to pay the bills presented to them.

How well Amanda remembered George Hollamby's reaction to the naming of Charles Edgar as a possible rival! His response, whenever his cousin's name was mentioned, was to fly into an uncontrollable rage. When he had calmed down enough to speak, he shocked his audience with a new revelation. Charles Crickmer Druce, the second son of T. C. Druce, George claimed, had in fact been illegitimate. He was the son not of Elizabeth Crickmer but of her sister, Mary (the sister who had witnessed Elizabeth's marriage to T. C. Druce before the Reverend Stocking, in October 1816). According to George Hollamby, T. C. Druce – the inveterate philanderer – had broken one of the strictest taboos by carrying on an illicit liaison with his wife's own sister, shortly after his marriage. Could this extraordinary story be true? If it was, then George Hollamby was indeed the legitimate and rightful heir to any titles held by T. C. Druce, his cousin Charles Edgar being barred by the illegitimacy of his grandfather, Charles Crickmer. Certainly, there were strange incidents which would tend to support George Hollamby's case. There was, for example, the odd addition of 'Crickmer' as Charles' middle name (not replicated for the other Druce children by Elizabeth

Crickmer), and the fact that Charles had received nothing in T. C. Druce's will. George Druce alone had received a legacy. This surely implied that he was T. C. Druce's only surviving legitimate son from his first marriage, and that Charles Crickmer and William (the gamekeeper's son) were illegitimate. In deposition evidence given in Australia, Charles Crickmer's daughter, Mrs Fanny Hughes, mentioned that she had heard her father and Uncle George speak of a 'short time between their births', and laugh over it.

The contention that T. C. Druce's second son Charles Crickmer was illegitimate served the purposes of George Hollamby's case admirably, save in one fatal respect: despite the circumstantial evidence, it could not be definitively proved. Realizing this difficulty, Thomas Coburn made despatch to Australia in order to secure a written undertaking from Charles Edgar in Sydney, that he would not dispute George Hollamby's claim to the title. By an agreement of 17 April 1905, therefore, George Hollamby and Charles Edgar Druce agreed an equal division between them of any property recovered, if the identity of the 5th Duke of Portland with T. C. Druce was proved. Although the written assurance from Charles Edgar that he would not pursue a separate claim failed to persuade the more sceptical investors, others, including Alfred Suart, were now convinced there was a valid claim to the Portland dukedom. Suart, like other investors in the Druce-Portland Company, was especially impressed by a large photograph shown to him by George Hollamby, said to have been taken from a portrait of the 5th Duke, which had been in the Crickmer family for the last thirty years. The original of the photograph, it was claimed, had hung in Welbeck

FAMILY TREE OF T. C. DRUCE AS REVEALED IN THE DRUCE–PORTLAND CASE

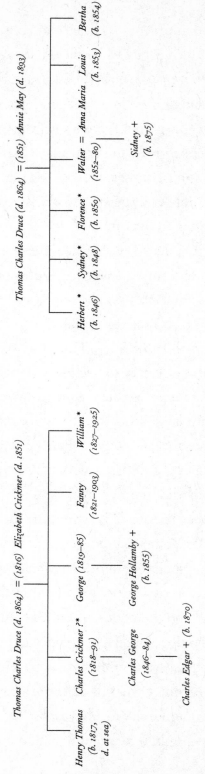

* illegitimate

\+ potential claimant to Portland title

Abbey until it was destroyed by a fire. George Hollamby, in talks with potential investors, would habitually compare this photograph with an uncontested photograph of T. C. Druce, complete with a bushy beard: the beard, he claimed, was clearly false, and there was an uncanny resemblance between the two men. They could only be one and the same person.

Suart was not the only eminent person who committed to the Druce case. The distinguished lawyer Thomas Edward Crispe, KC, was also a shareholder; and rumour had it that even an unidentified member of the Portland family held 1000 shares. Things did not, however, always run smoothly. One day, Amanda opened the door to an irate gentleman claiming to be a journalist by the name of John Sheridan, waving two commission notes in the air and demanding that George Hollamby recognize them. This George refused to do, and angrily turned him out. Later, he explained to Amanda that he and Coburn had granted an interest in the outcome of the case to Sheridan in exchange for raising funds, but he had not in fact raised one farthing to assist them.

As well as dealing with those involved in the financial running of the company, Amanda was also required to assist those who were preparing the Druce case for court. These included the rarely seen and permanently preoccupied solicitor, Edmund Kimber, along with a smooth-talking man called Kenneth Henderson. Henderson was a journalist who told Amanda that he was a great-grandson of T. C. Druce through his beloved daughter Fanny. He was managing editor of a publication called *The Idler*, which had produced a number of pamphlets advertising the Druce case. He showed several of these to Amanda. One, entitled *The Druce–Portland Case*, was on sale to the public for sixpence, and had gone through dozens of impressions. It featured on its cover portraits of the 6th Duke of Portland and George Hollamby, accompanied by the caption, 'Which is the Duke?' It also displayed a photograph of Welbeck Abbey next to one of an Australian settler slab hut. *The Idler* pamphlets included contributions from an anonymous member of the Cavendish-Bentinck family, who – Henderson told Amanda – supported the Druce claim and would, when the time came, make their support known. These contributions were mysteriously attributed to 'one who knows'. If Amanda had needed convincing about the validity of the Druce claim (which was doubtful, as she already fervently believed in it), the pamphlets fully persuaded her. Who, she reasoned, could question such plain and convincing evidence that Druce and the duke were one and the same?

For a start, there was the uncanny likeness between the photograph of T. C. Druce and the photograph alleged to be a portrait of the 5th Duke, which had been shown to prospective investors. (A number of persons to whom T. C. Druce was unknown, on being presented with several photographs, picked out that of T. C. Druce as the duke; a number of persons to whom the 5th Duke was unknown picked out a photograph of him as T. C. Druce.) Then there were the mannerisms. Those who knew T. C. Druce or the duke all agreed on the unapproachable and haughty manner of both men. Furthermore, the two men shared certain physical infirmities: the 5th Duke suffered from a skin disease that gave him a jaundiced appearance. T. C. Druce, likewise, presented a jaundiced complexion, and a number of his children and grandchildren were allegedly afflicted with the same skin condition. Druce and the duke were both also described as being about five feet nine inches in height, sturdily built and weighing about thirteen stone.

The two men also shared marked peculiarities of diet and habit. Both T. C. Druce and the 5th Duke were known to be abstemious with regard to alcohol and tobacco, were modest eaters, had an objection to butcher's meat, and a partiality for fish and chicken. Other unusual traits common to the two men included: a tendency to secrecy and reserve, together with a determined refusal to discuss their past or family background; a passion for subterranean wanderings; the wearing of wigs; methodical habits; unexpected appearances and disappearances for long periods of time; a desire to avoid sunlight (on account of the skin complaint); dislike of being personally addressed; and massive wealth. There was also the proximity in age between the two: Druce's given birth date, 1793, was just seven years before that of the 5th Duke, in 1800.

But in Amanda's eyes, the most convincing evidence for Druce and the duke being one and the same person was what appeared to be the virtually exact correspondence of the presence in public life of T. C. Druce with the disappearance from it of the duke, and vice versa. Thus from 1816 to 1818, T. C. Druce's name appeared in parish registers at Bury St Edmunds, as overseer of the poor. Family evidence showed that, during this period, his wife Elizabeth Crickmer lived with him in comfort and luxury, in the fine house on Great Market. This period would have corresponded with the 5th Duke's education, of which one would have expected to find records at a public school or university. But no record was given of him being educated at any college or other institution.

Then, suddenly, the name of T. C. Druce completely vanished from the records at Bury. In early 1820 Elizabeth was to be found living alone in a house rated at only £2 per year, having to be excused payments of 2 shillings annual poor rate owing to her poverty. Corresponding with the complete disappearance of T. C. Druce, however, abundant records of the 5th Duke appeared. In 1819 he was gazetted as an army officer, various records showing subsequent promotions. From 1824 to 1826 he sat as Member of Parliament for King's Lynn; and up to 1835, biographical accounts of the duke's brothers referred to him being associated with them.

But then, from 1835 onwards, all reference to the 5th Duke in public records seemed mysteriously to disappear. In 1854 the 4th Duke died, and the dukedom devolved on his surviving eldest son; and yet in *The Times* obituary of the 4th Duke, no reference was made to his heir. The funeral of the 4th Duke was attended by every male relation, except his successor. And at several social gatherings in 1846 attended by male members of the Bentinck family, the 5th Duke (then Marquess of Titchfield) was remarkably absent. In 1851 a Corn Exchange was opened at Worksop, the market town nearest Welbeck; the ducal family attended the event, all except the Marquess of Titchfield. On the other hand, this blank period in the duke's life corresponded with the time when T. C. Druce opened the Baker Street Bazaar and began his meteoric rise through the furniture business. It was the time of his setting up home with Annie May, starting his second family, and becoming a prosperous and well-known – albeit reclusive – figure in the London business world.

Then, in 1864, after Druce had ostensibly died, the 5th

1. Welbeck Abbey, Nottinghamshire residence of the Dukes of Portland, photographed in the early twentieth century.

2. 'Mrs Druce's Last Appeal Before Christmas': Anna Maria Druce and Chancellor Tristram in the Consistory Court at St Paul's Cathedral, December 1898.

3. Anna Maria Druce, February 1899.

4. A photograph alleged to be of the 5th Duke of Portland in disguise as the bearded Baker Street businessman, Thomas Charles Druce.

5. A photograph alleged to be of the 5th Duke of Portland as himself, clean-shaven with whiskers.

6. The North Lodge and tunnel entrance, Welbeck Abbey.

8. The 5th Duke of Portland from an old caricature drawing in the *Figaro*.

7. One of the many underground tunnels beneath Welbeck Abbey.

9. Holcombe House, Mill Hill, T. C. Druce's home from 1861.

10. The Baker Street Bazaar, T. C. Druce's
profitable London department store.

11. Annie May, whom T. C. Druce
married in 1851.

12. The Druce tomb in
Highgate Cemetery.

13. Elizabeth Crickmer.

14. The Reverend William Stocking of Bury St Edmunds.

15. Mr Justice Barnes (Sir John Gorell Barnes), who presided over the probate hearing *Druce* v. *Young* in 1901, in a *Vanity Fair* caricature, 1893.

16. George Hollamby Druce in an Australian bushman's outfit.

Which is the Duke?

The Present Duke.

The Claimant.

THE
DRUCE-PORTLAND CASE

Written by

THE CLAIMANT

The Only Authentic Account of

THE EVIDENCE

As told in "THE IDLER."

6^{D.}

Published exclusively by
"THE IDLER."

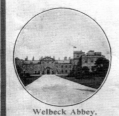

Welbeck Abbey.

Australian Slab Hut.

17. The cover of the 1907 *Idler* brochure devoted to the Druce–Portland case.

18. The police magistrate
Alfred Chichele Plowden:
'the Law in Marylebone'.

19. Horace Edmund Avory —
the 'acid drop' — in later life, as
a judge of the King's Bench.

20. William John Arthur Charles James Cavendish-
Bentinck, 6th Duke of Portland, c. 1900.

21–24. 'The Druce Case: examination of important witnesses': court sketches from the
Penny Illustrated Paper, 30 November 1907. From the top: Edmund Kimber; Miss Robinson;
Miss Maud O'Neill; Magistrate Plowden questions Mr Caldwell.

Duke suddenly reappeared in the records as mysteriously as he had vanished in the 1830s. This was the point at which he moved permanently from Cavendish House in London to Welbeck Abbey, and commenced the extensive tunnelling operations for which he was to become notorious. From now on, in fact, records relating to the 5th Duke were plentiful: right up to his death in 1879, and his discreet burial in Kensal Green.

In the course of her duties at the Druce office, Amanda also met some of the key witnesses in the case. They included an elderly and dignified gentleman with a stoop and a drooping white handlebar moustache, by the name of Robert Caldwell. Caldwell told Amanda the same story as he was subsequently to give in court. He informed her that he was a retired accountant, now seventy-one years of age. He had been born in Ireland, although he was now a naturalized American citizen and lived in New York. He had left Ireland in 1857 at the age of twenty-one, and had travelled via England as far afield as New Zealand and India, seeking a cure for an unsightly affliction from which he suffered – a condition then known as a 'bulbous nose' (and today known by the rather more technical term of 'rhinophyma').*

After a long and fruitless search for an effective treatment for his condition, Caldwell told Amanda that he had finally been cured of his ailment by a captain of the British Army in India, of the 3rd Foot Regiment, by the name of Arthur

---

* Characteristics of the condition include prominent pores and a fibrous thickening of the nose, commonly associated with the skin complaint known as rosacea.

Wellesley Joyce. He had then returned to England, where he demonstrated his cure to the eminent English physician, Sir Morrell Mackenzie. Impressed, Sir Morrell had introduced Caldwell to the 5th Duke of Portland, who suffered from a similar condition. Those events took place around 1864. Caldwell proceeded to treat the duke for his affliction, curing him in about sixty days. Over that period, he was paid handsomely in cash by the duke, and visited him both at Welbeck Abbey — where he saw the celebrated underground ballroom and picture gallery — and at the Baker Street Bazaar. Throughout his time with the duke, Caldwell told Amanda, it was manifestly clear to him that his Grace had a double identity as the furniture salesman, T. C. Druce. He had even seen the duke don a false beard when he visited him as 'Druce' at the Baker Street Bazaar. As the duke, he was always cleanshaven. Caldwell had also met T. C. Druce's/the duke's wife and children, at the Baker Street premises.

The final part of Robert Caldwell's story, however, had Amanda reeling in shock. In December 1864, he told her, he had been approached by the duke, who informed him that he wished to do away with his dual persona by 'killing off' his alter ego of Druce. To this end, the duke asked Caldwell to have a coffin made — or rather a box like a coffin, only not so tapered at the end — and to fill it with lead. This, claimed Caldwell, he duly did, with the aid of an old man and a carpenter, purchasing 200 pounds of lead and screwing it down in the coffin. He subsequently organized the mock funeral of T. C. Druce on 31 December: a splendid affair with many coaches. That was the last that Caldwell saw of the duke or of T. C. Druce; he remained in England for five or six years, finally emigrating to New York in 1871. He had contacted George Hollamby from the United States, he said, after reading about the case early in February 1907, in the newspaper the *New York World*.

Another key witness who was frequently to be seen about the Druce office was a dark-haired and sharp-featured lady from New Zealand, about fifty years of age, by the name of Miss Mary Robinson. She was always smartly turned out, with a neat, feathered toque perched upon her head, and normally accompanied by her 'lady companion', a younger and rather pretty lady called Miss O'Neill. Like Robert Caldwell, Miss Robinson told Amanda substantially the same story that she would later tell the court. She said that her father had been the owner, in the 1850s, of a tobacco plantation in Richmond, Virginia. When the American Civil War broke out in 1861, she was still a child. For her own safety, she left her homeland to come to England and stay with an aunt, arriving in August 1861. It was at this point in time that she began to keep a diary. While staying with her aunt in Tunbridge Wells, Miss Robinson had met Mr Druce as a guest at her aunt's house. He had told her, she recollected, that he lived in Nottingham, and kept tame foxes running about the woods on his estate.

About the middle of 1864, Miss Robinson told Amanda, she had returned to the United States. Here she had met the eminent author Charles Dickens, touring Boston in May 1868. Dickens, who according to Miss Robinson knew T. C. Druce, had suggested to her that she return to England, to act as Druce's 'outside correspondent' – a form of assistant or secretary, it appeared. It was Charles Dickens, Miss Robinson claimed, who told her that T. C. Druce of the Baker Street

Bazaar also lived at Welbeck Abbey and was, in reality, the 5th Duke of Portland. Acting on Dickens' suggestion, Miss Robinson had taken lodgings near Welbeck Abbey, staying with a family called Pearce at a house called 'Lady Hill'. Here, she had sent and received confidential letters on behalf of the duke – posting letters from him at the Post Office, and receiving letters intended for him at the Pearces' home, under the pseudonym of 'Madame Tussaud'. Much of the duke's clandestine correspondence that she fielded appeared to be with a mysterious Dutchman, by the name of 'Van Aish'. Throughout the time of her acquaintance with the duke, Miss Robinson declared, she had always addressed him as 'Druce'. The last she had seen of him was in late 1879, just before he died.

The third – and most enigmatic – of the Druce witnesses was a solemn and mysterious old lady in her seventies, who always appeared veiled in black (she had, for this reason, been dubbed 'the Veiled Lady' by Herbert Druce's lawyers, Freshfields). Mrs Margaret Jane Louisa Hamilton was quiet, well educated and had very good manners. It was she who had persuaded Sir Francis Jeune, president of the probate division, to grant preliminary 'letters of request' to Anna Maria Druce for the opening of the Druce vault back in 1898; and for many, it was her non-appearance at the subsequent trial of the matter before Mr Justice Barnes, that had been the principal reason for Anna Maria's dismal failure at that hearing.

Mrs Hamilton told Amanda that she had been born in Rome and was the daughter of Robert Lennox Stuart, an aristocratic and bohemian gentleman. Stuart had been a cousin and close friend of the 5th Duke, and his go-between in some of his amorous liaisons. Indeed, the duke had been her godparent.

Her father, she said, had taken her more than once to Welbeck Abbey, where she became a favourite of the duke (then Marquess of Titchfield), and learned from him that he was also T. C. Druce of Baker Street. After that, she had seen the duke in disguise as T. C. Druce at the Baker Street Bazaar, and had been told by her father of the duke's intention to destroy his alter ago by the pretended death of Druce, a mock funeral, and the burial of an empty coffin. She had recognized Druce at the bazaar from a photograph her father had given her of him, when she first came to London as a young girl, about the year 1844.

Mrs Hamilton recalled a number of vivid instances of clashes between T. C. Druce and his second wife Annie May, as a result of his double life. On one occasion, for example, Annie May had been audacious enough to embroider a ducal coronet on the corners of her handkerchiefs. This act had enraged the duke/Druce, who promptly snipped off the corners and threw them in the fire. She also remembered the many shadowy lady friends of T. C. Druce, including a mysterious Frenchwoman by the name of 'Madame Eloise', the object of a number of secret assignations.

Such, in essence, was the heart of the case that T. C. Druce was the 5th Duke of Portland. It now remained only for George Hollamby and Thomas Coburn to decide how they were to frame their claim. This was a subject of lively debate in company committee meetings. The position was complicated by the fact that the 4th Duke of Portland had taken care to protect the position of his daughters, so often left penniless under the traditional rules of primogeniture. Under the terms of the 4th Duke's will, the English provincial estates of the family (including Welbeck Abbey) followed the title, and were limited to the male heir. These estates therefore devolved, on the death of the 5th Duke without an apparent male heir, on his distant cousin William, who became the 6th Duke. However, a hugely valuable portion of the 4th Duke's properties – the London estate, which included vast swathes of Marylebone – was settled on the 4th Duke's issue, his four daughters succeeding (to equal quarter shares) in default of male heirs. Thus when the 5th Duke died, ostensibly unmarried, the Marylebone estates devolved on to his four sisters. The eldest sister, Lady Harriet, was unmarried; the next, Lady Ossington, was married but childless; the youngest was unmarried and predeceased the 5th Duke. The third sister was Lady Lucy, who in 1828 had married Charles Ellis, the 6th Baron Howard de Walden. It was her heirs, therefore, who inherited the priceless parcel of a large part of north-central London.

The Druce claimants thus had two potential estates they could choose to pursue: the Welbeck estate, then owned by William, the 6th Duke of Portland, or the Marylebone estate, at that point owned by Thomas Evelyn Scott-Ellis, 8th Baron Howard de Walden, the descendant of Lady Lucy. After much discussion, it was decided by the company committee that the claim would be brought against Lord Howard de Walden. A further action could be commenced against the 6th Duke of Portland and the Welbeck estate at a future date, if the first were successful.

A claim against the vast resources of the de Walden estates was embarked upon, but it soon became clear that to carry such a claim through to conclusion would be a lengthy and expensive process. Something more manageable was required. A softer target was therefore decided upon: a private prosecution for perjury would be brought against T. C. Druce's son Herbert Druce, who had testified during the course of the proceedings commenced by Anna Maria Druce, almost a decade ago, that his father T. C. Druce had died and was buried in December 1864. If T. C. Druce had indeed been the Duke of Portland in disguise, then Herbert must have lied. And winning the case against Herbert would be a major step towards victory, the real prize that beckoned with tantalizing elusiveness: the Marylebone estates, Welbeck Abbey and, ultimately, the Portland dukedom.

Yet again, therefore, clerks scurried to the Inns of Court with briefs for leading counsel; advertisements for witnesses were placed in newspapers around the world; proofs of evidence were prepared; witnesses gathered. The Druce case was once more ready for the road.

Marylebone Police Court

October–December 1907

He who states his case first sounds right,
until the other comes and examines him.

The Holy Bible, Proverbs, 18:17
(Revised Standard Version)

Marylebone Police Court, 2 Seymour Place, W1, was an imposing, two-storey Italianate building in white brick and Portland stone. On most days, it was surrounded by a rabble of vagabonds and pickpockets, plus the odd policeman on the beat. But this day – Friday, 25 October 1907 – was different. True, the courtroom was besieged as usual, but not by the usual crowd. For on this damp, wet and dreary morning of an exceptionally wet and dreary month, an impressive queue of smart carriages jostled for space in front of the courtroom doors, disgorging onto the muddy thoroughfare an array of fine gentlemen and fashionable ladies.

Those lucky enough to push their way through the clamouring crowd, past the narrow scrutiny of the burly policemen stationed at the court entrance, and into the crowded courtroom, would have discovered an even more unusual spectacle. This was the surreal sight of the Marylebone police magistrate, the bespectacled and grey-haired Alfred Chichele Plowden, surrounded by a cluster of titled females, the delicate scent of rose water that wafted from their collective presence mingling with the more familiar police court odour of old rags, tobacco, stale beer, sawdust, turpentine and cheese. Not that Mr Plowden objected to these charming invaders of his court. Throughout his life, he had been very susceptible to the charms of women. As he frequently said himself, the passages in his life which he most loved to recall were those in which the 'blue or black eyes of some goddess or other had played a leading part'.

Alfred Chichele Plowden was, perhaps, typical of a police magistrate of his day. He had been born in Meerut, India, and sent to school in England for the Spartan form of schooling then considered obligatory for his class, at the hands of a cane-wielding vicar. An education at Westminster and Oxford had followed, after which he had trained for the Bar. He was descended from the illustrious Sir Edmund Plowden of Plowden Hall: the great Tudor lawyer and advisor to Elizabeth I, whose legacy survives to this day in the splendid architecture of Middle Temple Hall. But Alfred Chichele Plowden would be the first to concede that he had not matched the high achievements of his famous ancestor. After a desultory career as a barrister on the Oxford circuit and part-time law reporter for *The Times*, he had narrowly lost the opportunity of a judicial appointment – by just three votes, he was at pains to point out – and had been obliged to settle for the much less prestigious post of a magistrate within the seedy confines of Marylebone Police Court. He often complained that it was like 'playing Hamlet in a barn'. 'Anything less like a Temple of

Justice', he would lament, 'can hardly be imagined. Marylebone compares favourably with some of the police courts in London, but with its sickly blue tiles running round the walls and its hideous wooden fittings, a stranger entering for the first time might feel puzzled to say whether he was in a lavatory or a conventicle.'

Plowden was especially incensed by the fact that, at this point in time, a police magistrate was not admitted to the hallowed ranks of the judiciary. Bereft of wig or gown, he was given no uniform or external badge to signify his position. 'It is almost of the essence of justice', he would complain, 'that it should at least look wise, and never has anything been better designed for this purpose than a judicial wig. There is no face so wise to look upon, that it may not be made to look wiser still in the framing of a wig. As his sword is to an officer, or his gaiters to a Bishop, so is the wig to a Judge.' Nevertheless, the twinkling-eyed and discontented would-be judge was known for the efficiency of his dealings with the ragged crowd of London's flotsam and jetsam that regularly found its way before him. Plowden was, quite simply, the Law in Marylebone.

On that October day, Mr Plowden's courtroom presented a crowded scene. On the defendant's side sat Herbert Druce, the accused, his head bowed. He had been spared the ignominy of the dock owing to his status as a gentleman. Close by sat the pale figure of the 6th Duke of Portland, who kept vigil day in and day out, alone amidst the brightly coloured throng of chattering ladies.

The task of Mr Plowden at this hearing was not fully to try the case, but rather to decide whether there was sufficient evidence to justify the committal of Herbert Druce for trial on the charge of perjury. The case was opened for the private prosecutor, George Hollamby, by the eminent barrister and Member of Parliament, Llewellyn Archer Atherley-Jones, KC. Atherley-Jones, who was later to become a judge, was also a leading Liberal politician. A dreamy idealist, his primary calling was to politics more than the law. His father, Ernest Jones, had been a leader of the Chartist movement in the 1840s, and had devoted his life to improving the conditions of working men. A man of affluent birth, Ernest Jones had given up his personal fortune to tour the country in worn-out shoes, campaigning for the rights of the poor. His inflammatory rhetoric had even landed him in prison, where he had continued unrepentantly to write polemical poems in his cell, it was said in his own blood. His son Llewellyn was to carry on his father's progressive battle, albeit in a less colourful fashion. As a lawyer at the Bar, he authored several handbooks on the rights of miners, and as a judge in later years he was to become famous for his leniency towards homosexuals. He was not a man to shrink from the prospect of representing an Australian bushman who claimed to be a duke.

Atherley-Jones' first task was the rather delicate one of explaining to the court that the defendant, Herbert Druce, was the son not of Thomas Charles and Mrs Druce, but of Thomas Charles Druce and a woman named Miss May.

'Illegitimate?' The magistrate's blunt question cut through the charged courtroom atmosphere like a knife. Herbert Druce's head hung even lower.

Counsel for the defence shot up from his seat like a bolt. 'He was the son of the second wife!' snapped Horace Avory, KC, representing Herbert Druce.

Horace Edmund Avory had been almost born into the Old Bailey. His father, Henry Avory, had been the chief clerk there for many years, and was said to know more law than many of the judges. Avory had therefore grown up surrounded by the cut and thrust of litigation. To the right of the legal spectrum and a fanatical advocate of the death penalty, Avory was a ruthless lawyer who, in later years, was to become the most feared of the 'Hanging Judges'. He was well aware of his reputation, which he regarded with a certain amount of black humour. In his later years, when an acquaintance passed him by in the street as an old man and asked him how he was doing, he is said to have replied: 'Oh, just hanging on, you know.' Small and wiry, with a mummy-like, expressionless face, Avory was described as 'the Sphinx of the courts' by the *Law Society Gazette*. 'Emotionless, austere, he holds the scales of justice in skinny, attenuated hands. One tries in vain to read the workings of the mind behind that mask-like face.' To the witnesses he cross-examined and those in the dock that he was later to judge, Avory was known as 'the Acid Drop'. Others described him as not so much dry, as 'desiccated'.

The latest instalment of the Druce saga opened with the shocking revelation that the diary kept by Miss Mary Robinson – a key document in George Hollamby's case – had, within the past few days, been stolen. Miss Robinson's account, which was supported by her lady companion, Miss O'Neill, was that she had been shopping in a London street, when a man came up and told her there was a spider on her shoulder. She had put down her handbag, which contained the diary, to glance at her shoulder, only to reach for the bag a few moments later and find that it had gone. The incident was all the more suspicious since Miss Robinson had already complained to the police about the theft of several other letters and papers during the course of her voyage to England from New Zealand. Notices had been posted in the newspapers, offering a £100 reward for information leading to the diary's return. But there had been no positive leads so far. Who had stolen the diary? Accusing fingers pointed at the agents of Herbert Druce and the 6th Duke of Portland.

George Hollamby's solicitor, Edmund Kimber, next gave evidence to the effect that he had sought an expert opinion on the age of the paper on which the diary had been written. He had been informed that the paper could well date from before 1860. This accorded with the dates when Miss Robinson claimed she had kept the diary. Miss Robinson then declared that she had made a copy of the diary prior to it being stolen. Application was made to admit the copy in court in place of the original, but – after a great deal of legal wrangling – the copy was ruled by Plowden to be inadmissible in evidence. Miss Robinson, it was concluded, would have to rely on her own recollection of events when it came to her turn to give evidence, without any *aide-mémoire*.

Llewellyn Atherley-Jones then finally got to the substance of the case, with a lengthy restatement of the facts, including a summary of the events at the trial before Mr Justice Barnes in the probate court six years earlier. He explained that evidence had then been adduced as to T. C. Druce's death and burial in 1864 by Herbert Druce, the nurse Catherine Bayly and Doctors Shaw and Blasson – Dr Blasson having died in the intervening years.

'I think', remarked Atherley-Jones, glancing at Horace

Avory, 'that my learned friend will probably assent to my statement that Dr Blasson is now dead, and has been dead for some time.'

'Nothing,' remarked Mr Plowden, with a twinkle in his eye, 'is to be taken for granted in this case.'

Atherley-Jones went on to explain that the prosecution's case was that Herbert Druce had lied on oath during the proceedings in the probate court before Mr Justice Barnes, when he had stated that T. C. Druce had died and was buried in 1864. The prosecution intended to prove this by calling witnesses who would testify to seeing Druce alive after 1864, to the fact of a 'mock' funeral, and to the fact that T. C. Druce and the 5th Duke of Portland were one and the same person.

The first witness for the prosecution was then called. This was the grave, elderly gentleman Robert Caldwell, who had told the secretary Amanda Gibson of his time spent treating the 5th Duke for his 'bulbous nose', and how he had been referred to the 5th Duke on the recommendation of the renowned medical man Sir Morell Mackenzie. Caldwell repeated his evidence in court in much the same terms as he had told his story to Amanda. Shown a number of photographs, he identified a large photograph of a clean-shaven man with large side whiskers as the 5th Duke of Portland, and two smaller photographs of a man with a bushy beard also as the duke, only this time posing as T. C. Druce in disguise.

It was now the turn of Horace Avory to cross-examine the witness. Even without the lawyer's garb of wig and gown – this being a mere magistrates' court – the stern face and skeletal figure of the future 'hanging judge' caused a hush of expectation as he rose to his feet.

'Mr Caldwell.' Avory's voice was low, but keen as a knife. 'Are you known in America as the "great American affidavit-maker?"'

The courtroom was suddenly very quiet.

'Certainly not!' replied the witness, highly affronted.

'They do not think much of your affidavits there?'

'I have only made two in my life!' exclaimed Caldwell.

'That is, one in this case and the other in the affairs of a Mr Stewart?'

'Yes.'

'You think that the one in this case is the most important? The most to come out of it?' Avory asked coldly.

'I do not understand.' The witness looked baffled, but an uneasy glint came into his eye. He shuffled and looked down at his feet.

A further barrage of questions from Avory revealed that Robert Caldwell had, just four years before, attempted to sell an affidavit he had sworn to the *New York Herald* for the colossal sum of $10,000. The affidavit claimed that a New York judge, Henry Hilton, had embezzled money from the widow of an American millionaire, Alexander Stewart, by forging her late husband's will. Remarkably, the lurid drama of the tale Caldwell had told in this first affidavit included another case of the theft and exhumation of a corpse – this time the body of the millionaire Stewart, which Judge Hilton had allegedly dug up and reburied in a cellar. The story in Caldwell's affidavit had some basis in truth, as the Stewart case had indeed been the subject of notorious wrangling in the New York courts. Alexander Turney Stewart was an Ulster-born entrepreneur who had settled in the United States in the 1820s, and made an immense fortune from running some of the world's first department stores. His death provoked a flurry of litigation on the part of various branches of his family, including allegations of fraud against his close friend and the executor of his will, Judge Henry Hilton. However, there was no doubt that the more outlandish claims in Caldwell's affidavit could only have been a fabrication. The information about his attempts to sell his version of the Stewart story to newspapers in the United States had been obtained by an agent of the 6th Duke of Portland, and passed on by the Duke's solicitors to those acting on behalf of Herbert Druce.

'They say of you over there,' Horace Avory began quoting from an American newspaper headline that he brandished before the court, "Mr Caldwell deals only with men who are dead." Have you noticed that peculiarity about your affidavits?'

'No, Sir!' The reply was unconvincing.

Next, Avory confronted Caldwell with the proposition that he was in fact in Ireland, employed as an accounts clerk in Londonderry for a man called Mr Christy, during the period from 1863 until 1871. This was the very time that he had claimed, in his sworn testimony, to be treating the duke for rhinophyma at Welbeck. Worse, Avory asked Caldwell whether it was not the case that he had been discharged from Christy's in disgrace, for embezzling his employer's money. Was this not the real reason why he had left for New York in such haste in 1871?

For a moment, the witness seemed to be hunting for a response to the allegations thrown at him. 'I know what you are driving at!' he exclaimed at last. 'I had a brother who was for some years with Christy. It is a case of mistaken identity.'

'Was he a twin?' Avory asked sarcastically.

'Not that I know of,' the witness replied.

Caldwell proceeded to explain that his brother was named William and he Robert, and that because neither of them liked their first names, they exchanged them. It was his brother, not he, who had embezzled Christy. The deed of assignment fraudulently conveying his employer's property that was shown to him by Avory was signed 'Robert Caldwell' by his brother, not himself, as they had changed names. However, the story of a *doppelgänger*, or double, who had supposedly committed the various crimes of which Caldwell stood accused by Avory, became harder and harder to maintain as the cross-examination continued. Especially when Avory called out for a gentleman named Mr Ballantine to stand up in court. Mr Ballantine – a tall, burly man with an Irish lilt – rose to his feet and confirmed that the man in the witness box was indeed Robert Caldwell, whom he recalled from his days as an accounts clerk in Christy's at Londonderry. Yet Caldwell doggedly persisted with his increasingly dubious story of a fraternal alter ego.

'My brother wrote like me, talked like me, and looked like me!' he said, flustered.

'Was he as truthful as you, or more so?' Avory shot back. The question raised raucous laughter from those assembled in the courtroom.

'I am truthful!' cried the witness.

All was now lost for Caldwell, however; whatever

credibility his story might once have had was in tatters. It only remained for Avory to twist the knife.

'You say that in 1855 you consulted Sir Morell Mackenzie. Are you aware that Sir Morell Mackenzie was then only seventeen or eighteen years of age?'

'I do not mean to say I saw Sir Morell Mackenzie then,' Caldwell replied hastily. He went on to explain that he was given a recommendation to Sir Morell in 1857, but carried it about with him for several years, before presenting it. The courtroom tittered. Caldwell, however, obstinately stuck to his story that he had treated the 5th Duke for a bulbous nose in the 1860s, and that he visited him both at Welbeck and the Baker Street Bazaar. He distinctly remembered the underground picture gallery and ballroom at Welbeck. He had also had dinner and stayed overnight at the Baker Street Bazaar, as the guest of the duke (disguised as Druce) and his family.

'And suppose those underground rooms, picture gallery and ballroom were never constructed until 1872, your whole story must be untrue?'

'Well, I am not to suppose anything at all; but I do not accept it as a fact,' the witness replied.

'And if there was no bedroom, kitchen nor dining room at the Baker Street Bazaar, your story must be untrue?'

There was a long pause. Finally, the reply came: 'I should say so.'

But Avory was not yet finished. Next, he confronted Caldwell with the fact that there was a tombstone erected in a Londonderry cemetery to a child of his called Caroline. Caldwell attempted to assert that this child was also that of his brother William, despite the inscription on the tombstone, which stated: 'Sacred to the memory of Caroline Matilda, the dearly-beloved child of Matilda and Robert Caldwell, who died 18 June, 1867, aged seven months.' Eventually, however, he was obliged to admit that the child was his own. The ruse of the 'twin brother' had finally been shattered.

'Now we have got it, definitely!' Plowden exclaimed.

Horace Avory smiled to himself. It was the answer for which he had been waiting. The Acid Drop had his first victim.

The second witness for the prosecution was Miss Mary Robinson – the lady from New Zealand, whose diary had been so shockingly pillaged from her handbag in a London street. She told essentially the same story that she had related earlier, to Amanda Gibson. She had been born, she said, on a negro plantation in Virginia, the daughter of wealthy plantation owners. She had been sent to England for safety during the American Civil War. She had known T. C. Druce in the 1860s, through her aunt at Tunbridge Wells. Mr Druce frequently talked to her about his country estate. She became on intimate terms with him, and he frequently joined in with their family events. In the summer of 1862, she said, Druce had attended a children's party with her in Rochester, where there were private theatricals. They had performed *Little Red Riding Hood*, and Mr Druce played the grandmother. He wore a nightdress, with a grandmother's cap tied with strings. She also told the story of how she became T. C. Druce's/the 5th Duke's amanuensis or 'outside correspondent', through the mediation of the writer Charles Dickens. She had met Dickens, she said, when he was on a tour of Boston. For several years she had acted as a 'go-between' for the duke at Wel-beck, accepting letters on his behalf which were addressed to her under the pseudonym 'Madame Tussaud'.

When it came to Horace Avory's turn to cross-examine Miss Robinson, he remarked contemptuously that he had some doubt whether he ought to cross-examine the witness at all; but lest any wrong inference might be drawn, he would put a few questions. He turned first to the alleged appear-ance of T. C. Druce/the duke at the children's party in 1862, expressing a certain dry surprise at the spectacle of the 5th Duke of Portland dressed up as the grandmother in *Little Red Riding Hood*.

'Supposing Mr Druce was being operated on by the sur-geon Sir William Fergusson at that time, he could not be the man who was at the children's party?'

'You only say suppose,' the witness replied coolly. But she had got her dates fatally wrong.

'Did he look like a man who had been seriously ill?' probed Avory.

'He did not do anything particular at the party,' came the witness's stonewalling response.

Avory then dealt with the issue of Miss Robinson's alleged relationship with Charles Dickens. Dickens, it appeared, was – according to his authorized biography – in Liverpool in May 1868. If this was the case, how was it to be reconciled with Miss Robinson's story of meeting him in Boston at that time? No reply was forthcoming.

'Are you aware', continued Avory, 'that it has been pub-licly proclaimed by the Dickens family that Mr Dickens had nothing to do with the duke?'

'When?' For the first time, Miss Robinson's confidence seemed to falter.

'A few days ago.'

The novelist's family, in fact, had been scandalized that the sacrosanct name of Charles Dickens was being dragged into the ignominious battle over the Druce case. Dickens' sister-in-law, Georgina Hogarth, had informed Freshfields that Dickens was acquainted with T. C. Druce as a superior tradesman and considered him a man of ability, but was never a friend of his. Mr Druce, she said, used to personally serve Mr Dickens when he went to Baker Street.

The cross-examination was beginning to have a strange effect on Miss Robinson. Appearing faint, she declared that she could not collect her thoughts, and that her memory was going. She sat still with her eyes closed.

'I cannot tell you anything now, I feel very unwell,' she murmured.

The hearing was therefore adjourned.

When the cross-examination resumed, things continued to go badly for Miss Robinson. Presented with letters written by T. C. Druce and the 5th Duke, she was unable – somewhat oddly for Druce's/the duke's amanuensis of eleven years – positively to identify any of them. She also seemed to think that 'Madame Tussaud', the name under which the Duke's letters were supposedly addressed to her, was normally spelled with a single 's' as 'Madame Tusaud'.

As the days of the court hearing went by and the witness evidence continued to unfold, the features of George Hollamby began to register increasing anxiety; while a glimmer of hope lit up the face of the 6th Duke of Portland.

Mrs Margaret Jane Louisa Hamilton – or the 'Veiled Lady', as Freshfields called her – was the last of the prosecution's key witnesses to give evidence in court. She, of all the witnesses, was the one whom Freshfields had most feared. Despite being tailed almost constantly by private detectives, she had hardly put a foot wrong. Her evidence had withstood formal cross-examination before Sir Francis Jeune in 1898, by the eminent Bargrave Deane, QC. It had also withstood informal cross-examination in chambers almost ten years later, by the equally eminent barrister, Thomas Edward Crispe, KC, before whom she had been brought by prospective investors in the Druce case. Crispe had marvelled at the coherence of Mrs Hamilton's story, and concluded that she was an 'honest witness.' (In fact, Crispe had been so convinced by her evidence that he bought shares in G. H. Druce, Ltd, himself. He was at that moment watching the proceedings in Marylebone Police Court on behalf of the company's shareholders.) Mrs Hamilton now repeated to the court the same story she had told Amanda Gibson – of her aristocratic upbringing and of her father Robert Lennox Stuart's close friendship with the 5th Duke. Could Mrs Hamilton stand up to an assault by Horace Avory?

When Avory rose to open his cross-examination, it was to confront Mrs Hamilton with a certificate of baptism showing that she was not the daughter of an aristocratic cousin of the Cavendish-Bentincks by the name of Robert Lennox Stuart, as she claimed, but rather the daughter of Robert and Isabella Atkinson of Westmorland. Mrs Hamilton's response was immediate and fluent. She accepted that she had been brought up by the Atkinsons, but she insisted that they were not her parents. Her father was indeed Robert Lennox Stuart, a close friend of the 5th Duke. A chink, however, had appeared for the first time in the armour of the Veiled Lady.

Mrs Hamilton had stated in her evidence that she had seen a photograph of T. C. Druce in 1844, before being introduced to him by her father at the Baker Street Bazaar. Her father, she claimed, had told her all about the duke's double life as T. C. Druce. Avory proceeded to show Mrs Hamilton the same photographs that Robert Caldwell had been shown, asking her which it was that she had seen prior to recognizing T. C. Druce in Baker Street. Mrs Hamilton confidently picked one of the photographs: a small one of T. C. Druce with full beard, sitting down at a table. She was sure, she said, that this was the photograph of Druce that she had seen, in 1844.

'Supposing such a photograph was not produced until 1850, what have you to say?' Avory asked.

'Well, I know the one I had was exactly like this.'

'You still stick to that?'

'Yes.'

On re-examination by Atherley-Jones, Mrs Hamilton refused to revise her story about the photograph. This led to an expert witness being called, to testify as to the age of the various photographs that had been produced in court. Mr William Debenham, former member of the Council of the Royal Photographic Society, began by setting out a brief history of the development of photography in the nineteenth century. The early form of photograph, he explained, was the 'daguerrotype'. This was current in the 1840s, and involved fixing the photographic image on a metal plate. Later, Henry Fox-Talbot invented the 'calotype', the first process of printing images onto paper. The Fox-Talbot process had been patented in 1841, and images produced by it were commercially available from 1847. None of the three photographs of the alleged duke and T. C. Druce, however, were Fox-Talbot-type photographs. Rather, they were photographs produced on albumenized paper, a later technique. The first – the large photograph of the clean-shaven man with whiskers, alleged to be the 5th Duke as himself – dated from 1855–1865. The two small photographs of a bearded man, said to be of T. C. Druce, were of the 'carte de visite' type – a form of photograph that had not become popular until 1859.

Avory's cross-examination of Mrs Hamilton had exposed flaws in her account of her family history and the genuineness of her story; to say nothing of the unmitigated disaster of Robert Caldwell's evidence and the dubious tale told by Miss Robinson, the amanuensis who could neither spell nor recognize her own master's handwriting. The few minor witnesses left to testify for the prosecution did little to repair the damage done to George Hollamby's case.

A Mr Marks, a fishmonger from Baker Street, testified to seeing lead put in T. C. Druce's coffin in December 1864 – he remembered it very particularly, as just beforehand he had been married and returned from his honeymoon. The only difficulty, as Avory was quick to point out, was that – according to his marriage certificate – he had in fact been married *after* the death and burial of T. C. Druce, in 1865.

A Mr Batt, the duke's former tailor, testified that a coat produced in court belonged to the 5th Duke of Portland; he failed, however, to demonstrate that it was the same coat as that worn by T. C. Druce in the photographs. There was also the niggling question of how the Druce party could have obtained a coat of the 5th Duke of Portland's in the first place. On the death of the 5th Duke, his clothes had been inherited by his old valet, John Harrington. How could one of his coats have ended up in the hands of George Hollamby? The 6th Duke of Portland immediately instructed his land agent, Thomas Warner Turner, to make extensive inquiries in order to find out how this could have come about.

After Batt, an engineer called Rudd testified as to the similarity of the large photograph of the bewhiskered, clean-shaven man with a portrait of the 5th Duke that he had seen at Welbeck Abbey; but he did not think the original portrait of the 5th Duke sported such large whiskers as in the photograph. When cross-examined, the only 'mystery' surrounding the 5th Duke's life that Rudd could think of was what he darkly referred to as the existence of a secret 'lady fraternity' at Welbeck. This sent a *frisson* around the courtroom. What could the 'lady fraternity' of Welbeck possibly have been? The 5th Duke of Portland, it appeared, had almost as many secrets as T. C. Druce; but leading a double life as a tradesman in Baker Street appeared to be less and less likely to be one of them.

On 13 December, the prosecution closed its case and it was time for Atherley-Jones to make his closing submissions. At

this point, George Hollamby's barrister took a highly unusual course of action: he disowned his own star witness. The doubts cast on the integrity of Robert Caldwell, he said – particularly as to his presence in Ireland when he claimed to have been treating the Duke at Welbeck, and his likely fathering of the child buried in the Londonderry cemetery – were such that he, Atherley-Jones, could no longer in conscience place any further reliance on his evidence. Avory had therefore scored a triumph, and a serious blow had been struck to the case for the prosecution.

The announcement that Caldwell's evidence was to be withdrawn caused a general stir in court, in the midst of which sharp-eyed observers would have spotted Edwin Freshfield exchanging whispered words with a solid-looking man sitting next to him. The man, who had a moustache and was wearing a blue serge suit, had only appeared in court late in the proceedings. He inclined his head towards Edwin and nodded. The pair then hastily donned their top hats, and slipped silently out of the courtroom.

It was now time for the defence to present its case. The witnesses called on Herbert Druce's behalf created a powerful impression. Catherine Bayly, the now elderly nurse who had attended T. C. Druce in what the defence alleged to be his last illness, and who had given potent evidence of his final hours at the hearing before Mr Justice Barnes, came to give evidence once again. Now nearly seventy-seven years of age, her evidence was as simple and powerful as it had been before. T. C. Druce had died on the night of 28 December 1864, just before 2 a.m., in his bedroom on the second floor of Holcombe House. She herself had held his hand as his life ebbed away.

He had been attended by the doctors Shaw and Blasson, along with two hospital nurses. One of the nurses had contracted blood poisoning from tending him, and had subsequently died. Shortly after T. C. Druce died, Herbert Druce entered the room. Druce's wife Annie May also came in, but did not stay — for the complaint from which T. C. Druce was suffering caused such a putrid smell that it was extremely unpleasant to stay in the room. After Druce's death, Dr Shaw had come to the house, and he and Nurse Bayly had laid the body out. Because of its offensive condition, it was wrapped in chloride of lime, before being placed in a double shell and sealed in the wooden coffin. Cross-examined on the question of why she locked the doors of the room in which the coffin lay, the nurse denied that this was to keep out the Crickmer children, or that T. C. Druce's daughter Fanny had been refused admission to see the body. Her evidence, when read out together with her testimony to the probate court in Anna Maria's case, had barely altered since 1901.

'You made the same statement then as you make today?' Horace Avory asked her.

'Yes, of course,' came her cracked and worn reply. 'I said the same thing then as I have said today. There was nothing else to say.'

The proceedings were now interrupted by a new sensation. Horace Avory passed a piece of paper to the magistrate. Glancing at its contents, Mr Plowden did not seem at all displeased. The note read that Herbert Druce — exhausted, presumably, by the endless years of litigation — had finally given permission for the Druce vault to be opened. In coming to this decision, Herbert had no doubt been encouraged by the opinion of Mr Plowden, who had remarked during the course of the hearing that it would be a very desirable step, in the interests of justice, for the grave to be opened. The 6th Duke of Portland, through his solicitors, had also been pressing Herbert Druce to consent to the opening of the vault, and had offered to pay the costs of doing so. A further factor that may have influenced Herbert was the excited state of public opinion, which was now at a peak of hostility towards him and his perceived unreasonable refusal to put an end to the affair by the simple act of opening the vault. The court proceedings would now therefore be held over, the magistrate announced, until the vault had been opened and its contents examined.

And so, after ten long years of battling through the courts, it seemed as though Anna Maria Druce's petition was finally to be granted. The Druce grave at Highgate was, at last, to yield its long-buried secret.

The Druce Vault

December 1907

Dead men tell no tales.

English proverb

Before dawn on the morning of Monday, 30 December 1907, a small group of men had already taken possession of the seats positioned before the gates of Highgate Cemetery. A biting wind swept the heights of north London that day, accompanied by cutting particles of sleet. And yet the inclement weather conditions had not deterred curious members of the public, who flocked to the cemetery to witness the most momentous event of the old year passing.

By daylight quite a crowd had assembled, and at 5 a.m. the main gates were opened to let in the electricians who were responsible for the special lighting arrangements. In order to ensure absolute privacy for the exhumation, a vast shed had been constructed over the Druce vault to conceal the operations, with no windows save skylights. It was a structure that some observers could not help but comment on with grim amusement: after all, the 'underground duke', with his aversion to daylight, could not have dreamed up a more appropriate backdrop for his putative exhumation.

Two hours after the electricians had departed, a covered van drove up containing the men who were bringing the tools necessary for the disinterment. Later still, three other vehicles arrived, conveying the officials authorized to attend the great occasion: solicitors, surveyors and other professionals representing the various parties. There was a significant police presence at the cemetery – officers were stationed at both the main entrance and the cemetery superintendent's lodge, and a mounted patrol stood guard at the perimeter fence.

Chief Inspector Walter Dew of Scotland Yard, the officer in charge, glanced at his pocket watch. He was not in the least disconcerted by the high level of public interest in the event. As a seasoned member of the Metropolitan Police Criminal Investigations Division, he had been involved in some sensational cases in his time. He had had the luck – or ill luck – to have been employed as a young detective constable in the Whitechapel division of the CID during the Ripper murders, twenty years previously. Those crimes, with their sequence of grisly finds in the form of horribly butchered human remains, were unsolved to this day. For Dew, the murders had turned into a morbid obsession. Jack the Ripper remained, among his many subsequent successes, his one haunting failure.

Born in humble circumstances – he was one of ten children, his father a guard on the railways – Walter Dew had joined the Met at the age of nineteen in 1882. He had worked his way up the force the hard way. Balding, stolid and with a well-clipped handlebar moustache, his plain habit of dress – he wore the same blue serge suit every day – had earned him the punning nickname 'Blue Serge' by his colleagues. For many, the swift ascent through the ranks of this rather bland man was a source of bafflement. But in a newspaper feature on the 'Twelve Greatest Detectives in the World' eight years later, a journalist argued that the secret to Dew's success lay in the very innocuousness of his appearance:

> If a 'swell' mobman had to be shadowed the usual order was 'Send Dew. He doesn't look like a policeman,' and Dew went into fashionable houses, restaurants, and theatres. He mixed in society without the slightest difficulty, for no one could suspect the faultlessly dressed, military-looking man of being an emissary from Scotland Yard. Certainly his appearance has helped him considerably.

The article continued:

> Mr Dew suggests the retired army officer rather than the detective. Imagine a man just above medium height, with a dark moustache, hair turning grey, a strong face tempered with a pair of kindly eyes, a clear-cut figure reminiscent of the barracks, and you have Mr Dew as he is today at the age of fifty-three. A major in mufti is as good a description as any. You will find many like him in the famous military clubs in West End London.

But whatever the secret of Dew's success, no officer could equal him for staunch loyalty to the only institution that had given him a chance in life – the Met, which he was later to describe as 'the finest police force in the world'.

Dew had been drafted into the Druce case at a late stage, when it appeared increasingly likely that perjury proceedings would be brought by the Crown against key witnesses for the prosecution such as Robert Caldwell, Mary Robinson and Mrs Hamilton. He had attended the later court hearings at the Marylebone Police Court, reporting back to Scotland Yard in his neat, round handwriting. He had also attended at St Paul's Cathedral three days before the day scheduled for the exhumation, on 27 December, when Chancellor Tristram – frail and white-haired now, requiring an arm to lean on as he walked unsteadily along the pavement – had once again heard the petition for a faculty to open the Druce grave. It was now ten years since Anna Maria Druce's original petition. This time, the sunlight bouncing off the statues of Carrara marble in the cathedral precincts highlighted not the worn and angular features of a middle-aged woman, but the portly figure of William Dankwerts, KC, arguing on behalf of the London Cemetery Company for a faculty to open the grave. The various legal arguments droned on at somewhat superfluous length: after all, the chancellor had heard them all before. The faculty was, for a second time, duly granted by the chancellor. This time, no one appealed against it.

Dew's opinion had recently been sought when Mr Edmund Kimber, solicitor for George Hollamby, had complained to Scotland Yard about a plot afoot surreptitiously to open the Druce grave, 'to defeat the ends of justice'. Kimber, citing rumours of such a conspiracy in the press, had demanded police surveillance of the grave. Dew had advised against it; the Druce claimants, he argued, could easily employ private detectives themselves to watch the grave, and the request for the police to do so appeared to be an attempt to induce the police to take sides. Dew had adopted the same approach when Kimber later demanded police protection, after the theft of Miss Robinson's diary. Dew was deeply suspicious, in any event, of Kimber's part in these matters. Was it not a coincidence that the diary had 'disappeared' the very moment it was required to be produced in court? Mr Kimber, in fact, seemed to make the loudest noises of protest when the conduct of his own side appeared the most open to question. Did he, for example, know rather more about a plot to dig up the Druce grave than he made out? Dew suspected that it was Kimber himself – or, at least, members of the Druce camp – who were behind a conspiracy to dig up the grave. And then there were the other dubious figures – members of London's twilight world whom he knew only too well – who hovered around George Hollamby like moths drawn to a candle flame: the crooked City wheeler-dealer Henry Marlow, with his grey beard and gold-rimmed glasses, and the sharp journalist Sheridan. In recent weeks, the shadowy figure of a woman dressed in black had been seen flitting around the tombstones of Kensal Green cemetery, in the vicinity of the old 5th Duke's grave. Who she was nobody knew, as she always vanished into the bushes when anyone tried to approach her. It was rumoured that she was Anna Maria Druce, escaped from the asylum in which she had been locked to haunt the 5th Duke's grave in her dementia. Such claims were almost certainly nonsense, as far as the matter-of-fact Dew was concerned. Still, they were evidence of something peculiar being afoot, all the same.

There was one aspect of the case, however, that was a source of great anxiety even to the pragmatic Chief Inspector. For it seemed that the Druce party was employing, to frame its dubious case, one of the greatest CID officers of the time. This was Chief Inspector John Conquest, a man who, in his day, had acquired a name as one of the ablest detectives in Europe. Now retired from the force, he was operating a private detective agency. Before his retirement, however, he had practically run Scotland Yard.

The stories of Conquest's achievements as a detective would fill a dozen exciting volumes. One of the most famous was his arrest of the burglars Charles Russell and William Whistler, whose most notorious heist involved the theft of £3000 worth of jewellery from a lady's bedroom in a house in Audley Square, off Park Lane. Russell, dressed as an old country squire, would visit West End estate agents and view houses for sale in wealthy neighbourhoods, so that he could draw a plan of the interior of any other house in the terrace, always particularizing the lady's bedroom. A small boy in Russell's employ would then slip along the roofs into the garret window of the intended house, and proceed to rob the bedroom while the family were at dinner. A code of signals, consisting of striking matches, was arranged, and it was by spotting these signals that Inspector Conquest got on the burglars' track. He identified about fifteen or twenty burglaries of this type in three months, all carried out by the same boy under the instructions of Russell and Whistler. The pair were arrested and tried at the Old Bailey, and sentenced to fifteen years' imprisonment.

Conquest's exploits also included shadowing Mr Gladstone, when threats were made against the Liberal prime minister during the 1880s. As the Grand Old Man's bodyguard, Conquest had stuck like a limpet to his charge, despite Gladstone's efforts to elude his protector.

The thought of investigating the conduct of such a hero,

and a fellow police officer to boot, was anathema to Dew. He could not – indeed, dared not – imagine that Inspector Conquest's conduct had been anything other than right and proper in the matter of the Druce case. He was a member of Dew's beloved Met. How could it be otherwise?

The clatter of approaching boots woke Walter Dew from his reverie. In this most frustratingly tangled of cases, so many questions remained unanswered. But at least, the truth about the contents of the Druce family vault was about to be revealed. As the morning wore on, two officially authorized press representatives arrived – one from the Central News Agency, the other from the Press Association. Great care had been taken to respect the privacy of the proceedings. Only authorized ticket holders were allowed into the cemetery, and entry permission had even been refused to an anonymous newspaper, which had offered in excess of £1000* to the London Cemetery Company for exclusive access to the exhumation. But the hounds of the press were not to be deterred. Later, it was discovered that an ingenious journalist had devised a scheme to communicate the outcome of the disinterment to the outside world, by waving different coloured handkerchiefs. Another pressman attempted forcibly to break his way into the site, but was barred at the gates.

It had been announced that George Hollamby, who had himself issued the summons for perjury against Herbert Druce, would arrive at the cemetery gates at 8 a.m. and request permission to attend the exhumation. This he duly did, presenting himself at the superintendent's quarters at

* Over £100,000 in today's money.

the appointed hour. He was, however, refused permission to enter, the reason given being that he was not one of the named persons authorized to be present in Dr Tristram's order. Retreating to the cemetery gates, George Hollamby issued a press statement: 'I have been refused admission, and I have lodged a protest.' He then left the cemetery to mingle with the assembled crowd, sidelined as a mere spectator of the drama that he himself had helped to create.

Within the interior of the shed, the only natural light was the grey sky glimpsed through the roof skylights. This was punctured, however, by the searing glare of naked electric bulbs suspended from the shed's ceiling. In the sharp reliefs of light and darkness thrown up by the arc lamps over the small knot of assembled men in top hats, word was finally given to commence the operations. A tarpaulin was spread over a portion of the floor, along with two pairs of trestles, on which a board was placed to make a table top. The layers of black mould and earth had already been dug up. Expertly, the workmen lifted the heavy flagstones with crowbars, and pushed them away on rollers. The vault – a glare of white-painted bricks – was thereby exposed, as far down as the marble slab which acted as a shelf for the coffin of T. C. Druce's second wife, Annie May. An electric light was hung over the grave, and a ladder lowered into the gaping hole. Then the workmen descended gingerly, passing ropes underneath the coffin and raising it to the surface. Next, they descended again into the vault to number the slabs making up the stone shelf, with a view to their exact replacement. The cement joints between the slabs were cut, to expose a coffin on the right-hand side; but when the workmen attempted to clear the dust and dirt off the face of the coffin, they were stopped and ordered to remove all the slabs that made up the shelf. As they chiselled away, large lumps of lime and stone fell on the coffins. But at last, the whole of the bottom level of the vault was exposed. On the right side lay the coffin of Anna Maria's husband Walter Druce, together with the tiny coffin of a baby – the dead child of Sidney Druce, T. C. Druce's second son by Annie May. On the left side was the coffin of Thomas Charles Druce himself. There then followed a long and expectant pause of whispering and shuffling of feet, as everybody awaited the arrival of the physicians, who were to inspect the contents of the coffin.

At 10.20 a.m. precisely the medical men arrived: Dr Augustus Joseph Pepper and Sir Thomas Stevenson. Dr Pepper came with a recommendation from the Home Office, and was a surgeon and pathologist of considerable distinction. Sir Thomas was a well-known toxicologist and forensic chemist, who had served as expert in a number of famous poisoning cases, including the Pimlico Mystery, the case of Florence Maybrick and that of George Chapman.

When the medical men arrived, the workmen once again descended into the vault, and hoisted up T. C. Druce's coffin with ropes. It was a large, old-fashioned coffin, approximately six feet five and a quarter inches in length, covered in blackish-coloured cloth and studded with brass nails. Of the six brass handles, one had come off, but the coffin was otherwise in remarkably good condition, save for some fraying at the sides and wasting at the edge of the lid. Once the nameplate on the coffin was carefully washed, the inscription became clearly visible:

THOMAS CHARLES DRUCE,

Esqre.,

Died 28th Decr.,

1864,

In his 71st year.

Above the inscription was a trefoil brass cross, and below it a Maltese brass cross. Robert Caldwell, in his evidence, had been adamant that there was no inscription on the coffin. If the age stated was correct, it would have made T. C. Druce's birth date 1792 or 1793 – seven years before the birth of the 5th Duke of Portland.

The diggers then left. Two workmen entered the shed bearing powerful pliers, with which they unscrewed the lid of the oak coffin. Within the coffin, there was found to be a leaden shell, bearing the same inscription as the outer coffin of oak. The lid of the leaden shell was then cut away, taking with it an inner, wooden casing. An electric light was suspended above the exposed contents of the coffin, the glare of the beam bouncing wildly as it swung over the expectant group. All craned to get a glimpse inside the coffin. A collective gasp rippled around the enclosed confines of the shed.

The Police Court

One week later

One of the most serious and cruel cases which have
been brought before a Court of Justice.

MR JUSTICE GRANTHAM
with reference to the Druce–Portland case, May 1908

O
n Twelfth Night, 6 January 1908, the Druce–
Portland case came up – this time at the Clerkenwell Police Court – for its fourteenth and last court
hearing. The witnesses of the exhumation of the grave at
Highgate were called immediately.

First in the stand was Mr Leslie Robert Vigers, a member
of the Institute of Surveyors. He had made a careful preliminary examination of the site prior to the exhumation, and
it was under his supervision that the monument had been
removed. He testified that the marble slabs and York stones
covering the grave had been lifted on the morning of Monday, 30 December. First to be exposed had been the coffin
of Mrs Annie Druce, T. C. Druce's second wife, resting on
a floor consisting of eight York stone slabs about one and a
half inches in thickness. When these slabs were raised, a vault
consisting of two compartments was revealed. The coffin containing the body of Thomas Charles Druce had been lifted
out of the vault. The floor of the grave was made of bricks,

pointed up and whitened. In the half of the vault from which
T. C. Druce's coffin had been removed, a sample of bricks was
lifted and the soil beneath tested with a crowbar, driven in as
far as a man was able in two places, to see if the clay beneath
had been disturbed. It was found to be quite solid: so-called
'virgin clay'. There was no lead to be found anywhere in the
vault or near the coffin. In fact it was clear, Vigers said, that
the soil of the vault had not been tampered with, and that the
grave and coffin appeared to have been undisturbed since
1864.

Next in the witness box came Dr Augustus Pepper, who
had attended the exhumation as a medical expert along with
Sir Thomas Stevenson. He had arrived at the vault at 10.20
a.m. on the morning of Monday, 30 December, to find it
opened and three coffins lined up on the floor of the grave.
The coffin bearing the inscription of Thomas Charles Druce
was raised under his supervision. The three layers of wood,
lead and inner casing of the coffin were then opened up. In the
inner shell there was the shape of a human body, covered by a
shroud of white cambric.

'Was there anything over the face?' demanded Horace
Avory. The atmosphere in the police court suddenly crackled
with electricity.

'A linen handkerchief about the size of a pocket handkerchief,' came the response.

'Any mark on it?'

'The initials "TCD", and the figure "12".'

'And on removing the sheet in which the body was
wrapped, what did you find the body to be?'

There was pause. 'A male body, aged... ,' came the reply.

Dr Pepper went on to estimate that the age of the body was about sixty-five to seventy-five. It was extremely well preserved. The skin was broken on only one part of the body. The doctor had with him at the scene one of the 'carte de visite' photographs of Thomas Charles Druce that had been produced earlier in the proceedings, showing the bearded Druce in a standing position. He was of the view that there was a 'striking general resemblance' between the photograph and the features of the corpse. The head was covered with scanty reddish-brown hair, the eyebrows thick and wavy. The beard was very bushy and the hair was coarse. It was natural hair, still attached to the skin, and had not fallen off anywhere. When Dr Pepper examined the body, he found there to be a marked difference between the upper and lower regions. In the lower parts of the trunk, there was extreme decay. This was consistent, he said, with the presence of abscesses or a destructive disease of some kind.

A peculiar feature of Dr Pepper's evidence was that, although a police photographer had been present at the time of the exhumation, no photographs of the grave or its contents were produced in court, or published afterwards in any newspaper. Had photographs of the coffin and remains been taken? If so, what did they show, and what had happened to them? Why had they been suppressed?

The final witness was George William Thackrah, a partner in the firm of Messrs Druce & Co. He had joined the firm in 1860, and had seen T. C. Druce almost daily until his death in 1864. He had been present at the exhumation and had seen the body in the coffin when the shroud was removed. He recognized the face distinctly as that of the late Thomas Charles Druce.

'You recognized him beyond a shadow of a doubt?' the magistrate asked keenly.

'Oh yes, beyond a shadow of doubt,' came the reply. 'There is no doubt whatever about it.'

There was silence in the courtroom as Llewellyn Atherley-Jones rose to his feet.

'Sir,' the advocate began, clearing his throat with a hint of nervousness, but nevertheless looking Mr Plowden steadily in the eye, 'I wish to give very shortly the views of the prosecution with regard to this case. You were good enough, when the question of the exhumation was first mentioned, to ask me – in a certain contingency – what view the prosecution would take of the case. I then answered that in my judgment, it would be practically impossible for the prosecution to proceed. Deliberation and anxious consideration since the happening of the event have confirmed the view that I then entertained.'

Pausing for an instant, he glanced towards the seated figure of Horace Avory, counsel for the defence. 'Sir,' he continued, 'I therefore have no hesitation in saying, speaking for myself and for those instructing me – that I now withdraw the prosecution.'

From the press gallery came murmurings, and a stifled exclamation. One of the fashionable ladies seated next to the judge fainted. Herbert Druce suddenly lost his stoop, and sat bolt upright. And, for the first time, the face of the 6th Duke of Portland lit up with a smile. For Atherley-Jones, the admission of the prosecution's defeat seemed a blessed release, and he appeared finally to relax. Horace Avory remained stonily silent and inscrutable. Did he know more about the secret lives of his clients than he chose to show? He was soon to receive a strange letter that would have shocked even those closest to the case. But for the moment his face, as always, revealed nothing.

There was a pause, as everyone waited for Mr Plowden to look up from his notes and speak. When the magistrate finally did so, his voice was grave. 'Gentlemen,' he said, adjusting his spectacles with a light cough, 'this inquiry may have taken some time, but I do not think any impartial person will say that the time has been wasted. The bubble which has floated so long and so mischievously out of reach has been effectually pricked at last. No one can now doubt that Thomas Charles Druce existed in fact; that he died in his own home in the midst of his family; and that he was buried in due course in the family vault in the cemetery in Highgate. His existence stands out as clear, as distinct, as undeniable as that of any human being that ever lived.' Directing a stern gaze towards the assembled journalists, Plowden continued: 'How the myth ever arose that confused Thomas Charles Druce and the 5th Duke of Portland as the same personality it would be idle to speculate. Sufficient to say that this case is an illustration of the love of the marvellous which is so deeply ingrained in human nature, and is likely to be remembered in legal annals as affording one more striking proof of the unfathomable depths of human credulity. The case is dismissed.' Turning then to Herbert Druce, he said in a much gentler tone: 'I have only one final word to say. Mr Herbert Druce leaves this court with his character for truthfulness absolutely and conclusively vindicated. Mr Druce, you are now discharged.'

Thus ended – ostensibly – one of the greatest legal sagas of the early twentieth century. Ten long years had passed since Anna Maria Druce first appeared before Chancellor Tristram with her application to open the Druce vault. During those ten years, a dozen judges had presided over fourteen court hearings; hundreds of legal personnel, from barristers to clerks, had spun arguments and taken down testimony; armies of investigators had combed through archives up and down the land; witnesses from three continents had been examined, cross-examined, and re-examined. Family secrets had been unearthed, shameful conduct exposed, and the lies that lurked beneath the respectable façade of Victorian society had been ruthlessly exposed before the public. Most of all, the Druce case had provided the world with one of its first global media sensations — a long-running saga that held the public in thrall, played out from Asia to the Antipodes, featured in every newspaper from the *New York Times* to the *Wanganui Chronicle*.

But the wider story was far from fully played out. For although one mystery about the life of the 5th Duke of Portland had been laid to rest, the case had raised many other questions, including the enigma of the shadowy 'lady fraternity' at Welbeck. Had the bachelor duke had something to hide after all? Not an alternative identity as T. C. Druce, admittedly, but some other dark secret? Who in the Cavendish-Bentinck family had been helping the Druce cause, and why? Most important of all was the question of who was behind the conspiracy at the heart of the Druce claim. Could the tracks of the perpetrators of this enormous falsehood — as it was now revealed to have been — be followed, before they were covered over?

Act Three

REVELATION

Truth is the daughter of time.

Attributed to SIR FRANCIS BACON,
English philosopher and statesman

The scene immediately after the opening of the Druce vault
(the *Penny Illustrated Paper*, 4 January 1908)

London and Welbeck

December 1907

> Many people read about detectives, and they see
> things upon the stage about detectives, and they
> think it is a very good sort of life; but when they
> come to try it they find it is earning your livelihood,
> like lifting bricks and everything else, and they get
> tired of it.

SUPERINTENDENT JAMES THOMSON, 1877

With its revelation of a dead body corresponding to the physical description of T. C. Druce, the opening of the Druce vault on Monday, 30 December 1907 was a fatal blow to the Druce claim, which had been founded on the contention that T. C. Druce's coffin was filled with lead. However, the claimants' case could be said to have started to disintegrate two weeks earlier, on Friday, 13 December, when Llewellyn Atherley-Jones disowned his star prosecution witness, Robert Caldwell. At the moment when Atherley-Jones effectively conceded that a key witness had probably lied on oath, there was a great commotion in court. A jubilant cheer rang out from the ranks of the defendants. Even the 6th Duke of Portland, who had attended virtually the whole of the trial, lost his anxious expression briefly. This was also the moment — as we have seen — when Edwin Freshfield was observed to confer with, and then exit the court in the company of, a solid-looking man in a blue serge suit. Inspector Dew – for the moustachioed man was no other than he – was determined that the perjurer Caldwell, along with the other witnesses who had lied on oath, should be brought to justice. He and Freshfield were therefore soon rattling in a four-wheeled cab through the backstreets of London at a cracking pace. Their mission was to obtain an audience with the chief magistrate, Sir Albert de Rutzen, at Bow Street Police Court. For it was from Sir Albert that they had the best hope of obtaining an immediate warrant for Caldwell's arrest, on the charge of suspected perjury. Unfortunately, however, on arrival at Bow Street, it was discovered that Sir Albert had already left court for the weekend. There was therefore no option other than to make haste to the chief magistrate's private residence at 18 Cranley Gardens, South Kensington. As the last rays of the setting sun struggled to pierce the night fog that was already seeping into the alleyways of the city, the pair finally managed to accost the chief magistrate on the steps of his home. After a hasty conference between the three men, it was decided that the warrant for Caldwell's arrest should be issued promptly the following morning.

Walter Dew therefore presented himself at Bow Street Court at the first light of dawn the next day, 14 December, and obtained the warrant from the chief clerk, Mr Newton. He then proceeded by four-wheeled cab to 15 Albert Road, Regent's Park – the home of Elizabeth Crickmer's nephew John, with whom Caldwell had been staying. A stiff-faced woman opened the door. Mr Caldwell, she informed him, had left the house at 8 a.m. on the morning of 12 December, taking a cabin trunk with him. He had informed her that he was going to Waterloo Station, en route to Southampton, and that he was leaving for America that day. The woman said she believed Caldwell's ticket had been purchased from Thomas Cook by someone from the 'Druce Office', and that Caldwell had very little money himself.

Walter Dew must have been bitterly disappointed at the news that the canny old bird had flown, a full two days before his pursuers had even sounded the alarm. However, with stoic professionalism, he pursued the line of inquiry with Cook's. He found out from the travel agency that a second-class passenger ticket had been purchased for Caldwell, who had left Waterloo at 10 a.m. on the morning of Thursday, 12 December. He was, apparently, bound for the American liner SS *Kaiserin Auguste Victoria*, which sailed that day for New York from Southampton. Caldwell was seen at the station by a representative of the Hamburg American Line Company, and his Cook's ticket exchanged for a ticket of that company. The agent was positive that the man he saw was the Robert Caldwell for whom Inspector Dew was searching – not least because, when Cook's telephoned the Hamburg American Line Company and asked, 'Is this the Caldwell in the Druce case?' the reply received was an affirmative.

The SS *Kaiserin Auguste Victoria* was due to dock in New York the following Friday, 20 December. A coded message was accordingly sent to police in New York, to seize the passenger immediately upon disembarkation, with a description of the wanted man: age seventy-one, height five feet seven inches, pale complexion, very grey hair, with a moustache and receding hairline. All steamers that had docked at Cherbourg en route to New York after 12 December were to be

watched closely. If necessary, a lawyer named Selden Bacon –
whom the duke's solicitors had employed to shadow Caldwell
– could be called on to identify him. A briefing was sent by
Freshfields to Lord Desart, director of public prosecutions, in
order for his office to prepare papers seeking Caldwell's extradition, on landing, from the American authorities.

There was nothing further to be done, for the moment,
other than wait for the prey to walk into the trap. In any event,
Dew's attention was quickly diverted by another troubling
event. The 6th Duke's butler, Ballard, had recently observed
a shady-looking character hanging around his master's London residence. The man – about fifty years old, rather stout,
with a full grey beard and gold-rimmed glasses – had, on several occasions, knocked at the front door, and asked to see his
Grace. Dew went to interview the grave, reserved old servant. 'I didn't recognize the fellow,' Ballard told him. 'But he
said he was in direct contact with people his Grace might like
to know about. He claimed it was quite in his Grace's interest
that he wished to see him, and concerned no one else.' Walter
Dew sighed. Another headache to tax his already overloaded
brain. And yet, Ballard's description of the man called to mind
someone else who had been linked to the Druce case… Something to do with Anna Maria Druce… But for the moment, he
couldn't for the devil recall what it was. Ah well. He would
have to go through the files again.

As Walter Dew pored over his files on the Druce case,
attempting in vain to find a clue to the identity of the 6th
Duke's mysterious stalker, the duke's land agent, Thomas

Warner Turner, faced a problem of his own. A chubby and ebullient figure, Turner had served the Cavendish-Bentincks all his life, and was devoted to William, the 6th Duke. His father, F. J. Turner, had been land agent to both the 5th and 6th Dukes, and William had given him a touching credit for his forty-eight years of service at the 1906 Welbeck Tenants' Show:

> When I first came to Welbeck, now twenty-seven years ago, I was a mere boy, very ignorant of the ways of the world, and more ignorant still, if it were possible, of business habits and of the management of a great estate. I shudder to think what might have been my fate, and the sad fate of those dependent upon me, if Mr Turner and others, who guided my footsteps, had been different from what they proved themselves to be. It was in his power to make or mar the happiness and prosperity, not only of myself, but also of many of those who live in this district and who farm my land.

Turner was proving himself a worthy son to follow in his father's footsteps. In fact, he had already scored a triumph by discovering the ruse by which the 5th Duke's old overcoat had been acquired by the Druce party from its owner. On the death of the 5th Duke, most of his old clothes had been inherited by his trusty valet, John Harrington. When Harrington died, the clothes were divided between his children. On making inquiries, Turner had discovered that in the spring of 1906, a former abbey servant, Joseph Stubbings, had paid a call on Harrington's daughter, Bertha Lambourn. Stubbings had been accompanied by an unidentified man and woman.

The woman had told Bertha that she collected curios, and had an umbrella once owned by the Duke of Marlborough. Would Bertha be so kind as to show her some items of the late duke's clothing? After much pressing by the lady, Bertha had reluctantly brought out a shoe, a black coat and inverness cape* 'very much worn', an old umbrella, a night-cap and a wig. The couple wanted to pay her for them, but Bertha refused. Taking the items, the woman expressed her thanks, and said they would be valuable additions to her collection. She gave Bertha some silver for the children's money-box, and placed a sovereign on the mantelpiece. The trio then departed. According to Bertha's description, the man who accompanied Stubbings was tall, well-built and broad-shouldered with short grey hair, a grey moustache, a fresh face and a brusque manner. The woman professed to be the man's wife, but was very much younger than him, and although well-dressed with a seal-skin hat and plume, did not appear to Bertha to be a lady.

Turner was delighted with his uncovering of the subterfuge. 'I fancy my information will checkmate the blackguards and make John Conquest look small, as I firmly believe from the description given of the man who secured the coat that he is the scoundrel who smuggled it away by a trick,' he wrote triumphantly to the duke's solicitor, Horseman Bailey. 'And if you want some of the 5th Duke's coats to wear in court, I shall forward sufficient tomorrow morning to allow each member of your firm to appear in one!' He went on: 'I have been on the track all day, and I feel I am quite qualified for a leading position in the detective force at Scotland Yard!'

* A form of sleeveless weatherproof overcoat.

Turner's latest detective assignment for the 6th Duke, however, this December of 1907, was proving a much harder case for the estate manager-turned-amateur sleuth to crack. A key claim of the Druce camp had been that a large photograph of a clean-shaven man with whiskers – said to be a picture of Thomas Charles Druce, and to have been in George Hollamby's family for over thirty years – was a photograph taken from a portrait of the 5th Duke, alleged to have hung in Welbeck Abbey, until destroyed by fire. During the court proceedings before the magistrate Plowden in early December 1907, Nurse Bayly had voiced the opinion that this portrait was in fact a photograph of Thomas Charles Druce in his younger years, before he grew a beard. The Cavendish-Bentinck family had always denied that any photograph of the reclusive 5th Duke existed; and the only officially acknowledged portraits of his Grace were paintings by the portraitists Joshua Dighton and Leslie Ward, together with busts by the sculptors Sir Edgar Boehm and Henry Richard Hope-Pinker. Both the Leslie Ward portrait and the busts had been commissioned posthumously. In addition, there existed a marble model of the 5th Duke's left hand, based on a cast made upon his death, showing it to be one of remarkable fineness and delicacy.

In the run-up to the 1907 perjury trial, the 6th Duke had been anxious to acquire all the existing portraits of his predecessor. He had therefore instructed Turner to purchase any such portraits as he could find before they could be exploited by the other side. The Druce camp was desperate to do the same. The race to acquire portraits of the 5th Duke created a lively trade for art dealers, many of whom shuttled between one side and the other, in a bid to drive up prices. The 6th Duke was also eager to track down any pictures commissioned by his predecessor, including the portraits of Adelaide Kemble by John Hayter. In particular, he had told Turner that it was imperative to find a series of paintings of Adelaide in an opera with the enigmatic title of *The Secret Marriage*. (Adelaide had performed in an English version of Domenico Cimarosa's opera, *ll matrimonio segreto*, in 1842.) Strenuous efforts were therefore made to track down the *Secret Marriage* paintings, and when practically all of Hayter's paintings of Adelaide were finally found, they were kept under lock and key in the abbey.

How, Turner wondered, was he to prove that the alleged photograph of the 5th Duke touted about by the Druce contingent never hung in Welbeck Abbey? Certainly, it was not listed in any of the detailed catalogues of the Welbeck collection that had been produced by successive curators. The position was complicated by the fact that the 5th Duke – in characteristically eccentric fashion – had taken it into his head to make a bonfire of a sizeable number of the abbey paintings in 1864. Richard Goulding, the librarian at Welbeck, had been assigned the task of investigating the burning, and had calculated that approximately eighty to a hundred pictures had been torched. Most of those that had been burned, Goulding told Turner, were much dilapidated, or appeared to have represented nude figures. He showed Turner a pencilled note made by Charles Taylor, the Welbeck curator at the time, in the margins of a catalogue of the collection, next to the entry for a painting called *Nude Figures Sleeping*:

May 30th 1864. My son John tells me that the Duke is burning pictures; I suppose it will be such as this — which was
only fit to burn. It was more than I had power to do.

But Turner could see that it was going to be virtually impossible to prove that the portrait paraded by the Druce contingent
was not one of those that had gone up in flames. There was
no doubt that the 5th Duke detested being portrayed in visual
form: in 1876 he had even dismissed three workmen who had
dared send a caricature of him to a local newspaper. Sighing,
Turner turned his attention to a much more exciting prospect
— the promised visit to Welbeck, in the coming weeks, of the
famous detective, Walter Dew, to further his investigations.

The object of Turner's excited anticipation, meanwhile, had
just received a telegram that sent him immediately to the Home
Office. On 21 December 1907, Walter Dew was informed
that the SS *Kaiserin Auguste Victoria* had docked at Hoboken,
New Jersey, and that Robert Caldwell had been arrested on
disembarkation, at the request of the British authorities.

London and Worksop

January 1908

'Very strange things comes to our knowledge in
families, miss; bless your heart, what you would
think to be phenomenons, quite... Aye, and even in
genteel families, in high families, in great families...
and you have no idea... what games goes on!'

CHARLES DICKENS
Bleak House

Chief Inspector Dew's triumph at engineering the
arrest of Robert Caldwell on his arrival in America
was short-lived. For the old man, ever-resourceful,
managed to get himself released on $5000 bail, for reasons
of ill health. And worse was to follow. On 14 February 1908,
Caldwell's daughter filed a petition asking that her father
be declared a lunatic. On the same day, two doctors swore
before the Commissioner of Deeds in the city of New York
that Caldwell was insane. The doctors' reports were hardly
a ringing endorsement of Caldwell's reliability as a witness.
According to one, 'Robert Caldwell gave a history of suffering from hallucinatory episodes and described hallucinations
of fantastic and terrifying character.' The doctor was, moreover, of the opinion that he was 'suffering from paranoia, and
had been so suffering *for the past year or more*'. 'My father',
Caldwell's daughter stated, 'has always exhibited a marked

tendency to claim intimate and cordial relations with various prominent men, and to have knowledge of important facts regarding conspicuous trials or mysteries, which may have from time to time been given widespread notice in the public press.' She added that, when her father first told her about his intimacy with the 5th Duke of Portland and his curing of the Duke's diseased nose, she had thought him quite mad; but the fact that his story was corroborated by lawyers from England had convinced her that it was true.

The upshot was that far from being handed over to the British authorities for extradition and trial for perjury in England, Robert Caldwell languished in the sprawling, Gothic monolith of the Manhattan Hospital for the Insane on Wards Island, surrounded by the shrieks and groans of New York's demented. Meanwhile, the legal wrangling continued over whether he was in a fit state to be deported to England. Dr William Mabon, the superintendent of the Manhattan State Hospital, was an alienist of note and a plain-speaking New Yorker who was not about to be bullied by the British Consular authorities. 'Our examination of the patient', Mabon declared in his report, 'reveals a man in advanced years, who shows evidence of senile changes, namely, arterial thickening, muscular weakness, and such physical condition as requires his nearly continuous confinement to bed.' The patient made 'statements regarding the Druce case which appear to have some foundation, but, reasoning on false grounds, he has apparently taken on a well-fixed delusional formation'. Mabon added – apparently without a hint of irony – that Caldwell also had 'some defect in his grasp on recent historical events'.

Faced with the unattractive prospect of forcing the

extradition of a sick old man who might well expire on their watch and cause an embarrassing public scandal, the Home Office authorities – despite the strong protestations of Inspector Dew, Freshfields and the 6th Duke's solicitors – were inclined to back down. There were also the not insignificant costs of a protracted legal battle to consider, which the Home Office was reluctant to incur.

Dew paced the leafy embankment fronting New Scotland Yard, grimacing with frustration. A bitter January wind cut through the oil-cloth cloak that he pulled tightly around his hunched shoulders. Ahead of him, the River Thames was in even greater tumult than usual, heaving with a mass of barges and packet boats that were busy ferrying stocks and supplies to the newly established stadium at White City, built to host that year's Olympic Games. Dew glared at the river steamers that endlessly ferried thousands of London commuters to and from their daily business. The wretched old man, Caldwell, was a fraud – there was no doubt about it. Dew had just received a statement from a Mr Joseph Roulston, a fellow passenger on Caldwell's voyage from New York to England on board the SS *Minnetonka* in 1907, when Caldwell was coming to England to give evidence in court. The statement related that Caldwell had spent much of that journey talking about his time in Londonderry. Dew had also interviewed the daughter of the late Captain Joyce, the army officer whom Caldwell claimed had cured him of a bulbous nose in India. She was adamant that her father had never set foot in India, and the records showed that Joyce had been in Gibraltar throughout the time of which Caldwell had spoken. And then there was

Caldwell's preposterous claim of having been consulted by the then teenage surgeon-in-training, Sir Morell Mackenzie.

Dew shook his fist at a four-wheeled cab, which had carelessly splashed his blue serge suit with gutter water in passing. If the general public only knew how frustrating the detective business was, there would be none of this fascination with Sherlock Holmes and the like. But Dew was soon to have better success in his hunt for the conspirators. Another of the Druce party's witnesses was about to fall into his net.

Thomas Warner Turner beamed with satisfaction as he read over the telegram that was handed to him by Horseman Bailey, the 6th Duke's solicitor. He could hardly think of three words that would have given him greater pleasure. The telegram was from J. G. Littlechild, one of the private investigators tailing the Druce party on the Duke's behalf. It read simply: 'Woman just arrested.' The terse words glossed over the high drama of what had happened on Friday, 17 January 1908, in the normally quiet suburban streets of Lavender Hill, south London. That morning, a warrant had been issued for the arrest of Miss Mary Robinson, the second key witness in the Druce case. She it was who had testified to being the duke's amanuensis, or 'outdoor secretary', and to have seen Druce/the duke as Little Red Riding Hood's grandmother in a show of amateur theatricals. All that day, Detective Inspector Walter Dew had kept a close eye on the rented flat in Lavender Hill in which Miss Robinson and her companion, Miss O'Neill, had been staying. He was armed with his warrant. Finally, at 8 p.m., he and a fellow officer had forced their way into the property.

'Your name is Mary Ann Robinson,' Dew said, before reading out the warrant for the lady's arrest on the grounds of suspected perjury.

'Mary Robinson,' she corrected him. 'Well, now then, how have I committed perjury, that is what I want to know?'

'At the police court you said that your name was 'Miss Mary Robinson', that you were born in America and that your father was the owner of a tobacco plantation,' Dew replied. 'But it is alleged that your name is 'Mrs Mary Ann Robinson', that your father's name was Webb and that he was a police sergeant in the 'V' Division, for many years stationed at Mortlake.'

'Good God, who told you that?' asked the lady.

Dew remained unperturbed. 'That is what is said, and I have a photograph which is said to be you, and that you were married to a butcher named William Robinson at Leeds in 1863.'

At this, the woman sullenly stepped aside, and allowed Dew and his fellow officer to inspect the flat. Having confiscated a pile of documents, Dew laid a hand upon her shoulder. She did not resist. As she was led out, she whispered fiercely to Miss O'Neill: 'I won't say a word, I'll die first.' Her companion replied, with equal vehemence, 'Nor will I, they can kill me first!'

The next day, Saturday, 18 January 1908, 'Miss Mary Robinson' – or rather, to give her her true name, 'Mrs Mary Ann Robinson, née Webb' – appeared in court at Bow Street, charged with perjury. Walter Dew was not pleased to see that she was represented by Edmund Kimber, the solicitor who was acting at the helm of the Druce claim. Dew was convinced that Kimber was of the shadiest breed of solicitor, operating barely within the boundaries of the law. He had in the past been accused by one of his clients of committing perjury, and although he had been cleared, there was no smoke without fire, in Inspector Dew's opinion. A further stain on Kimber's character in Dew's eyes was the fact that he had also represented that archetypal fraud, Arthur Orton, the butcher from Wagga Wagga who had claimed the Tichborne title. Dew was sure that Kimber had only offered to represent Mrs Robinson to protect his own interests, and indeed the solicitor was even then busy writing letters to the newspapers claiming that the lady was mad. Kimber had gone so far as to write to the Lunacy Commission, stating that he was willing to make submissions in support, should they be so minded to commit Mrs Robinson to a lunatic asylum. How very convenient, Dew muttered to himself.

From his researches, Detective Inspector Dew was sure that Mrs Robinson was not mad. As to whether she was cunning and avaricious, of course, that was a different matter. Following his own favourite adage that 'dogged perseverance has brought far more criminals to book than flashes of genius', Dew had for months been supervising a detailed search of local records. Throughout the country, dozens of detectives had been conducting hundreds of personal interviews, trying to piece together the true story of the duke's self-professed 'amanuensis'. The turning point in this investigation had been the discovery of Mrs Robinson's long-lost younger brother, now an insurance agent in Barnes. From the identification evidence of the brother, Dew was satisfied that he could prove that 'Miss Mary Robinson' was in fact Mary Ann Webb, the daughter of a Metropolitan Police officer, who had married a butcher by the name of Robinson in 1863. Her so-called 'lady companion', Miss O'Neill, was in fact her daughter, Maud. The family had emigrated to New Zealand at some point in the 1870s, and in 1886 Mr Robinson had died. After this, mother and daughter had lived in various districts of Christchurch, finally settling in the coastal suburb of New Brighton in 1906.

Information that the Home Office had received from the Christchurch police and passed on to Dew suggested that Mrs Robinson and her daughter were a thoroughly bad lot. There was, for instance, the case of a mysterious fire that burned down the Christchurch house they had been letting in 1906 – an occasion for Mrs Robinson to make the then enormous claim of £400 on the household insurance policy, taken out to cover a collection of valuable jewellery and furniture, including a piano. The local police, Dew was informed, had always regarded the incident as highly suspicious, but the true cause of the fire had never been proved. Dew was fairly sure it had been started by the Robinson women themselves, in order to claim on the policy. Mrs Robinson had stated that everything in the house had been destroyed by the fire. How, therefore, could her diary – if genuine – have escaped intact? 'There is no doubt', wrote a Christchurch police officer to Scotland Yard, 'that Mrs Robinson is a fraud.'

The 6th Duke, only too delighted to facilitate the perjury prosecution, sent the Home Office a cheque for £500* to pay the travel expenses of any New Zealand police officers

* Equivalent to more than £50,000 today.

required to attend a future trial of Mary Ann Robinson. However, from the local knowledge demonstrated by some of her statements in court, it seemed likely that Mary Ann had, at some point, been at Welbeck. She referred, for example, to the town of Worksop in the same dialect as locals, as 'Warsop'; and her description of 'Lady Hill' corresponded with Lead Hill, an area of the town that was known to be a rough place. Neighbours in Christchurch also recalled that Mrs Robinson had talked a great deal about her time at Welbeck Abbey from the moment she arrived, and that she had adopted the most extraordinary airs and graces. The precise nature of Mary Ann's contact with Worksop had yet to be clarified. And so it was that Detective Inspector Dew travelled to the town on the afternoon of Wednesday, 22 January 1908, finally fulfilling a promise of long standing to visit the hub of the wheel around which the Druce case still so tantalizingly turned. His mission: to find out exactly what had been 'Miss' Robinson's business at Welbeck Abbey.

Thomas Warner Turner waited impatiently in the flock-wallpapered vestibule of the Royal Hotel on the Market Place at Worksop. He had some important news to tell Inspector Dew – information that he was bursting to impart. When the great detective himself appeared, descending the oak stairway that led down from the guest rooms, Turner was at first surprised by his appearance in the flesh. Could this bland and avuncular figure, the 'major in mufti' with a sandy moustache and dressed in a blue serge suit, really be the famous detective of whom he had read so much in the newspapers? Swallowing his surprise, Turner advanced with hand outstretched. It did not take him long to brief the inspector on his discovery. He had, that very morning, found out that Mary Ann Robinson's husband had been employed as a shepherd on the Welbeck estate, around the year 1872. If the inspector was so minded, they could interview the informant – an old shepherd still employed on the estate – that very day.

Soon Dew and Turner were rattling in a cart from Worksop to the neighbouring hamlet of Cuckney. There, on a windswept farm, they spoke with two elderly shepherds who recalled William Robinson quite well. He was employed by the 5th Duke for about a year, they said, and had been discharged because his dog had worried the sheep. They knew he had a wife, but could not recollect meeting her. She was known, they said, to 'be a loose character in Worksop'. The next day Mr Whall, a local solicitor who had been searching the registers of births, marriages and deaths on Turner's behalf, telephoned Dew at the Royal Hotel to say that he had found death certificates for a daughter named Kate Ellen Robinson, who had died at Lead Hill, Worksop, on 6 August 1870, at the age of six, from smallpox; and for a son named Frederick Robinson, aged three, also living at Lead Hill, and also suffering from the same disease. Dew, without a moment's hesitation, established that the signatures on each of the death certificates were identical to the one on the papers relating to the Christchurch fire insurance claim. So this was the reality of Mary Ann Robinson's connection with Welbeck: far from being the Duke's confidante and personal secretary, she had in fact been married to a shepherd who had worked, for barely a year, on the abbey farms.

While Inspector Dew was well satisfied at the day's outcome, Thomas Warner Turner was rather more circumspect. He had not told the inspector all that he ought to have told him. The cause of Turner's unease was the contents of a letter that he had received two months previously, in late November 1907, from a local businessman by the name of Arthur Markham. Markham was a conceited fellow, who had got himself into trouble with the local press in the past, on account of his overbearing behaviour. However, the information that he had imparted in his letter to Turner was troubling.

In his letter, Markham related how he had fallen into conversation recently with a local farmer called John Crowder. Crowder had been employed as the 5th Duke's foreman on the building works at the abbey. For the last four or five years of the duke's life, Crowder had seen him every day, reporting to nobody else. On his master's instructions, he had been given a lodge facing the old abbey, looking directly onto the duke's suite of rooms above the abbey entrance porch. From his window in the lodge, Crowder could even see the duke's bedroom. The duke, he said, was nearly always up at 5.30 in the morning, and he frequently saw his tall figure silhouetted against the bedroom window in the early hours.

Over the years, Crowder said, he had become extremely attached to and protective of his master. He recalled that the late duke would take long nightly rambles over the Welbeck estate, even in rain or hail. In particular, he liked to roam the rugged terrain of Cresswell Crags, a deep gorge nearby that cut through the gentle slopes of the surrounding Nottinghamshire countryside. Before striking out into the darkness, the duke would strap a large bull's-eye lantern on a belt round his body. Crowder, anxious for his safety, took to following him in these midnight rambles. He recalled how the duke once got into difficulty in boggy ground in the shrubbery in the early hours of the morning. Crowder was obliged to get hold of some planks to enable his Grace to clamber out.

Markham's letter also touched on questions he had put to Crowder concerning the duke's relationships with women. Crowder had been adamant that the duke saw no women whatsoever during the time that he served him, except a young lady called Annie Roper and her sister, Becky. They were the daughters of a baker on the Welbeck estate, and were both in their twenties. According to Crowder, the duke had a lodge built especially for the two young women. There were three keys to the lodge, one each for the two sisters and his Grace. The duke, Crowder said, used to 'go into' the lodge with these two women, at about seven or eight o'clock at night.

After reading Markham's letter, Turner interviewed Crowder personally. When questioned by the land agent, Crowder changed his story to say that he had merely seen the duke speaking to the two young ladies. However, when he interviewed the other servants, it became apparent to Turner that the duke did indeed have an intimate relationship with the two sisters. In particular, it seemed that he had been very fond of Annie Roper. Joseph Burns, an old employee on the building works, related to Turner that he remembered Miss Roper, and that he himself used to take books and sometimes notes to her from the duke, who would also tell him what to say, such as: 'Tell Miss Roper I shall be passing at six o'clock' (although he never said for what purpose). Once, Burns said, he saw the duke with Miss Roper when they were working near the lodge in which she lived. In fact, he thought that the work they were doing there was only being carried out as an excuse for the duke to speak to her. On at least one occasion, the duke went into the house with Miss Roper.

A former gamekeeper at the abbey, Bernard Boaler, also recalled Annie Roper. The duke, he told Turner, fenced off a plantation of evergreens of about four or five acres. There were three ways to get into it, but there was only one official entrance gate, which was kept securely locked. Nobody was permitted to enter the plantation, except the duke and Miss Roper. In its dark and secret depths was a little summerhouse. According to Boaler's account, Miss Roper always dressed well, appeared to have plenty of money, and used to go to London – thus fuelling gossip as to her relations with the duke, who was then well over sixty. Boaler added that the 5th Duke had also been associated with another woman, a cook named Jane Walton. But he left it cryptically at that, giving no further information about her. Further investigations revealed that Annie Roper had subsequently married a man named Baker, and moved north. Her sister, Becky, had remained a spinster.

Turner's interviews with the duke's old servants also shed light on the old rumours that his Grace was incapable of fathering an heir owing to an injury suffered in his youth. An old teller of underwood cuttings, who had married the daughter of the 4th Duke's stud groom, told Turner the story. 'I heard', related the old man, 'that the three young Lords, Lord John, Lord George and Lord Henry, were riding and larking across the country to Fitzpatrick the Tailor of Worksop. Lord John's horse stumbled, and he was thrown onto the pommel of the saddle, and as a result a London doctor said he would not ever be any good to a woman.' The duke's valet of ten years, Henry Powell, supported the old man's story. He would regularly rub down the duke with glycerine for his eczema, he told Turner, and 'when seeing him naked had observed that he was badly ruptured'. He also noticed that the duke's testicles 'hung down very much'. Furthermore, a man called William Higgs had also written to Baileys, Shaw & Gillett, the 6th Duke's legal advisors, in December 1907. In this letter Higgs stated that his father, a builder, had done a great deal of work for the 5th Duke, and on his Grace's death his butler, Lewis, had given him a truss for a rupture of the right side of the groin, for his own personal use. From this, it was apparent to Turner that the 5th Duke had suffered from an untreated groin hernia on the right side, which might well have prevented him from having children. The hernia would also explain his refusal to ride in later years, turning his back on a pastime that had been a passion of his youth.

Turner's interviews with the 5th Duke's old servants would provide useful ammunition for the defence of the Druce claim, and witness statements of their testimony were drafted accordingly. The fact that Crowder was prepared to swear that the 5th Duke saw no women other than the Roper sisters in the 1870s contradicted Mary Ann Robinson's claims to have been his 'outside secretary'. Similarly, the evidence that the late duke suffered from a groin hernia, rendering procreation unlikely, struck a blow to the very heart of the claim that he had married in secret under the guise of T. C. Druce, and fathered several children. On the other hand, as a gentleman born and bred, Turner found the thought of exposing the 5th Duke's private affairs abhorrent. The idea of such confidential information being mauled over by press hounds and paraded before the general public was unthinkable. Luckily for him, however, the problem was about to be solved by itself, without him needing to breathe a word of the duke's secret. For on Monday, 27 January 1908, the Home Office received the following message, transmitted via the Medical Officer at Holloway Prison:

To the Chief Inspector of Police, New Scotland Yard.

Mary Robinson would feel much obliged if the Chief would send an Inspector to see her at the above Prison.

(sgd) Mary Robinson.

A matter of days after his return from Welbeck, Inspector Dew found himself on the way to Holloway Prison. Mary Ann Robinson, it would appear, was about to make a confession.

Holloway Prison

January 1908

The criminal is the creative artist;
the detective only the critic.

G. K. CHESTERTON
The Blue Cross: A Father Brown Mystery

The four-wheeled cab pulled to a halt outside a pair of iron gates, which cast their shadow over the busy thoroughfare. Behind the gates rose a mass of Gothic battlements, towers and pinnacles. Holloway Prison, when it was built in 1852, had been modelled on the front of Warwick Castle. Originally envisaged as a mixed prison, it had over the course of the nineteenth century come to house predominantly women, in response to the increased demand for space to incarcerate the prostitutes, Molly cutpurses, thieves and drunks who constituted London's burgeoning female criminal population.

Accompanied by a fellow officer, Inspector Dew rang the doorbell, at which a wary eye appeared at the grating. Then, after a deafening clanking of bolts and turning of keys in ancient locks, the two officers were let in. A melancholy prison guard led them through a series of winding, gas-lit passages. They passed through a courtyard overgrown with weeds, and continued on to a large reception room, flanked by narrow

individual cells. The pale shafts of winter sunlight that struggled through the window casements made barely an impression on the dingy walls. Mary Ann Robinson awaited them in
one of the cells, accompanied by the prison matron and two
strapping female wardens. Dew barely recognized the confident woman who had given evidence scarcely a month ago in
the crowded police court. Now, she was pale and drawn.

As Dew had expected, Robinson announced that she had
decided to plead guilty to the charge of perjury, and to make
a full confession. She then went on to tell her story. It was an
extraordinary tale, even in the light of the bizarre revelations
that Inspector Dew had come to expect of the Druce case.

Mary Ann related how she had been living in 1906 as a
widow in the suburbs of Christchurch, New Zealand, with her
daughter Maud. One day, she saw an advertisement in a local
newspaper, seeking people who knew anything about the 5th
Duke of Portland. Having lived briefly on the Welbeck estate
thirty years previously, she responded to the advertisement.
About three weeks later, two men came to call on her. One of
them said that his name was Druce. When she subsequently
met George Hollamby in person, Mary Ann was positive that
he was not the man who had visited her in Christchurch in
1906. The two men, however, were extremely similar – the
visitor had the same blue eyes and bushy moustache as George
Hollamby. She believed the man may have been George Hollamby's younger brother, Charles.*

---

* The identity of the 'man named Druce' who visited Mary Ann in
Christchurch has never been established for certain. It is likely that he was
a relative of George Hollamby.

The 'man named Druce' told Mary Ann that he had heard she was clever at writing, and that if she did as he asked, she would receive £4000.* The task was easy: all she had to do was write down everything she knew about the 5th Duke from her time at Welbeck, and make it as attractive as possible, to help them get the funds to fight their case. The visitor explained in outline the Druce claim that the 5th Duke of Portland had led a double life as T. C. Druce of Baker Street. Mary Ann was, in any event, familiar with the case from the extensive reporting of the proceedings to date in the New Zealand newspapers.

Mary Ann immediately set to work. As her father's favourite, she had been privileged to receive an education at the progressive teacher-training institution, the Home and Colonial College. It was an unusual distinction for a policeman's daughter at the time. Gifted from her childhood days with a knack for telling stories, she did not find it difficult to amalgamate the information that had been fed to her by the visitor named Druce, the newspaper accounts of the Druce case, and her own recollections of her brief sojourn at Welbeck as a shepherd's wife in the 1870s, into a highly romantic and fictionalized account of a young girl's encounter with a mysterious and haunted nobleman, who lived a double life as a tradesman named Druce. As she compiled her story, George Hollamby and Thomas Coburn – who were then in England preparing the case – kept in touch with her by letter, sending her pamphlets with further information about the claim. Having written out her 'diary' on sheets of notepaper and being well

* More than £400,000 in today's money.

satisfied with the result, Mary Ann transcribed the pages into a copybook that she bought cheaply at an auction house.

Early in 1907, George Hollamby and Thomas Coburn cabled Mary Ann £250 to enable her to come to England with her daughter, Maud. On board ship, she took on the name of 'Miss Mary Robinson', and Maud posed as her female companion, 'Miss O'Neill'. When they disembarked at Plymouth, Mary Ann and Maud were met by the Druce party's legal men, Edmund Kimber and Thomas Coburn. Mr Kimber said to her, 'We want to make a sensation: there is nothing done without it.' On the train to London, there was a lot of talk about the Druce case. Kimber kept repeating to her, over and over: 'Stick to your tale, stick to your tale.' As they pulled into London, he told her: 'You will get your £4000 without a murmur, perhaps £5000, if you will stick to your guns.' Mary Ann also recalled that, during the course of the train journey, a strange incident took place. An unknown woman came up to her in the carriage and said, 'Mrs Robinson, beware.' Mary Ann later saw her in court, but she never found out who she was.

On their arrival in London, Mary Ann and her daughter were introduced to George Hollamby, whom everybody addressed as 'Your Grace'. Kimber took possession of the diary and Thomas Coburn told Mary Ann that she had been brought over to 'make a sensation'. He also told her that Mrs Hamilton was writing a life of the 5th Duke, which would cause 'another sensation', and for which she was to be paid £600. A few days later, Edmund Kimber told Mary Ann that he had read her diary, and that she should have been a historian: 'It will just suit our purpose!' he exclaimed. 'We can raise any amount of money on it.' He also told her that he would keep possession of the diary, that she should keep her counsel, and reiterated that she would get £4000, without a doubt. Mary Ann was insistent that the first time anybody had asked her any questions about the diary was when she was cross-examined in court by Horace Avory.

In the meantime, the diary did indeed seem to be making plenty of money – for some people. Whenever someone turned up at G. H. Druce, Ltd, and expressed an interest in buying shares in the Druce case, they were immediately taken to Kimber's office to be shown the diary. Each time this happened, Kimber charged the company commission – with the result that, as George Hollamby complained to Mary Ann, Kimber was making £50 (£5000 in today's money) or more a week out of it. Various newspapers also began to serialize the diary. Both George Hollamby and Thomas Coburn expressed annoyance to Mary Ann that they did not themselves have possession of the diary, and began to plot how to get hold of the elusive document with the unfailing Midas touch. In fact, it was clear that desire to gain possession of the diary was causing members of the Druce party to fall out with each other. But Edmund Kimber kept the diary under lock and key. Every day, Mary Ann would go to Kimber's office, where he would read out extracts from it and then ask her to make alterations, marked on pieces of paper. But he took care to take the pieces of paper away afterwards.

'Kimber and Coburn were constantly vying with each other, and running each other down,' Mary Ann related to Inspector Dew. Coburn, she said, had told her he came from Australia, that he was a practising lawyer of some standing, and had made £20,000 from the land boom, but that he had then lost it, and gone bankrupt. If George Hollamby lost the case, he (Coburn) would 'take good care that he did not lose anything by it, and that he would be worth a million, but if Druce got his rights he (Coburn) would be worth a lot more'. Like Kimber, he told her to stick to her guns, and she would get her £4000, which he described as 'a mere flea bite'. Coburn asked her repeatedly to request the diary back from Kimber, but Kimber refused to return it. Coburn also told Mary Ann that the Druce claimants would have to depend on their witnesses, as they did not intend to say anything in court themselves.

During their stay in England, the Druce party rented a flat for Mary Ann and Maud in Lavender Hill. However, they were usually late with paying the rent, and Mary Ann frequently had to chase Kimber for it. Kimber's chief clerk, Jenkins, would come over with the money, and used to mutter darkly that everybody involved in the conspiracy 'would sign their own death warrant'. George Hollamby, in Mary Ann's view, was a crude man, his behaviour hardly befitting the claimant to a dukedom. One day, he and one of his cronies exposed themselves to Mary Ann and her daughter by opening their trousers in front of them. Coburn also behaved lecherously towards them, running his hands up Mary Ann's and her daughter's clothes. When she complained about him to Edmund Kimber, he said he knew Druce was a 'low man', and asked if he or the others were drunk at the time.

Her suspicions of the Druce party growing deeper as the days passed, Mary Ann instructed her own solicitors, Oswald Hanson & Smith, and through them finally managed to recover her diary from Kimber. But the diary was subsequently stolen: the account of its theft in the street, which Mary Ann had given in court the previous October, was true. She did not know who stole it. 'I never actually told the Druce people I manufactured the contents of the diary,' Mary Ann told Dew. 'But I felt that they knew it, from the manner they treated me.' She had thought the diary was just to be used for the purposes of raising funds for the case, and never imagined she would have to appear in court. 'I told Coburn I should be no good, as I knew nothing about the lead in the coffin, and would not swear it for nobody,' she told the inspector. 'He then said I should only have to kiss the book and that it would be over, and that the others would swear to lead in the coffin. But when I read Nurse Bayly's evidence, my eyes were opened, and I could see that Druce was nothing but a base imposter. Then I made up my mind I would tell the police all about it. I know my father was a policeman, and I would rather tell the police than anyone else.'

Mary Ann related that shortly after she was remanded in custody following her arrest by Dew on 17 January, Edmund Kimber came to see her in Holloway Prison. She told him, defiantly, that she was minded to plead guilty, and 'show the lot of them up'. Kimber replied, 'Oh, you must not do that, if you do, they will give you seven years.' He then persuaded her to allow him to represent her, but at the same time was writing to all the newspapers claiming that she was mad.

Thus ran the substance of Mary Ann's confession.

Back in his office at Scotland Yard Inspector Dew sighed, leaning back in his black leather chair, studded with neat rows of brass nails. Ranged on the top of the leather-topped walnut desk, which was littered with papers, were souvenirs from some of the chief inspector's famous cases: a framed letter from the dowager Duchess of Sutherland thanking Dew for his efforts in capturing the international jewel thief 'Harry the Valet', and one from Parr's Bank expressing gratitude for his role in tracking down the notorious Russian fraudster Friedlauski, who had posed as a City gentleman under the name of Conrad Harms.

Dew thought it over carefully. Mary Ann Robinson was not a reliable witness, but somehow, he felt that the bulk of what she said was probably true. What, after all, had she to lose, now that she was pleading guilty? It seemed clear to him that her 'diary' was a clever fake, an amalgamation of personal recollections of Welbeck, newspaper reports of the case, and what the Druce people had told her about the claim, without their specifically directing her to make it up. The fact that the diary was a fabrication had been implicitly assumed by all the parties, but never openly discussed. Presumably, this was part of the strategy by which George Hollamby, Kimber and Coburn intended to avoid directly incriminating themselves in the fraud. In her confession Mary Ann had persisted with her claim that she did indeed know the author Charles Dickens, although she admitted that she had concocted the story of his introducing her to Druce/the duke. She had also hinted to Dew, although she did not put this in her official statement, that she had enjoyed intimate relations with the 5th Duke of Portland. This Dew considered utterly preposterous (he did not, after all, know of the 5th Duke's apparent penchant for servingwomen, as revealed to Turner). The 6th Duke also dismissed the idea of a liaison between Mary Ann and his cousin as ridiculous, highly amused at the 'old liar that she was'. Whatever the truth of the matter, it is a curious fact that Robinson – the wife of a lowly shepherd – possessed valuables, including jewellery and a piano, to the amount of £400* in her Christchurch house. These items were certified by the insurers, and subsequently made the subject of the fraudulent insurance claim.

Certainly, Dew had to admit that the lady had a gift for high-flown rhetoric. A cache of 'letters' to her from the 5th Duke, penned by her own hand, had been found in her flat, along with other correspondence. One of them read as follows:

My dear Mary,

Remember this that though you were not the wife of my youth, you are the joy of my life. You are the most worthy of my earthly comforts.

You possess what I most admire in womanhood, sweetness and cheerfulness mixed with gravity of manner.

For your studies I recommend some of the most useful parts of mathematics, as in my eye they are a special object of interest.

So farewell my dearest
From your faithful and dearest friend
John CS Bentinck

Welbeck Abbey. 1874.

* £40,000 in today's money.

Dew could not resist a chuckle. Why, in another life, the lady might have been a writer of romance. He had read worse among the cheap railway fiction paperbacks on the shelves of news stalls in railway stations. At least, however, the wretched woman had now dispensed with the services of that blackguard, Kimber: for even as Dew had been interviewing her in prison, a message had arrived for the governor of Holloway from Kimber, asking if Mary Ann wished him to continue to represent her. She had, at last, the wit to refuse. Dew thought that she would be immeasurably better off without him, especially as he had heard on the grapevine that she would likely be represented at her future court hearings by the formidable Sir Edward Marshall Hall (known as 'the Great Defender').

Inspector Dew's musings were cut short by the sudden, shrill ring of the black candlestick-and-wall telephone that was precariously perched on the piles of papers on his desk. He lifted the receiver to his ear. George Hollamby, he was informed, had that day publicly repudiated Kimber. At the same time, 'Miss O'Neill' had finally confessed to being Mary Ann's daughter, admitting that her real name was Maud Robinson.

In his estate office at Welbeck, Turner too was exultant. It appeared that the Druce show was falling apart.

'We just need to find some evidence getting Kimber and Coburn into our net,' he wrote to Horseman Bailey, echoing the 6th Duke's impatience to put the master puppeteers of the Druce charade behind bars as soon as possible.

Events now seemed to be gathering pace. In the ensuing weeks, the civil action that George Hollamby had commenced against the estate of Lord Howard de Walden disintegrated, like the perjury proceedings that had been brought against Herbert Druce. Only this time, rather than being voluntarily withdrawn, the case was dismissed out of court as 'frivolous and vexatious'. The evidence of T. C. Druce's body in the grave, the judge ruled, had finally laid to rest any doubt as to the matter.

Then, in early spring, the last of the key Druce witnesses was apprehended. On 7 March 1908, the mysterious Mrs Hamilton was arrested on a charge of perjury, and brought before the police court. The true identity of the 'Veiled Lady' – the woman in black who had testified both for Anna Maria Druce in 1898 and for the second Druce claim of 1907 – was about to be revealed.

A London Hotel

September 1898

It is perfectly obvious by the mere application of one's common sense to the problem before us, that this woman is the smallest possible component part of the great whole which constitutes this conspiracy.

SIR EDWARD MARSHALL HALL, KC
in defence of Mary Ann Robinson

Margaret Jane Atkinson – the woman who was in her later years to play a leading role in the Druce saga, as the mysterious 'Veiled Lady' – came from a family cursed by madness. Born in the 1840s in the town of Kendal, in Westmorland, her childhood was spent in a windswept valley of southern Lakeland. Much of the world in which Margaret grew up was grey, from the slate roofs of 'the auld grey town', as the locals called it, to the winding ribbon of the old Kendal canal with its barges drawn by packhorses, soon to be replaced by the new, steel-grey ribbon of the railway. Perhaps this was the reason she felt the need to invent a world of colour for herself. Certainly, she cut an eccentric figure in the old town, with her curious, old-fashioned stuff gowns and black ringlets. Rumour had it that the whole family was mad: Margaret's sister Isabella was incarcerated in a Carlisle asylum from an early age, and her uncle was known to the Kendal townsfolk as 'Silly Ned'.

Margaret herself was prone to wild fantasies. At some point in her youth, she took up with a dissolute married sailor by the name of Captain William Hamilton. She was subsequently to claim that they married on board ship, in a storm. Whether this really happened was doubtful, and was vehemently denied by Captain Hamilton's wife. What is certain, however, is that Margaret had two children by the captain and a third by a travelling scissor-grinder, whose baby she gave birth to in a barn.

When Captain Hamilton found out about his mistress' unfaithfulness he immediately returned to his wife, leaving Margaret to wander the country, supporting herself and her children by taking jobs as an itinerant housekeeper. Margaret's daughter became a prostitute in London, until she was 'rescued' by a worthy lady called Mrs Whingate. Mrs Whingate 'saved' Margaret's daughter by persuading one of the girl's former clients, a Mr Edward Mussabini, who went by the name of Edward Bower, to marry her. It was at the Bowers' home in Norwich in 1898 that Margaret, or Mrs Hamilton as she was now known, appeared one day, talking about Anna Maria Druce and the extraordinary claim to the Portland millions. Her late father had been intimate with the 5th Duke, she declared; and of course, Druce was the duke.

Whether or not Edward Mussabini strictly believed his eccentric mother-in-law's story, he was quick to spot an opportunity. He therefore paid a call on the barrister who was then representing Anna Maria Druce, Mr Arnold Statham. During his visit, a journalist by the name of John Sheridan knocked on Statham's door. 'Oh, here's the very man,' Statham exclaimed, and introduced Sheridan to Mussabini.

Sheridan wasted no time in setting up an interview with this intriguing new witness, and within a few days Mrs Hamilton found herself ensconced in a plush red velvet sofa in the cosy panelled dining room of Anderton's Hotel on Fleet Street, engaged in conversation with the charming young journalist before a roaring fire. Sheridan carefully recorded everything that Margaret said in his notebook, and promised that she and Mussabini would get £3000* each for the information.

'In fact,' Mussabini complained bitterly to J. G. Littlechild, the private investigator employed by Freshfields and the 6th Duke to investigate the case, 'he never gave her more than £1 after each interview, and not a penny more than £7 altogether.' Sheridan guarded Mrs Hamilton jealously, Mussabini continued. He kept the old lady to himself until he had exhausted all the stories she could tell, which he reported, with padding, in *Lloyd's Weekly Newspaper*. Finally, when he had got all he could out of her, he introduced her to Mrs Druce's solicitors. After Anna Maria's case collapsed in 1901, Sheridan 'took her with him' to George Hollamby, who paid him handsomely for the new and valuable witness. Asked by J. G. Littlechild if he actually believed his mother-in-law's story, Mussabini became evasive: 'My wife always found her mother reticent and mysterious,' he replied. 'She would often say to her, "Ah my dear, I have seen a bit of the world you know, and have had a good time in my day." But she never told her where or how she had the good time.' Mrs Hamilton spoke often of visiting Welbeck, but whether this was imagination or reality, they had no idea. 'From past experience,' Mussabini mused, 'I think she is

---

* That is, over £300,000 in today's money.

quite capable of imagining a thing, putting it forward as truth, and coming in time to believe it herself.'

The information about Mrs Hamilton's true identity and background had been gathered painstakingly for some months before her trial by J. G. Littlechild. A former Scotland Yard officer, now retired and going it alone as a private investigator, like John Conquest, Littlechild had conducted a very thorough search into the 'Veiled Lady's' past. In doing this, he had been helped in no small measure by his previous acquaintance with Margaret's son-in-law Edward Mussabini, whom he knew by his real name, Giuseppe Mussabini, probably from his time in charge of criminal foreigners at Scotland Yard. Littlechild had unscrupulously blackmailed Mussabini into persuading his mother-in-law not to give evidence on behalf of Anna Maria, by threatening to reveal dubious goings-on from the Italian's criminal past. Mussabini's report back to Littlechild left little doubt as to the heavy-handed tactics that had been used to scare the old woman into silence:

> I gave her the strongest points I could, and laid stress upon the horrible ruin she would bring upon her daughter and myself if the facts, which would be wrung from her in cross-examination, were to reach the ears of my people. That all would be well if she would upon leaving her present employ next Monday take a small room somewhere in London, and live in complete obscurity, until it was safe for her to join us here.

On the basis of Littlechild's research, it was clear that Mrs Hamilton's evidence had been the stuff of fantasy from start to finish – from the tale of her father being an aristocratic friend of the 5th Duke's by the name of Stewart (he was, in fact, called Atkinson), to her being 'Mrs' Hamilton (it looked very likely that she had never been married at all). The firm of Kendal solicitors who had acted for the Atkinson family for many years, and who knew both Margaret Atkinson and her sister Isabella well, had remarked in a letter to Bailey's: 'After reading her evidence as given in the newspapers, and in particular her cross-examination, we can only say that her story seems to us to be a tissue of lies from the time of her alleged birth at Rome onwards.' It was also now known that it was Mrs Hamilton who had haunted the 5th Duke's grave at Kensal Green dressed in black, laying a wreath on the tomb before fleeing the approaching journalists.

On reading Littlechild's reports, Inspector Dew was of the opinion that Margaret Hamilton was a fantasist and hysteric. He had no doubt that she would be convicted of perjury in her forthcoming trial, as would Mary Ann Robinson, but the likelihood was that the judge would impose a reduced sentence on account of Mrs Hamilton's advanced age.

The real question, Inspector Dew mused, was how to catch the bigger players who stood in the shadows behind these two mad old women. Robert Caldwell, he could see, was likely a lost cause. The head of the New York asylum in which he had taken refuge, Dr Mabon, still refused to certify him as being in a fit condition to be extradited, and the New York court was showing no inclination to go against Mabon's judgment. It was, however, becoming increasingly clear that Caldwell had been mixed up with the set of City sharks that had hung around both Anna Maria and George Hollamby. Only a few months beforehand, in November 1907, a gentleman called Thomas Wyatt had written to Freshfields, stating that Thomas Marlow – one of the Marlow brothers, both of whom were notorious figures in the City underworld – had gone to America with Caldwell in 1871, and had become great friends with him in New York. Caldwell, Wyatt said, was what was known in New York as a 'petty fogger' – that is, someone who 'would do anything for money'. Moreover, having painstakingly trawled through his case files for a matching description, Dew was virtually certain that the man who had been shadowing the 6th Duke was the other brother, Henry Marlow. Presumably, now the bubble had burst, he had been hoping to obtain money out of his Grace in return for blowing the whistle on former chums such as Caldwell. But even Caldwell and the Marlow brothers had been but puppets to the masters of the show.

It was the question of how to snare the blackguards Kimber, Coburn, George Hollamby and Sheridan that was now taxing Inspector Dew. Coburn and George Hollamby had been too wily to be directly involved in the evidence-gathering, relying instead on intermediaries and middlemen. The role played by the solicitor Edmund Kimber in the conspiracy was beginning to look very black indeed. Mary Ann Robinson had already given a flavour, in her confession to Dew at Holloway Prison, of Kimber's decidedly questionable methods of manipulating evidence in the form of additions and alterations to her diary. It seemed to Dew that the 'theft' of the diary was very likely his work. And Dew's investigations were uncovering further evidence of wrongdoing on Kimber's part. During the hearing before the magistrate Plowden, Kimber had given evidence that he had sought an expert opinion on the age of the paper on which Mary Ann Robinson's diary had been written, and had been informed that it 'could well be before 1860'. In fact, Dew found out from his subsequent investigations, Kimber had been told precisely the opposite. A few months previously, Fresh-fields had received a visit from a man called Charles Botten, manager of the City stationers Dixon & Rowe. He told them that Kimber had come to see him in November 1907, seeking an expert view as to the age of the diary. Botten had declared that he was far from an expert, but that in his view, the paper likely dated from *after* 1861. A few weeks later, Kimber had returned to Botten's office, declaring that he had been put in the witness box by Atherley-Jones, and asked questions about the diary. He told Botten: 'I'll just put a few things down on paper, and send my clerk, Fletcher, to you with them tomorrow.'

The next day, Fletcher had come to see Botten with a writ-ten statement. Botten had not kept it, but to the best of his rec-ollection it said 'that I as an expert was thoroughly conversant with paper that was made in America fifty years ago'. Botten told the clerk he was nothing of the sort, as in fact he knew nothing of what America produced fifty years ago. Fletcher ran his pencil through that sentence. The next sentence was: 'That I had been all my life in the paper trade, that I was an expert and thoroughly knew what I was talking about.' Botten retorted that this was patent nonsense – that he was a dealer in paper, and did not claim to be an expert. Fletcher ran his pencil through that sentence also. Botten then said to the clerk, 'I will tell you what I did tell Kimber. I said that I thought it very doubtful whether that class of paper was made in 1861, or that period.' Fletcher took this down in shorthand. Botten then told the clerk he was minded to go and see Messrs Freshfield about it. Fletcher put no more questions to him after that. In his subsequent interview with Freshfields, Botten continued:

> 1861 or 1862 was the year when the duty came off paper, and I personally doubt whether paper as common as this was made at the time. It was a cheap engine-sized paper, I think. I did not examine enough of the paper to see if there was a watermark or not. Pages of a book of this size would be cut from a larger sheet of paper, in cheap paper like this sometimes 8 times as large as the page. You might examine 20 sheets and only find a watermark on the 21st. In common engine-sized writing paper like this, the manufacturer does not put a watermark in unless it is ordered.

The way in which Kimber had treated Botten's 'evidence' and misrepresented his statements recalled, to Dew's mind, what Mary Ann Robinson had told him about the solicitor's amendments to her diary.

As for the journalist John Sheridan, the account that Edward Mussabini had given to J. G. Littlechild of his dealings with his mother-in-law, Mrs Hamilton, suggested flagrant manipulation of the evidence of a key trial witness. And more evidence against Sheridan was emerging. In the course of his investigations, Dew had interviewed Edward Phillips, the former managing clerk of Macarthurs & Co., the solicitors originally employed by Anna Maria Druce to fight her case in 1898. Macarthurs, along with her barrister Arnold Statham, had withdrawn from the case after Mrs Druce insisted on issuing bonds to raise funds. According to Phillips, John Sheridan had introduced Mrs Hamilton to Macarthurs after he had interviewed her with Edward Mussabini in Anderton's Hotel. After hearing Mrs Hamilton's story, Phillips asked Sheridan not to publish any details in a newspaper, as it might harm Anna Maria's case. However, he later found that Sheridan had published a lengthy interview with her in *Lloyd's Weekly Newspaper*. Phillips also told Dew that he had received one day a letter from a man describing himself as Robert Caldwell, claiming to have an intimate knowledge of the 5th Duke. He had shown it to Arnold Statham, who had dismissed the letter as 'one written by a maniac'. Phillips had granted Sheridan access to his files in return for him helping with his research. On going through his files after Sheridan's visit, he found that the letter from Caldwell had disappeared. He was sure, he told Dew, that Caldwell's letter had been taken from the file by Sheridan, who had subsequently sold it to the Australian party when they took over the claim after Anna Maria's case collapsed.

The problem with all of this, as Inspector Dew well knew, was that so much of it was speculation, based on innuendo, circumstantial evidence and unreliable witnesses. The most damning evidence against Kimber and Sheridan, after all, came from Mary Ann Robinson and Margaret Hamilton – who were themselves on trial for perjury. As for John Sheridan, Dew had recently had an interview with the Official Receiver's Office (which was looking into the role of the journalist in the affairs of the various Druce-Portland companies, by then bankrupt). According to the official receiver, Sheridan had submitted a doctor's letter to the

Commission, certifying that he was suffering from tuberculosis of the lungs and throat, that his condition was most severe, and that it was necessary for him to have a rest from business affairs, most particularly from speaking. How very convenient, Dew muttered to himself.

Most perturbing of all, however, was the role that appeared to have been played in the conspiracy by a man whom Dew himself had always held in the highest regard: retired Chief Inspector John Conquest, formerly of Scotland Yard's Criminal Investigation Department. It was an undisputed fact that Conquest had helped the Druce party in putting together its case. If the evidence unearthed by the 6th Duke's land agent, Thomas Warner Turner, was correct, it would appear that Conquest had been involved in acquiring by deception some of the 5th Duke's old clothes from the family of his former valet, with the fraudulent purpose of passing them off in court as heirlooms supposedly possessed by the family of George Hollamby. Brought against a high-ranking former police officer, such a charge (that of effectively conspiring to pervert the course of justice) was of an extremely grave nature indeed. The British public of the period idolized the amateur detective, epitomized by the ultimate gentleman sleuth, Sherlock Holmes. However, the professional plain-clothes policeman – meddling in the affairs of ordinary people – had been traditionally regarded with deep suspicion. Dew was old enough to remember from his teenage years, when he was a humble railway porter harbouring dreams of joining the Metropolitan Police Force, the notorious police coruption case known as the Turf Fraud Scandal. In *1877* three senior police detectives – Inspector John Meiklejohn, Chief Inspector

Nathaniel Druscovich and Chief Inspector Palmer – had been accused of accepting bribes from a pair of City swindlers, Harry Benson and William Kurr, for keeping them informed of police movements to track them down. Benson and Kurr had stolen over £30,000 from a Parisian lady, Madame de Goncourt, in a scam involving horseracing bets. Nobody could work out how the pair of crooks always managed to remain one step ahead of the police – until the mystery was revealed. The ensuing 'Trial of the Detectives' had been one of the most sensational court cases of the 1870s. Meiklejohn, Druscovich and Palmer had been found guilty and sentenced to two years in prison. Public outrage at the scandal had led to a Committee of Inquiry, which resulted in the reorganization of the police force, including the replacement of the former Detective Branch by the CID.

If Bertha Lambourn, the daughter of the duke's valet Harrington, who had been swindled into selling his clothes, identified the man who called on her as John Conquest – as seemed likely to be the case – the conduct of the retired chief inspector would be exposed, and another public scandal would certainly ensue. Dew's spirits sank at the thought. Public confidence in the plain-clothes police force would be rocked again. The Metropolitan Police CID – an institution that had raised him from a humble railway porter to a member of the respectable middle class, which had opened doors to him in the highest echelons of society, and which he revered as the greatest police force in the world – would undoubtedly suffer lasting damage to its reputation.

In London, as the months rolled on, Inspector Dew continued to worry about the far-reaching implications of the Druce investigation. In the meantime, spring had come to Welbeck Abbey. For the first time, a delicate tracery of tiny green buds appeared on the branches of the ancient beeches and tall hedgerows that lined the avenues of the estate. Snowdrops, crocuses and even the earliest daffodils pushed through the soil. As the days became warmer and brighter, the 6th Duke and Thomas Warner Turner also seemed to grow lighter in spirit, exchanging pleasantries with the workers on their rounds of the estate. Perhaps this was due to more than just the change of season: for they were also becoming more and more confident of victory. Events were finally taking a turn in their favour.

Mrs Hamilton's trial began in April, and being prosecuted by the pitiless Horace Avory, her defence stood little chance of success. She was duly found guilty by the jury and convicted in May, although – as Dew had predicted – she was granted a relatively lenient sentence of eighteen months' imprisonment because of her age. Mary Ann Robinson's treatment was less sympathetic. Despite her guilty plea and a skilful defence on the part of her Counsel Sir Edward Marshall Hall – who took great pains to point out that she was but a puppet in the affair – she was convicted in April, and sentenced to four years' penal servitude. Caldwell continued to languish in the New York asylum, eluding extradition by the British authorities, until the Home Office finally gave up on him, as a lost cause, in June.

The convictions of Mary Ann Robinson and Mrs Hamilton gave a taste of sweet vengeance to the 6th Duke and his advisors, but it was not enough. 'His Grace', Turner wrote to Horseman Bailey in January, 'is on the whole happy with the

outcome of the case, but is desirous of dealing in a strong manner with all persons who should be brought to book.' Turner
reminded Bailey that the duke was happy with progress so far,
but was 'very impatient for action to be brought against Coburn
and the whole crew'. The 6th Duke even went so far as to ask if
steps could be taken to prevent Llewellyn Atherley-Jones from
being appointed a recorder in Newcastle because of his role
in the matter, but was tactfully dissuaded from such a course
by Turner and Horseman Bailey. It seemed, however, only
a matter of time before Kimber, Coburn, George Hollamby
and Sheridan were put in the dock. Thomas Warner Turner
rubbed his chubby hands in glee. The moment was drawing
ever nearer. What joy to witness the scoundrels cower in the
witness box – the very spot that they had been cunning enough
to avoid thus far, getting their lackeys to do the dirty work for
them – and pay the price! But then a thunderbolt struck.

On 1 June 1908, Horseman Bailey received the following letter from Lord Desart at the office of the Director of Public
Prosecutions:

The Director of Public Prosecutions

Treasury Chambers, Whitehall, London S.W.

1st June, 1908

Gentlemen,

Re DRUCE

With reference to your application to this Department that
a prosecution should be instituted by the Director of

Public

Prosecutions against George Hollamby Druce and a number of other persons on certain charges of misdemeanour, I have this day received from the Attorney-General directions that such a prosecution is not to be conducted by this Department. It will not be necessary to point out to you that this decision will in no way prevent the institution of criminal proceedings at the instance of a private prosecutor.

I have the honour to be, Gentlemen,
Your obedient servant,
Desart

Bailey, Turner and the duke were aghast. They simply could not believe it. The entire Druce affair had been summarily dropped from further public investigation.

Sledmere House, East Riding

1870s

Laws, like the spider's web, catch the fly
and let the hawk go free.

Spanish proverb

For several days after the surprise determination of the Director of Public Prosecutions not to proceed with any further prosecutions in relation to the Druce affair, there was a flurry of activity from the duke's advisors to try to get the government to change its mind. Horseman Bailey replied to Desart's letter immediately, the hurt tone of his response conveying a stinging rebuke:

5, Berners Street,
London,
June 3rd, 1908

My Lord,

<u>Re DRUCE</u>

We have to acknowledge receipt of your Lordship's letter of the 1st instant informing us of the decision come to that a Prosecution is not to be conducted by your Department against George Hollamby Druce and other Persons.

We regret the decision arrived at, as we cannot but feel that the prospects of bringing the Guilty to Justice in any proceedings our Client might be advised to take must be diminished by the fact that, notwithstanding that the Treasury have taken Action against certain of the witnesses who gave evidence in the recent Proceedings, they have refrained from prosecuting the Persons chiefly concerned in promoting what Mr Justice Walden described as a monstrous Claim.

We have the honour to be,
My Lord,
Your Lordship's very faithful servants,
Baileys, Shaw & Gillett

The next day, Horseman Bailey obtained a joint legal opinion from the barristers R. B. Finlay, Horace Avory and S. A. T. Rowlatt. The opinion justified a charge of champerty* and conspiracy to prejudice the due course of justice against George Hollamby, John Crickmer, Thomas Coburn, John Sheridan and Edmund Kimber, but not against Fanny Druce's grandson, the journalist Kenneth Henderson (the role of Inspector Conquest was not, it appears, discussed). Further representations were made to the public authorities. But it was to no avail. The Druce case, as far as the government was concerned, was a book that was now firmly shut.

* Champerty is an illegal agreement, by which a person (with no previous interest in a lawsuit) finances it, with a view to sharing the disputed property if the suit succeeds.

Chief Inspector Dew was not as surprised as the Duke's advisors to find that the Druce case was closed. In fact – although he hardly dared admit it, even to himself – he was, perhaps, even slightly relieved. It never did any good to attack the reputations of one's fellows in the profession. Dew did not know for sure who had ensured the dismissal of further proceedings in the Druce case. There were any number of interested people who could have found a sympathetic ear in which to whisper in the cosy bars of one of the many gentlemen's clubs scattered over London. Retired Chief Inspector John Conquest – who had a lot to lose from further investigations of the fraud – still had many friends in high places. Edmund Kimber had the powerful solicitors' association, the Law Society, to back him up. A number of peers and other establishment figures – including Lord Deerhurst and the leading barrister Thomas Crispe, KC – had either toyed with investing, or actually bought, Druce company shares, and stood to lose professional credibility if they were exposed as investors in a fraud. It was in the interests of all these people that the Druce case was buried as quietly as possible. The Druce affair, in fact, became messier the closer one got to the heart of the matter. Better to stop with the two mad old women, who had been convicted and were even now toiling in penal servitude, and about whom nobody cared two hoots.

Mad women, in fact, seemed to be something of a feature of the Druce case, in Dew's estimation. There had been, to start with, the crazed Anna Maria Druce, who had unleashed the whole affair in the first place. How, or where, the idea that the 5th Duke of Portland was the same man as T. C. Druce had originated, other than in her diseased brain, he had no idea. Then there had been the two crazy female witnesses, Mary Ann Robinson and Mrs Hamilton, who had concocted the fabulous stories about their experiences with Druce as the duke. And in only a month's time, the name of yet another woman was to be dragged into the affair; only this woman was of an importance on a scale entirely removed from the others. She was, in fact, a member of one of the most powerful and ancient aristocratic families in England. She it was who had been the mysterious member of the Cavendish-Bentinck family whom George Hollamby and Coburn had darkly hinted at, as someone who supported their case and who would come forward 'when the time came'. Brilliantly witty and a serial seductress, she had already scandalized society in one of the most famous trials of late Victorian England. Her family were desperate that she should not do so again.

It was Amanda Gibson – the secretary who had worked for the Druce company – who dropped the bombshell when Inspector Dew interviewed her in July 1908. Although the official police investigation was closed in June, Dew continued for a few months to carry out inquiries privately on behalf of the 6th Duke's representatives, with a view to establishing whether a private prosecution for perjury against the major culprits was worth pursuing.* 'Lady Sykes', Amanda told Dew, 'was providing information at

* Metropolitan Police detectives were, at this time, permitted to carry out assignments on behalf of private clients if this did not interfere with their official police duties.

this time to the journalist Kenneth Henderson about the Portland family, and Henderson paid her.' As we have seen, Henderson was then general manager of *The Idler*, which had published a series of pamphlets produced by the Druce camp to set out and advertise their case. The information that Lady Sykes gave Henderson, Amanda told Dew, related to the Duke of Portland's family, and the articles were signed under a *nom de plume* as 'one who knows'. Dew probably knew little about Lady Sykes, other than that she had been involved in a spectacular court dispute with her husband, Sir Tatton Sykes, in the 1870s. He was unlikely to have known that she was connected with the Cavendish-Bentincks, having scant contact with high society outside his immediate professional duties. He needed to find out more.

Dew's subsequent researches would have revealed a tangled web of dashed hopes, wasted talent, greed, decadence and despair. Lady Christina Anne Jessica Cavendish-Bentinck – 'Jessie' to those who knew her – was the daughter of George 'Little Ben' Cavendish-Bentinck, MP for Whitehaven, and a granddaughter of the 4th Duke of Portland. A spirited young woman, Jessie was handsome rather than beautiful: she was striking with her square jaw, sparkling dark eyes and mass of curly black hair. A victim of her ambitious mother's social scheming, she was married off in 1874, at just eighteen years old, to Sir Tatton Sykes, heir to the fabulously wealthy Sykes family that had for centuries dominated the landed gentry of Yorkshire. The Sykes lorded over their environs from the gloomily palatial splendour of the family seat, Sledmere House, in the chilly wolds of the East Riding.

The Sykes marriage was not a happy one. Thirty years

Jessie's senior, Sir Tatton had established a reputation for eccentricity that rivalled even that of the 5th Duke of Portland. A disappointment to his father and ignored by his mother, he had developed a reclusive, hypochondriac disposition, with a marked distaste for the female sex. Among his many odd traits was a hatred of flowers: he deplored them as 'nasty, untidy things', and would not rest until he had raked over the beautiful gardens he inherited at Sledmere, right up to where they met the house. Sir Tatton absolutely forbade the cultivation of flowers in the gardens of the cottages on the Sledmere estate, with the exhortation, 'If you wish to grow flowers, grow cauliflowers!' He was even known to have taken a cudgel to offending blooms, if any of his tenants dared to disobey his command. Another peculiarity of Sir Tatton's was an aversion to workers' cottages on his estate having a front door. (It was speculated that he hated the sight of women gossiping in the porch.) Cottages on the Sledmere estate, therefore, were only permitted false front doors, with their real entrances at the side or the back. A further oddity, which uncannily echoed one of the 5th Duke of Portland's own, was Sir Tatton's firm belief that the body should always be maintained at an even temperature, with the result that he possessed a series of coats designed to be worn on top of each other. A vicar of Sledmere explained Sir Tatton's singular practice thus:

> On two chairs outside his special den were arranged different coats. On one there were heavy overcoats, on the other four covert coats, all of different colours and each was a perfect fit, made to go one over the other, and allowing for size. He sometimes wore six coats. I have seen him in church

gradually strip off four covert coats and Ulster, and he still had a coat on.

A vivacious and intelligent eighteen-year-old girl and a cantankerous old man whose behaviour became increasingly peculiar as time went on were unlikely to form a marriage made in heaven. By his latter years, Sir Tatton lived mainly on a diet of milk puddings and chewed-up meat (he would chew the meat, swallow the juices and regurgitate the rest). Eventually, Lady Tatton Sykes installed herself in London, while her husband remained at Sledmere. She began to entertain a series of lovers at lavish parties, earning herself the rather unkind moniker of 'Lady Satin Tights'. Owing to her extravagant lifestyle, Jessie ran up a series of enormous debts, which the tight-fisted Sir Tatton wished to avoid having to pay off. It was then that he hit upon the novel idea of using the Married Women's Property Act 1882 to that end. The primary purpose of the Act was to improve the lot of married women, and it certainly went some way to assisting abandoned wives like the unfortunate Elizabeth Crickmer. However, the Act also contained the stipulation that a husband would no longer be liable to pay his wife's debts, if he publicly advertised the fact. Sir Tatton therefore made legal history – and broke a gentleman's code of honour – by being the first man to do just that. The advertisement read as follows:

I, SIR TATTON SYKES, Baronet, of Sledmere, in the County of York, and No. 46 Grosvenor Street, in the County of London, hereby give notice that I will NOT be RESPONSIBLE for any DEBTS or ENGAGEMENTS which my wife LADY JESSICA CHRISTINA SYKES, may contract, whether purporting to be on my behalf or by my authority or otherwise.

Of course, this simply brought all Jessie's creditors crawling out of the woodwork, desperate to prove their debts. The result was one of the most notorious trials of the 1890s, when a major moneylender attempted to sue Sir Tatton for his wife's debts. Sir Tatton's defence was that the signature on the promissory notes was not his own, but forged. This argument was accepted by the jury, who found Sir Tatton not liable for the debt. The obvious question implied by the verdict, but left unresolved and hanging in the air, was: who had forged the signatures? To which, equally obviously, there could be only one answer. Fingers were pointed, accusingly, at Lady Sykes. She became a marked woman – disowned by her relatives, shunned by respectable society, drowning in a cycle of increasing drunkenness, gambling and debt. It was even said that her alcohol dependence reached the point where her old and faithful maid began hiding bottles of perfume from her inebriated mistress, for fear that she would drink them.

Following Jessie's pathetic career after the trial, Dew could see how she was tempted into helping the Druce party by writing articles for *The Idler* in return for money. Various attempts had been made to come to a settlement with Sir Tatton for the payment of alimony, brokered by Jessie's long-suffering son Mark, but all collapsed; by the early 1900s she was left struggling to maintain her own drinking, gambling and extravagant lifestyle by attempts at writing books and forays into journalism. None of this was, in itself, particularly shocking to Dew's mind, nor indeed any worse than what had already been said about the unruly lady. In fact, Horseman Bailey had informed him that Lady Sykes had admitted to them that she had written articles for *The Idler*, and that the 6th Duke had reprimanded her with the wish that she had 'left the matter alone'. However, there was something else – a statement made to Inspector Dew by Mary Ann Robinson in Holloway – which was a different matter altogether. Something that made even the laconic chief inspector take a sudden intake of breath. Something that, if it got out, would cause the devil of a scandal, making the Sykes trial of the 1870s appear as tame as a boundary dispute between neighbours.

'Soon after I came here, Mr Henderson told me to go and see Lady Sykes,' Mary Ann had told Dew. According to Mary Ann, the purpose of the visit to Lady Sykes was for Mary Ann to tell her that she 'knew the duke's two wives, and she [i.e. Lady Sykes] would try to get a settlement for G. H. Druce out of the Duke of Portland'. When Mary Ann protested that she knew nothing of the duke's two wives, Henderson said, 'Well, it is useless to have brought you over if you won't do as we tell you, and if you don't mind you won't get your £4000.' Mary Ann therefore had little choice but to accompany Henderson to see Lady Sykes, a journey that took place in an unmarked cab. 'I went to see a lady,' she told Dew, 'and she asked me if I knew the duke's two wives. I said no, and she said "She is no use." I described the duke to her, and she said I was all right.'

Inspector Dew could barely believe his ears. Was Lady Sykes actually getting mixed up in trying to extort a settlement from the 6th Duke of Portland, on behalf of the Druce party? He had asked Robinson to describe the lady she had met. 'She was a thickset lady with a heavy jaw, about fifty years old,' came the reply. Lady Sykes would then have been fifty-two years old and her square jaw had always been a distinguishing feature. Dew sighed. Things did not look good for Jessie. And, it had to be conceded, they did not look good for the honour or the privacy of the Sykes family. Disgusted at the humiliating publicity of the debt trial, Sir Tatton had been keeping an even lower profile than usual in recent years, escaping abroad on tours of the Middle East and concentrating on his pet hobby of demolishing and rebuilding churches in the East Riding. The last thing the Sykes family needed was another sensational trial involving Sir Tatton's wife. Nor would the 6th Duke of Portland, eager as he was to have the real culprits brought to book, have relished the prospect of the Cavendish-Bentinck name being dragged through another media circus. And Jessie, whatever her many faults, was, after all, a Cavendish-Bentinck. Yet another reason, Dew thought, why the Druce affair was very likely to be buried. Quickly, discreetly, and with as little sensation as possible.

And that, in fact, is precisely what happened. Shortly after his interview with Amanda Gibson, Dew's instructions to investigate the Druce matter on a private footing appear to have been withdrawn. Over the summer of 1908, the Druce affair began slowly but surely to drop out of the newspaper headlines of which it had been such a dominant feature throughout the previous decade. The eye of the fickle newspaper-reading public was turning elsewhere: to the increasing excitement of the 1908 London Olympics; to the race that summer between the Wright brothers and the French to be the first to achieve powered flight; and then, in the autumn, to the gathering clouds looming over the Balkans with the first annexation of Bosnia-Herzegovina by the Austro-Hungarian Empire, the initial warning shot of a conflict that was soon to change the old hierarchies for ever.

To be sure, the odd event in the aftermath of the Druce affair was reported in the ensuing years, as a footnote to what was becoming increasingly regarded as a bizarre curiosity in the annals of British legal history. Thus, on 13 January 1911, the *New York Times* reported that Robert Caldwell, 'notorious as a maker of false affidavits', had passed away in the insane asylum on Ward's Island where he had been incarcerated ever since slipping back to America after the trial in London. According to the newspaper, he had been 'suffering from a twist of the brain'. Edmund Kimber continued to practise as a solicitor in southeast London, dying in Lewisham in 1934 at the ripe age of ninety. Coburn, who fled back to Australia immediately after the collapse of the case, returned to England for his retirement many years later, when all the fuss had died down, and the case was forgotten. He died in Kerrier, Cornwall, in 1952 at the age of eighty-seven. George Hollamby emigrated to Oakland, California, where in 1913 he told a journalist from the *Oakland Tribune* that there was a tunnel between the duke's London mansion, Harcourt House, and the Baker Street Bazaar, and that the coffin in the Druce vault contained only a dummy. He claimed that he had been offered 'ample funds' by wealthy women to continue to fight the case in return for his hand in marriage, and that he would be returning to England to revive his claim. However, he remained in Oakland, working as a carpenter and janitor. By 1937 he was living in a rooming house on 723 Sixth Street, blind and on a pension. He died in 1942.

Around the same time as the reports of Caldwell's death in January 1911, two curious articles appeared in the press relating to Anna Maria Druce, the woman who had started off the whole affair, and who had so mysteriously disappeared after the collapse of her case in 1901. The first article, published in the *Daily Express* on 3 January 1911, announced Mrs Druce's apparent death in London. A brief summary of the Druce affair was given, but no details of Anna Maria's funeral or burial. On the very next day, however, an article appeared in the *Daily Telegraph*, quoting Anna Maria's daughter Marguerite, who claimed that her mother was perfectly alive and in her usual state of health. Had Anna Maria had one last grim laugh at everybody's expense, by staging her own death before retreating into the shadows? The truth was not to be established until many years later.

The 6th Duke, in the meantime, stoically acknowledged defeat in his attempts to bring the main players to justice. He appears to have thrown in the towel and moved on with the many challenges that awaited Welbeck in the new century. He did not, however, forget to reward those who had assisted him in the bitterest battle of his life. The faithful land agent Thomas Warner Turner received a monetary gift, as did the old servants of the 5th Duke who had assisted with the compiling of witness testimony. The 6th Duke also sent a cheque for £100* to Inspector Dew, together with

---

* Equivalent to £10,000 today.

smaller sums for the other officers involved in the case. He thanked them all, and in particular Dew, who, he said, had 'throughout dealt with the case and its innumerable ramifications in the most thorough way'. He then turned the page on this particularly distasteful episode in the family history, and moved on to shooting, stalking and suchlike more pressing matters.

Did Chief Inspector Dew proudly display a souvenir of the Druce case on his desk? Somehow, it seems unlikely. Within just two years of the closure of the Druce file, Dew was to become one of the most famous detectives on earth, applauded the world over for his pursuit and capture of the murderer Hawley Harvey Crippen, in a transatlantic chase that held the world in thrall. As a result of detective work by Dew, Crippen was caught and convicted of murdering his second wife Cora, having allegedly buried parts of her dismembered body in the basement of his house before attempting to flee the country with his lover, Ethel Le Neve. He was hanged in Pentonville Prison in 1910.

The Crippen affair made Dew a household name. It was the case by which he liked to define his detective career. Even his autobiography, published many decades later in 1938, was triumphantly entitled *I Caught Crippen*. As the *Saturday Post* commented dryly in 1916:

> Ask the average person who Walter Dew is, and he will answer, 'The man who arrested Crippen.' Some will cut down the answer to 'Crippen Dew.' Such is fame.

There were those who speculated, as indeed had been the case throughout his career, that Dew, the bland and avuncular 'major in mufti', had a certain amount of luck; that it was the wireless telegraph message from the canny skipper of the ship on which the murderer had fled that really turned the tables on Crippen. To any such insinuations, Dew was quick to protest loudly, firing off lengthy letters to the offending newspapers, with threats of libel action. Like J. G. Littlechild and John Conquest before him, Dew followed the venerable path of becoming a 'Confidential Agent' on his retirement from the force, which he announced immediately after the conclusion of the Crippen case in 1910. From 1928 he lived out his retirement in a bungalow in the stolidly respectable seaside town of Worthing, West Sussex, where he blended imperceptibly into the crowds of other pensioners reading newspapers in deck chairs and strolling the windy esplanades. The only matter worthy of note relates to Dew's rather curious household arrangements: a widower since 1927, Dew shared his little bungalow with two women, a widow called Florence Idle and her spinster sister-in-law. (Dew was to marry Florence, twelve years his junior, in 1928.)

In marked contrast to the Crippen case, Dew was forever to maintain a mysterious reticence with respect to the Druce affair. He skirted around it in his autobiography, with the excuse that he did not wish to comment on it, for fear of causing pain to the relatives. But – as Dew's biographer Nicholas Connell has pointed out – this excuse could just as easily have applied to many of the cases that Dew *did* cover in his autobiography, in graphic detail. Was it that he simply did not wish to reveal too much about this particular investigation?

In any event, there was a good reason why he could not have done so, even if he had wanted to: the fact that, for the next eighty years, a number of the key police files relating to the Druce fraud investigation were classified. Whatever secrets they held, therefore, were under lock and key, and could not be revealed until many decades later.

A Library in Nottingham

October 2013

Very, very deep is the well of the past.
Shall we not call it bottomless?

THOMAS MANN
Joseph und seine Brüder (Joseph and his Brothers)

The atmosphere in the Manuscripts & Special Collections reading room was suffocatingly hot and stuffy. Hunched at the wide tables arranged in rows beneath the glare of the strip lights, bespectacled researchers pored over cracked, ancient manuscripts propped on great foam cushions, held open by leather weights and beaded chain bookmarkers. There were sumptuous illuminated medieval manuscripts, early drafts of classic literary works in the authors' original handwriting, nineteenth-century legal documents painstakingly written out by clerks in laborious copperplate. Aloof and above them all, a marble bust of the Duke of Wellington – a somewhat random and incongruous figure in this harshly modern setting – frowned at some unspecified spot in the middle distance. The only sound was the intermittent tap, tap, tap of the librarian's fingers on a computer keyboard, and the angry buzz of a trapped fly periodically hitting the glass windowpane.

Feeling a headache coming on, I sighed. My throat was parched from the heat, dryness and dust of the atmosphere: new dust from the concrete and asphalt motorway network that surrounded the warehouse in which the library was housed, old dust from the ancient tomes that were, in many instances, seeing the light of day after decades in sunless storage. The reason I was here, whiling away the hours at the Manuscripts & Special Collections department at Nottingham University, was that this was the place where the most important collection of contemporary documents relating to the Druce case was to be found. For by a combination of bequests, auction sales and transfers in lieu of death duties, the vast bulk of the archives of the Dukes of Portland – archives running to tens of thousands of documents, spanning over three hundred years – had ended up in the possession of the University of Nottingham. The documents included the private and estate correspondence of successive dukes, the correspondence of their solicitors, Baileys, Shaw & Gillett, in relation to the Druce case, private investigators' files, court papers and a comprehensive collection of newspaper cuttings. The documents had been carefully and accurately catalogued, but many had clearly never been reviewed before. Some were simply rotting away: pieces of the past that were mouldering to extinction, disintegrating in my hands as I placed them gingerly on the foam reading pad.

This was my last visit to Nottingham, ending several weeks during which I had been steeped in the Portland archives. Like most days of archive research, it had been a mixed day. In the course of the week I had waded through a good part of the correspondence of Baileys, Shaw & Gillett and many court documents. The earlier court documents about the case – dating from the late Victorian period – were in fading, yet still beautifully engraved, copperplate script. Later documents, from the Edwardian years, began to appear in early, rudimentary typewritten form. In trawling through the records, even I – a trained lawyer – found it a challenge to keep up with the twists and turns of this most complex of cases: the multiple hearings in different divisions of the civil and church courts, the endless interlocutory applications, the interminable legal arguments, the hundreds of pages of affidavit evidence. In all my research, however, I had not found the jewel for which I was so eagerly searching: the missing photographs taken by the police photographer at the opening of the grave. That they had existed at one time was not in doubt – Edwin Freshfield had referred to them in a letter to the Home Office. They had certainly never been published, however, and indeed, it appeared that they had been suppressed at the time. In the absence of any evidence to the contrary, I could only assume that they had been destroyed.

Having trawled through the court papers and correspondence, I was now working my way through the proofs of witnesses in the civil proceedings of *Druce* v. *Howard de Walden*. These were statements taken on the duke's behalf from witnesses with a view to their appearance in the civil case against Lord Howard de Walden that had been started by George Hollamby. In the event, the proofs had never been made public, as the case was dismissed before it came to a hearing, after the grave had been opened. The witnesses, therefore, were never called to give evidence in court. Their statements, however, made fascinating reading. Many were old servants of the 5th Duke, and as I read them, I caught glimpses of an aloof, haughty, yet ultimately lonely and vulnerable man. With the exception of a few close friendships with some of his female relations – his sister, Lady Ossington, being perhaps the most dear – the 5th Duke appeared alone and alienated from his class. If he was close to any human beings, he seemed closest to his servants: his valets, the tenants on the Welbeck estate and the hoards of navvies that he employed on his endless building projects. Many of these told affectionate and touching stories of their master. Seventy-two-year-old Henry Powell, for example – the duke's valet from 1852 to 1862 – recalled a fire in the vast downstairs bathroom at Harcourt House. The duke, ever ailing, had been taking a bath for the cure of sciatica, trying out an improvised arrangement of blankets hung around the bath on clothes horses to try to trap the heat. An oil lamp had set fire to the blankets. Powell had returned to find his Grace shivering and alone, wrapped in a blanket at the top of a staircase.

Other estate workers suggested that the duke was not unaware of his reputation for eccentricity. Seventy-year-old Joseph Burns, for example – employed by the duke's contractors for the fitting up of iron fencing round the abbey park – stated:

The late Duke well knew the opinion of the outside world concerning him. Upon this his Grace once questioned me, and as I did not wish to answer him, he said the lightest opinion was that he was a Welbeck oddity, while others would go so far as to say that 'he was covered with leprosy and not fit for a human eye to gaze upon.' 'It would be well,' he said, 'for the working class if England possessed a few more oddities like me and with no more leprosy than I have, which is none.'

What was immediately apparent from the mass of evidence gathered by Baileys, Shaw & Gillett, in preparation for the defence of the civil proceedings of *Druce* v. *Howard de Walden*, was the enormous amount of work the firm had done in establishing the Duke and Druce's separate identities by an analysis of their movements. Of course, this evidence had never been made public, as the proceedings were dismissed after the opening of the Druce vault. Effectively, every single documented location in which T. C. Druce and the 5th Duke had spent any time in their lives, was minutely diarized in handwritten record books split into double columns, to enable the ready identification of any dates on which there was clear evidence of them being in different places. The comparison made it abundantly clear that T. C. Druce and the 5th Duke could not possibly have been the same person. For example, on 15 October 1856, there was documentation recording T. C. Druce in Torquay, Cornwall. At this point in time, there was incontrovertible evidence that the 5th Duke was in Paris. In September 1857, T. C. Druce visited northern Europe – including Brussels and Paris. In the same month, the 5th duke's daily correspondence located him firmly at Welbeck.

I had already made a search of the nineteenth-century census records, which indicated that T. C. Druce and the duke had been in different locations on census nights. In the 1851 census, for example, the 5th Duke (as Marquess of Titchfield) was recorded as being at Harcourt House, while T. C. Druce was recorded in his then residence at Richmond. In the 1861 census, the duke was recorded again as being at Harcourt House, while T. C. Druce was recorded at his then address at 58 Finchley Road, St John's Wood. In the 1871 census, after the death of T. C. Druce, the duke was recorded as being at Welbeck Abbey. However, while apparently persuasive evidence, the census returns were not totally conclusive, as anyone leading a double life could easily have lied on his returns. This point was made by Baileys after the Druce case failed, when an action was brought against the 6th Duke by a researcher called Mr Haworth. Haworth claimed remuneration for research as a result of an idea he had proposed, of establishing the separate identity of the 5th Duke and T. C. Druce based on the census returns. Quite apart from the point – reasonably made by Baileys – that anybody could have had the idea, they also made the argument that the census returns did not provide conclusive proof, by themselves, of separate identity. The voluminous correspondence anchoring the duke and Druce in different locations, however, was a different matter. Here were real letters, stamped and postmarked, sent at the same time from different continents. That would have been pretty hard to fake.

Interestingly, despite the extensive and painstaking research that had clearly been carried out by Baileys into the lives of the two men, there remained two unexplained 'gaps' in T. C. Druce's life that were unaccounted for. The first was the period prior to 22 September 1815, the date of the first written record for T. C. Druce, when he appeared on a rate book in

Bury. This was a year before he married Elizabeth Crickmer. Before September 1815, Druce's life was a blank page. The second unexplained 'gap' was the decade between 10 September 1818 (the last recorded entry for Druce in the Bury rate book) and 1829 – the year in which he first appeared at Graham's in Holborn, signing invoices, prior to moving to Munn's. While T. C. Druce was patently not the 5th Duke of Portland, he remained a man of mystery. Where had he come from? What was he doing for the first ten years after abandoning Elizabeth Crickmer?

There was one statement, however, for which I had not been prepared, and which came as something of a shock. It was that of sixty-four-year-old William Kerridge, the 5th Duke's valet from 1859 to 1860. According to Kerridge, when he first went to Harcourt House, the furniture in the reception room was packed in the middle of the room and covered in dust sheets. This was because the duke had given orders that the furniture was to be looked over and cleaned, the renovation work being given to Druce & Co. of Baker Street. Then came the surprise. According to Kerridge, he clearly recollected one occasion when T. C. Druce was in the house, and the 5th Duke upstairs. In fact, he had left Druce in the reception room, talking to Lewis the butler, when the duke rang his bell to order his dinner. On descending the stairs after seeing the duke, he had found Druce still in conversation with Lewis.

If it were true, William Kerridge's statement was the only eye-witness account of Druce and the duke being effectively together in one place, at the same time. Of course, Kerridge might not have been telling the truth. His statement had never been subjected to the test of cross-examination in court. But

I did know that T. C. Druce had done work for the 5th Duke, from the existence in the duke's papers of a trade circular from Druce & Co. dated 15 October 1869, which I had already seen. This implied that the duke had indeed been a customer of Druce's at one time or another, prior to this date. There was nothing unusual or suspicious in this. Druce & Co. were a leading firm of house decorators and furniture suppliers, counting among their clients the French Embassy in London, Buckingham Palace, and many establishment figures from Charles Dickens to Albert, the Prince Consort (who was said to be a frequent visitor to the bazaar).

Other witness statements were tantalizingly suggestive. For example, both Leslie Ward – the *Vanity Fair* artist who had been commissioned to paint a posthumous portrait of the 5th Duke – and the sculptor Henry Hope-Pinker, who had made a posthumous bust of him, submitted proofs testifying to the existence of two death masks of the duke. Leslie Ward stated that he had instructed a professional caster, an old Italian who used to work for Sir Edgar Boehm, to take a cast of the duke's head shortly after he died, at Harcourt House. The caster described the duke's features as being of 'the most regular and delicate type', and did not notice any evidence of skin disease, although he did notice that there was 'a little sign of eczema on the duke's chest'. After the picture was finished, Ward sent the cast to Sir Edgar Boehm to assist him in making his bust. He did not know what subsequently became of it, and feared it had been broken up when Sir Edgar's things were disposed of, after his death. Henry Hope-Pinker stated that he had cast the duke's head himself. He had made a very close inspection of the duke's face in death, and found no evidence of skin disease. The duke was, on the other hand, very pale, with refined features, and had no eyebrows or hair. Intriguingly, Pinker said that he still had the death mask he had made in his possession, and that he intended to produce it as evidence in court. Yet there was no record of a death mask of the 5th Duke in existence. What could have become of it?

Every day, therefore, brought resolutions of old mysteries, and the appearance of new ones. The frustration of searching what appeared to be an endless haystack was more than made up for by the sheer delight of finding – buried among the acres of dross – the occasional, glittering gem for which I had been looking. The conflicting newspaper reports of Anna Maria's alleged 'death' in 1911, for example, led me to search through the official death records, where I found a death certificate for an Anna Maria Druce who died at a London asylum in 1914, having been transferred there from the Marylebone Workhouse. The dates fitted with Anna Maria's age. What a grim irony it was, that the woman who dreamed of being a duchess ended her days in the very workhouse from which she had started her journey. Mr Justice Grantham had been all too correct when , in dismissing the civil proceedings against the de Walden estate, he described the Druce case as 'one of the most serious and cruel cases which have been brought before a Court of Justice'.

The reasoning that had led Anna Maria to link T. C. Druce with the 5th Duke of Portland in the first place remained frustratingly elusive. Was she simply mad? The idea that ten years of bitter and hugely expensive litigation could have been triggered by the fantasies of a crazed woman beggared belief. On the other hand, nobody had ever been able to identify the parents of T. C. Druce or the circumstances of his birth, and there had been persistent rumours that he came from aristocratic origins. A former salesman at Druce & Co., Joseph Elliott Lawledge, for example, told Freshfields that it was generally believed that Mr Druce was the 'offspring of a ducal house', and that he 'had been born on the wrong side of the blanket'. It was not, therefore, beyond the bounds of possibility that T. C. Druce was in fact of aristocratic birth, possibly illegitimate, and that this was the basis for Anna Maria's misguided conflation of him with the Duke of Portland. The tissue of lies and deceit that Druce had woven around his life compounded the confusion. His concealment of his first marriage and his refusal to discuss his family or his past, created an aura of mystery that fed local gossip, fuelling the wildest imaginings of a neurotic woman.

The reasoning and motives of the later players in the Druce saga – Kimber, Coburn and George Hollamby– were equally hard to fathom, especially those of George Hollamby. After all, he had at one point rejected an offer of today's equivalent of £5.1 million to drop the case. For a carpenter hailing from the suburbs of Melbourne, such a sum would have been like winning the lottery. And then there was his single-minded determination to have the Druce vault opened. George Hollamby's rejection of the huge offer to drop the case and his insistence on having the grave opened could be consistent only with a belief that the grave was indeed empty or filled with lead. He might have used fraudulent *means* to obtain his ends, putting forth false witnesses, but he must surely have believed that, when the tomb was finally laid bare, Anna Maria's story would prove correct. Edward Swift, a commission agent and one of the salesmen of Druce company bonds, informed investigators that George Hollamby had told him that his brother had tried to convince him to accept the offer to drop the case, but that he had refused, saying that 'if it was worth what they offered him, it was worth fighting out'. The writer and journalist Bernard O'Donnell, who shared lodgings with George Hollamby in London during the 1907 perjury trial, was also convinced that George fully believed in his title to the Portland estates. According to O'Donnell, George was:

> a quaint little fellow, as eccentric as his grandfather, Thomas Charles Druce, and at the time I knew him used to spend all his spare time at his workshop, trying to perfect a perpetual-motion machine which he had invented. But he was quite convinced that his grandfather was one and the same as the Duke of Portland, and he took himself very seriously in this belief.

As with Anna Maria, any motives or misconceptions of George Hollamby's must ultimately have stemmed from the callous and deceitful behaviour of T. C. Druce. By deserting his first wife and children, burying the fact of their existence and so obviously favouring his second family, Druce created a deep-felt anger and resentment that was to be passed down through generations to come. How many of George Hollamby's actions could be attributed to a desire to take revenge on the man who had rejected his father?

Whether the lawyers Thomas Coburn and Edmund Kimber had as fervent a belief in the genuineness of the Druce claim as George Hollamby is doubtful. Coburn was well known as a sharp practitioner, who as a twice bankrupt didn't have much to lose; and Kimber must have profited handsomely from the fees he charged his client, as well as the commission he presumably obtained from the newspaper serialization of Mrs Robinson's notorious 'diary'. George Hollamby, it seems, was a stooge to his canny partners-in-crime.

My review of the correspondence of Baileys and Freshfields further revealed that some events that had seemed highly suspicious at the time – such as the unexplained transferral of the title to the Druce vault from Anna Maria's son Sidney to Herbert Druce – had quite an innocent explanation. In this case, Freshfields had originally been advised that the vault was legally defined as land or 'real property' (in which case it would devolve on the legitimate heir, Walter), but were subsequently told that it was defined as a 'chattel' or personal property, which meant it was included within the residuary estate that devolved on the named executor and residual legatee, Herbert Druce. Other documents were intriguing in the possibilities they suggested. Included among the 5th Duke's papers, for example, was a plan and 'specification of Works to be done in Erecting and Completing a Sub-Way connecting Harcourt House with the stables in Wimpole Street'. The plans were signed by one George Legg of 14 Westbourne Place, Eaton Square, SW, and were dated May 1862. There was also a letter from William Cubitt & Co., Gray's Inn Road, offering to undertake the contract for the 'sub-way at Harcourt House' for £883. Was the 5th Duke planning a maze of underground tunnels under Harcourt House, like those he was constructing at Welbeck Abbey?

These were interesting questions, but they paled into insignificance next to the extraordinary discovery I made one afternoon, as I was trawling patiently through the correspondence received by the lawyers during the perjury trial. The Druce affair being the sensation that it was, Baileys, Freshfields and Horace Avory received a deluge of letters from the public during the course of the case. Some letters contained hints and advice about the case and possible witnesses, of varying degrees of usefulness; many were begging letters addressed to the 6th Duke; a fair number were from people who were clearly stark raving mad. One letter, however, was different. It was faded, written in the crabbed script of a middle-aged person. I almost missed it, buried as it was in the boxes of paperwork that I was working through. It read as follows:

Great Mongeham
Nr Deal, Kent
November 3rd 1908

To H.E. Avory, Esq

Sir,

Will you please excuse this liberty I am taking in writing to you? For one reason that you may know where I could be found if I should be required. Formerly Fanny Cavendish Bentinck, known as Fanny Ashbury since between 4 and 5 years of age. Now Mrs Fanny Lawson, and the only daughter of the Fifth Duke of Portland. My circumstances prevented me from coming over when the case was on in

Court. I should like to know who is receiving the money
my mother's father tied on me as a child. I don't know if my
grandfather is living or my mother's sister. I should be very
pleased Mr Avory if you could tell me anything about them
or my two brothers William and Joseph. The Ashbury family kept me in the dark concerning my own people.

I remain, dear Sir, very truly,
F. Lawson

My immediate reaction to the letter was one of incredu-
lity. How could the 5th Duke of Portland possibly have had
any children? Had he not been advised by the doctors that
he was 'no use to a woman', on account of having suffered a
groin hernia? In any event, how could the existence of a child
born to such a prominent personage possibly have been kept
secret? Dismissing the letter as the production of yet another
deluded crank, I continued with my review of the correspondence. But then, a few letters on, I came across a second letter,
written a month later, in the same hand:

Great Mongeham
Nr Deal, Kent
December 4th 1908

H.E. Avory Esq, KC

Dear Sir,
[sic] May I trouble you to forward the inclosed [sic] to
Messrs Bailey Howard [sic] & Gillett the solicitors? And
many thanks for sending me their names. My place here is

a little thatch bungalow, one of two little dwellings at the precinct and would not be noticed very much from the road. I have two sons the oldest George married with a little son two months old, a petty officer at Portsmouth, and Bert, a marine Lance Corp. at Chatham, just joined the HMS Inflexible stationed at Chatham, he was born on the Welbeck estate at the Ashburys. The old couple are dead. The HMS Inflexible leaves in a few weeks for foreign service.

Attached to this letter was a statement that read simply:

Will Messrs Bailey Howard [sic] & Gillett please send to Mrs Fanny Lawson statement of what her father left to her credit in their care and oblige. Her father the Fifth Duke of Portland and also address of her brothers William and Joseph. To the Thatch Bungalow…

address, etc

I reread the letters several times over. Somehow, they did not strike me as being the product of a diseased brain. The writer was clearly at least middle-aged – the handwriting was evidence as to that – and the spelling and punctuation errors indicated a lack of education. But mad, no. And the information was too specific to be fabricated – there were Fanny's sons' names, George and Bert, and details of their positions in the armed services. There was a genuine sense of personal loss in the letters that touched me, too. These were not mere begging letters. They were letters beseeching the recipient for information, for news of what had happened to the writer's maternal grandfather, aunt, and most of all, two lost brothers. It seemed that the writer, Fanny, had been kept away from virtually her entire family. There was also the slightest hint of subterfuge, in the reference to her cottage being one that 'would not be noticed very much from the road'. Was Fanny hinting that she was expecting a personal visit from the 5th Duke's lawyers?

My head was in a whirl. Could the 5th Duke of Portland really have fathered two sons and a daughter? Could they have been brought up secretly, separated from each other, the daughter raised by a local Welbeck family called the Ashburys? It seemed, on the face of it, incredible. What Horace Avory would have made of such a letter, when he received it ten months after the Druce trial, I could only speculate. Somehow, I suspected it would have prompted a raised eyebrow, even on that mask-like countenance.

Incredible or not, I had to find out more. I sent a request for information to a medical acquaintance of mine, a member of the Royal College of Surgeons. Was it possible, I asked, for a man suffering from an untreated groin hernia to father children? I then set to work looking up any records of Fanny that might exist. If – as Fanny intimated – she and her two brothers, William and Joseph, were indeed children of the 5th Duke who had been brought up by a local family, surely there would be records relating to them in the Portland archives: correspondence regarding the terms on which they were handed over to the Ashburys, details of any sums of money transferred to them for the children's maintenance. However, a thorough search of the papers in the archives drew a complete and utter blank. If any documents relating to Fanny or her brothers had once existed, they must have been destroyed.

The two letters I had found had clearly slipped through the net – presumably because they had been filed with seemingly innocuous correspondence with the public in the aftermath of the perjury trial. It seemed, in fact, that I only knew about Fanny's existence because somebody in the lawyers' offices had not been careful enough.

Since the Portland papers were not of assistance, I turned to the public records. Surely there must be some reference to Fanny in the official registers of births, marriages and deaths, or the census returns? After some searching, I found that a Fanny Ashbury was registered as born to a couple named George and Hannah Ashbury in 1855, in Whitwell, a village on the Welbeck estate. The couple were clearly of lowly stock. George was a joiner and Hannah was illiterate, marking Fanny's birth certificate with a cross as her signature. The same Fanny was listed as living with the Ashburys at Whitwell, aged six years, in 1861, along with a brother, William, then aged nine. Could this be the Fanny Lawson who wrote to Horace Avory, and was this William the brother she had mentioned in her letter? If this was indeed the Fanny for whom I was looking, she would have been fifty-three years old when she wrote to Avory. In the 1871 census, the sixteen-year-old Fanny reappeared, working as a servant in the household of a man called Calvert Bernard Holland, a manager in Sheffield. But then, she seemed to disappear from the records. What could have happened to her?

Realizing that I would have to spread the net wider, I began to search the census records for Scotland and Ireland. I also searched the emigrant passenger lists of persons on outbound ships in the 1870s and 1880s to Canada, Australia and New

Zealand. Finally, I struck gold. Trawling through the Scottish marriage records, I discovered that a Fanny Ashbury had married a George Lawson in Edinburgh in 1880. The couple were subsequently recorded in the Scottish census records until the end of the century, living in Midlothian. The Scottish census records also contained vital information that proved I had indeed found the Fanny Lawson who had written to Horace Avory in 1908. For they recorded, as members of Fanny's household, her sons George and Bert, referred to in her letters ('Bert', in fact, turned out to be short not for 'Robert', but for 'Bertram'). George, the elder son by just one year, was born in Midlothian in 1884; and true to Fanny's letter, Bertram, the younger son, was born on the Welbeck estate, in the village of Norton Cuckney, in 1885.

By the turn of the century, Fanny had disappeared from the Scottish records. The 1901 and 1911 censuses showed her as a widow living in various villages in Kent, not far from the village of Great Mongeham, from where she had written her letters to Horace Avory. Curiously, while Fanny had given her birthplace as Whitwell in the earlier censuses, in these later records, her birthplace was simply listed as 'not known'. George and Bert, just as Fanny had written, were destined for careers in the Royal Marines. In 1911, George – at the age of twenty-seven – was a petty officer on HMS *Albemarle* at Weymouth. At just sixteen years old, Bertram was already a bugler on HMS *Wildfire* at Sheerness in Kent; and by 1911, aged twenty-six, he was a Lance Corporal at the Royal Marine barracks at Chatham. According to the England & Wales death index, Fanny Lawson died in 1917, in Portsmouth, at the age of sixty-two.

Curious to find out more about Fanny's sons, I contacted a specialist military researcher, to see if it was possible to track down the boys' service records from the information given in Fanny's letters. These, I reasoned, might well shed more light on Fanny and her family. I also put in a tentative request to visit Welbeck Abbey: perhaps someone there might know something, if anybody were willing to talk. I had, in any event, been intending to visit Welbeck for some time, and now seemed an ideal moment to take my research to this next stage. Having put out these feelers, there seemed little more to do, other than to wait and see what happened.

By this time, the reading room had closed, and I had headed back to my sparsely furnished but comfortable hotel room, with its wide window overlooking the grey slate roofs, red-brick warehouses and smoking factory chimneys of Nottingham's old industrial Lace Market district. A light, sooty drizzle was falling from the scudding clouds. Somewhat wearily, I began to look through images of documents relating to the Druce police investigation held by the National Archives at Kew. To save time and extra travelling, I had obtained several volumes of these on a computer disc. My vision began to blur as yet again, pages and pages of yellowing briefs, opinions and interview notes, mostly in faded copperplate script, passed in succession before my eyes – this time, somewhat incongruously, on a flickering computer screen. Perhaps it was time to call it a night. On the verge of switching the machine off, I suddenly sat bolt upright as I found myself clicking through a series of photographs that I had not seen before: a grave, staked off with cordons... the inside of a vault... a large, dusty coffin swathed in a black cloth... an open coffin lid... the outline of a shroud...

I was looking at the police photographs that had been taken when the Druce vault was opened.

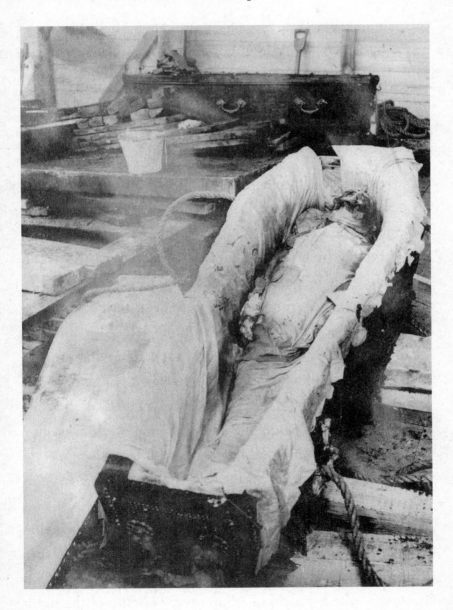

Welbeck Abbey

October 2013

It began in mystery, and it will end in mystery, but
what a savage and beautiful country lies in between!

DIANE ACKERMAN
A Natural History of the Senses

I t was a crisp, cold, misty October morning when I
stepped onto the platform at Nottingham City Station to
take a train to Welbeck. The station, in the middle of a
major refurbishing programme, was not an attractive sight.
Scaffolding and temporary façades covered over the old, red-
brick Edwardian baroque building, with its terracotta walls,
slate roof and art-nouveau-style wrought-iron gates. Most of
the people at platform 4 – where I stood, stamping my feet
in the cold and blowing my fingers – were waiting for the
fast train to King's Cross. Only a few remained on the platform afterwards, awaiting the local train that would travel the
length of the 'Robin Hood line', the track that runs through
the remote, hilly region north of Nottingham to the town of
Worksop.

The train was one of those ambling, rickety affairs that
stopped at every village station. I therefore had ample leisure
to review the astonishing photographs from the National
Archives, which I had pulled up on my computer the night

before. There were six photographs in all, just as Edwin Freshfield had listed them in his letter to the Home Office. The first three showed the exterior of the Druce grave ready for the exhumation, surrounded by the high walls of the temporary shed that had been constructed around it to protect the privacy of the proceedings. The fourth showed the open vault, with the outline of two adult coffins side by side. A tiny baby's coffin was clearly visible, to one side. The fifth photograph showed the coffin of T. C. Druce: a heavy, old-fashioned affair with a great plaque and brass handles, adorned with two crosses, exactly as Inspector Dew had described it. The sixth and final photograph was the most eerie of all: it revealed the open coffin, with a shrouded fig-ure bundled inside. The face, beneath the shroud, was indis-tinct; but it was just possible to make out the outline of a beard. A pencilled note with the photographs, headed 'Mr May – Registry' and dated 30 January 1932, read:

I have turned out these photographs. They are of the Druce grave opened by S. of S.'s authority early in the century. They are not for general consumption. They might be put away with papers which I suppose are preserved about this cause célèbre.

It therefore appeared that, even as late as 1932 – twenty-five years after the events – the police photographs of the Druce grave had been hidden away, considered by the authorities as unfit for public consumption.

My attention was suddenly caught by the fact that the train was approaching its final destination. I now saw that the nature of the countryside had changed dramatically since leaving the outskirts of Nottingham. No longer dense and cluttered, it had become wild and open, a chill wind whipping the lean grass in the meadows and the forlorn leaves that still clung to the trees. The few villages that we passed were remote and grim, clusters of small stone cottages hugging the windswept slopes. My guide at Welbeck for the day was to be Derek Adlam, the long-serving curator of the Portland Collection at Welbeck Abbey. He had, by an odd coincidence, asked me to meet him at Whitwell – the stop before Worksop, and Fanny's birthplace.

Alighting from the train, I could not help but look curiously around me at the village that – ostensibly, at least – was the place of Fanny's birth. But Whitwell had the same shut up, reserved expression of so many villages of this region: a tiny community fallen on hard times, closed in on itself, jealous of its secrets. I was met at the station by Mr Adlam, a charming gentleman with an encyclopaedic knowledge of the Welbeck estate.

'How long have you been here?' I asked, as we drove through winding country roads, through shafts of glancing sunlight.

'Oh, about thirty years,' he replied, with a smile.

'Does all this land still belong to the Welbeck estate?'

'Most of it.'

The extent of the terrain was impressive. I knew that the Portland London estates had already been split off from the Welbeck and other provincial estates, under the terms of the 4th Duke's will. The London estates had passed through the 4th Duke's daughter, Lady Lucy, by marriage to the de Walden family, who own a significant portion of Marylebone to this day. The gloomy palace of Harcourt

House was demolished in 1906, its vast bathrooms, trap-doors and glass screens making way for a block of expensive flats. As for the Welbeck estate, that had passed to the 6th Duke of Portland, who died in 1943. His son, the 7th Duke – known as 'Chopper' Portland – was described by the Duke of Bedford as 'a pompous-looking man with a moustache'. He had two daughters but no sons. On his death, therefore, the Portland dukedom passed to a remote kinsman who claimed his descent from the 3rd Duke, Ferdinand Cavendish-Bentinck, who became the 8th Duke of Portland. The last Duke of Portland was Ferdinand's brother, the 9th Duke, William Cavendish-Bentinck: after he died in 1990 without a male heir, the dukedom became extinct. Many years before this, however, 'Chopper' Portland had stripped the title of assets, ensuring that his daughters obtained the benefit of Welbeck Abbey and all the treasures within. The descendants of those daughters live at the abbey to this day, which remains a private residence. I was, I knew, extremely privileged to be allowed a glimpse into this closed world.

Our arrival at the abbey was announced by the giving way of country roads to a wide avenue trimmed with smart, clipped box hedges. The car drew to a halt on a gravel pathway. Leading me through a series of arches into a warren of passages, Mr Adlam said, 'This is all the 5th Duke's work.'

I took a sharp intake of breath. I was in one of the duke's underground passageways. The scale was, quite simply, enormous. Passages branched out in every direction. Running along one was a set of tracks, laid in the floor – the very tracks along which the 5th Duke's dinner had made its lonely, rattling journey from the abbey kitchens to the dining room. Most of the duke's vast network of underground tunnels on the Welbeck estate is today caving in and abandoned. Locked gates and 'Keep out' notices bar the old entrances and exits, stone slabs cover the roof skylights, and security cameras blink warning lights to discourage the inquisitive. However, in places where sections of the underground network underlie public footpaths – such as the 'Robin Hood Way' – the path overground is still punctured by moss-covered stones at regular intervals, blocking the skylights that originally lit the tunnels beneath.

Turning down a side passageway, Mr Adlam led me deftly through a maze of corridors, opening out into an enormous room that was flooded with light from huge skylights in the ceiling. This was the underground ballroom that had been constructed by the 5th Duke, originally intended as a church – unique, in its day, for possessing the largest unsupported ceiling in the world. Next came the room that had actually been the ballroom in the 5th Duke's time: the splendid, mirror-lined room with a ceiling painted in sunset colours, as the child Ottoline had remembered it almost a hundred and forty years before. Now, it was a deserted library. Empty bookcases lined the walls, and a newer, albeit very fine, Arts-and-Crafts ceiling had replaced the Duke's painted sunset.

'This', I could not help saying, 'is, quite simply, extraordinary.' And indeed it was: the vastness in scale, the melancholy grandeur, the echoing desolation of the cavernous spaces, were all but overwhelming.

'Aha.' Mr Adlam seemed mildly amused at my reaction. 'Just wait for this!' Leading me down a further set of echoing corridors, he brought me into a large, oak-panelled gallery with a solid, Arts-and-Crafts square staircase.

'Meet the 5th Duke!' said Mr Adlam.

I turned round to find myself looking straight in the eye of the bust of the 5th Duke by Eric Boehm: the very one that had been produced in the legal proceedings as evidence of his appearance. Flanking the bust of the duke were two others of Adelaide Kemble by the sculptor Jean-Pierre Dantan. She was a strangely masculine-looking woman with a strongly aquiline nose, and her great attraction for the duke had always struck me as something of a mystery.

'How strange, that this is virtually the only likeness of the 5th Duke,' I mused, walking round the bust.

'Not quite… ' Mr Adlam was looking at me oddly.

'You mean you have something else? What?' I asked.

'We have something,' Mr Adlam replied. 'I'll show you in due course. But I'm not sure *what* it is.'

My curiosity piqued, I followed the curator back to his office, in a large and echoing basement room. He pulled me up a chair.

'We have all John Hayter's portraits of Adelaide,' he said, opening a file on his computer. There, in succession across the screen, flashed literally hundreds of portraits of Adelaide Kemble in different operatic roles: Adelaide in *Semiramide*, *Norma*, *La Somnambula*, *Le Nozze di Figaro*… even Adelaide in *The Secret Marriage*.

'But then,' Mr Adlam went on, 'we also have this. I'm not sure what it is, as the label has been lost.'

Another image flashed on the screen. It was the shrunken figure of a head, couched in a simple, soft-wood box, on a piece of what looked like old curtain fabric. I knew, immediately, exactly at what I was looking.

'That must be the death mask made by the sculptor Henry Hope-Pinker,' I exclaimed, and recounted to Mr Adlam what I had read in Pinker's witness statement about the mask he was willing to produce in court. 'There was another made by Leslie Ward and used by Sir Edgar Boehm, but that was believed to be destroyed.'

'I do remember having a bit of a turn when I discovered it,' Mr Adlam remarked. 'I just opened this modest, nondescript box in an attic in the abbey, and found the duke within it, so to speak! The problem was I could not identify what it was, as the label had long been lost. How remarkably interesting.'

Half an hour later, Mr Adlam and I were ensconced at lunch in the 5th Duke's great gasworks, built to power the gaslights that flared in the maze of underground passageways beneath the abbey. Now, however, it was the Lime House Café, a buzzing tearoom offering organic ginger beer and the local speciality of Stichelton blue cheese.

We had been talking for some time about the 5th Duke.

'I read something', I told the curator, 'about the 5th Duke having had an illegitimate child. Does that mean anything to you?'

Mr Adlam frowned. 'I did hear', he replied, 'some gossip, that he had an illegitimate daughter by a servant, who was subsequently raised on the Welbeck estate. But that was thirty years ago, that I heard it. Anyway, I simply don't believe it to be true.'

'Why not?' I asked.

'Because,' he replied, 'it doesn't fit the character of the 5th Duke. If he had an illegitimate daughter, he would have had her brought up in the class to which she belonged. He would not have let her grow up as a servant.'

By the time I left Welbeck, it was already late afternoon, and the sun was beginning to fade before the rising mist as I shivered on the Whitwell Station platform, waiting for the rickety train to take me back to Nottingham. I had promised to send Mr Adlam the document catalogue numbers of the witness statements made by Leslie Ward and Henry Hope-Pinker, to help him identify the 5th Duke's death mask with greater certainty. Even as I waited, I turned over what the Welbeck curator had said in my mind. Was it not in keeping with the 5th Duke's character to have allowed his illegitimate daughter to be brought up on the estate, like a servant? Did the 5th Duke care about such things? From what I could surmise of his behaviour, he seemed to prefer the company of servants to his social equals. I was not sure that he would have considered a lowly life so very distasteful. He seemed to have wanted nothing more than to disappear into the crowd.

I arrived back at my hotel room to find a reply from my surgeon acquaintance to my query, waiting in my inbox. It was unequivocal:

There are a number of types of groin hernia (or inguinal herniae) – the main ones are 'direct' and 'indirect'. They vary in size and magnitude: one allows intestines to descend into the scrotal sac, while the other is predominantly a weakness of the abdominal wall and doesn't facilitate translocation of the bowel into the scrotal sac. In either case, there may potentially be damage to the nerves that travel and/or vessels that travel to the scrotum, but they don't often affect the testicle itself, and therefore don't affect the ability to produce sperm significantly. Irrespective of whether the hernia was indirectly affecting the testicle or not, or the hernia was so large that it had to be surgically repaired with removal of the testicle, the other testicle can still produce sperm (unless there was a double hernia or bilateral hernia affecting both sides, which is unusual).

I therefore think it unlikely that a hernia would have affected the Duke's ability to father a child – I find it likely that he still would have been able to father one or more children following that accident.

I already knew the duke had suffered from a hernia on the right side, not both. It seemed, therefore, that – contrary to the advice given the duke by his doctors – he was capable of, and indeed probably had, fathered at least one child. But who was the mother? Mr Adlam had mentioned local gossip of her being a servant. Fanny was born in 1855. This discounted the Roper sisters as possible candidates, as they were too young, and were not linked with the duke until the 1870s. Racking my brains, I recalled another name that had been mentioned in connection with the duke, by the gamekeeper Bernard Boaler – a cook by the name of Jane Walton. Looking up the census returns, I found that there was indeed a Jane Walton – then a twenty-one-year-old kitchen maid – on the staff at Welbeck in 1851, when the Duke was still Marquess of Titchfield. Her father had been a farmer in the Nottinghamshire parish of Greasley. Intriguingly, his name had been Joseph, as was that of one of Jane's brothers. Another of Jane's brothers was called William, suggesting that both Joseph and William were Walton family names.

For twenty years Jane had stayed on at Welbeck, promoted to the status of cook by 1871. By 1881 – two years after the 5th Duke's death – she was fifty years old and still unmarried, living as a modestly prosperous farmer with thirty-five acres of land. Her younger brother, Joseph, was the farm bailiff. Could Jane, the cook at Welbeck Abbey, have been the mother of Fanny and her two brothers? Interestingly, Bernard Boaler – the only witness to refer to Jane Walton, and the most frank in his description of the duke's affair with the Roper sisters – had caused Turner some concern. Before interviewing Boaler, Turner had written anxiously to Baileys, Shaw & Gillett in these terms:

I find out from Mr Bernard Boaler's cousin that he would not be at all a desirable man to approach, in fact, he would most likely do everything he could to 'upset the applecart'.

Why was Turner worried that Boaler might 'upset the applecart'? Was he fearful that Boaler, with his forthright testimony, might go a bit too far – that he might, in addition to the Roper sisters, mention one of the 5th Duke's mistresses which the defendants to the Druce claim wished to keep hidden away? A key argument of the defence to the claim that the 5th Duke of Portland had led a double life as the tradesman

T. C. Druce was that, as a result of the duke's riding accident, he was unable to father children. If it were to be made public that, on the contrary, the 5th Duke *had* fathered several children, that argument would collapse. If Jane Walton was the mother of Fanny and her brothers, she and her children were potential dynamite to the defence of the Druce case. The fact of their existence must be suppressed.

By now, I had obtained the military service records of Fanny's two sons, George and Bertram. George, the elder son, had joined the Royal Navy in 1899, at the age of sixteen. He was promoted steadily through the ranks and continued to serve in the Gunnery Branch of the Royal Navy, including in the Persian Gulf and the Mediterranean. In 1921 he was commissioned (in the rank of Commissioned Gunner), serving successively in HMSs *Surprise*, *Excellent* and *Champion*, where his ability was assessed as 'Exceptional'. On 4 May 1920 his Captain's report stated: '...I should be very pleased to have him as one of my Lieutenants any time. Specially recommended for advancement.' He received a personal commendation for salvaging an aircraft off Malta on 4 December 1931, and was promoted to Lieutenant Commander in 1933.

George retired from the Royal Navy in 1933, at the age of fifty. However, he re-enlisted at the outbreak of the Second World War. He was discharged in 1946 and released in 1947 (aged sixty-four), five days after being promoted to Commander. He was awarded the Distinguished Service Cross, and had the further distinction of a Mention in Despatches in the New Year's Honours List of 1 January 1941. Altogether, George Lawson would have earned at least eight medals for his service during the two world wars. He died in 1970, at the age of eighty-seven.

Fanny's younger son, Bertram, had been enlisted at the age of just fifteen as a Drummer in the Royal Marines, Chatham Division. A short lad, he was only four feet eight and one-eighth of an inch in height (five feet six and a half inches when he was discharged from the Navy as a grown man). He served as a Bugler until 1907, when he became a Private. He was then promoted through the ranks to Lance Corporal, Corporal and then Sergeant, in which rank he served for the duration of the First World War. Throughout these twenty years of service, he was invariably assessed as being of 'Very Good' character and 'Very Good' ability. In 1920, he was promoted to the rank of Colour Sergeant. Like his brother George he received an impressive number of decorations during his period of service, including a Bronze Medal for Military Valour in 1918, a Meritorious Service Medal in 1919, three First World War medals and a Mention in Despatches in September 1918. He died in 1954, at the age of seventy.

It appeared, therefore, that Fanny's two sons – the putative grandsons of the 5th Duke of Portland – had both had exemplary careers in the military. They were, in fact, war heroes. Looking at the successive reports over the years by their commanding officers – invariably in the same neat, army script, invariably repeating the same remarks such as 'VG', 'Excellent', 'Exemplary' – I was struck by how different the approach of Fanny Lawson's family to exclusion and rejection was from that adopted by the first family of T. C. Druce, the Crickmer-Druces. While the Crickmer-Druces had thought only of revenge for the wrongs done to them, of looking back to the past to reclaim a misconceived heritage, the members of this small family had looked to the future, and dedicated themselves to the service of their country.

I then turned my attention to the two 'brothers' mentioned by Fanny in her letter, William and Joseph. If William was indeed the nine-year-old boy listed in the Ashbury household along with Fanny in the 1861 census, the records showed that he had died a young, and presumably tragic, death in 1870, at just eighteen years old. This was the period when Fanny was out at service with the Holland family in Sheffield, so it was perfectly possible that she had not known about his death.

Of the other brother, Joseph, I could find no trace. A handwritten note of a meeting with Thomas Warner Turner at the offices of Baileys, Shaw & Gillett dated 17 April 1907, which included a reference to Annie Roper, also contained the cryptic words '<u>In Joseph</u>', heavily underlined. The note, however, gave no further details or information. Other than this, I drew a blank.

The lack of information about Joseph's fate left me with a feeling of frustration. I had sensed the desperation in Fanny's letters. She had wanted, so much, to know what had happened to her brothers, to the family from whom she had been separated as a child. Irrational and illogical though it was, I felt I had let her down. As far as I could see, Joseph had vanished for ever: he had been excised by the hand of Victorian censorship, wiped clean from the slate of history. Did a vital clue lie buried in some obscure archive or pile of letters, hidden in a long-forgotten drawer or crumbling to dust in an attic? For the present, I could not tell. The figure of Joseph remained an obstinately elusive question mark, hidden in the inscrutable folds of the past that blanketed him like a pall.

An Obscure Grave

London, December 2013

I had now come to the end of my investigation of the Druce affair. Or perhaps, it would be more correct to say, I had reached the furthest point I could. For the picture I had uncovered was not so much in the form of a puzzle, to which there was a neat solution, merely requiring the finding and replacing of missing pieces. It was more like a reflection seen through a glass darkly, growing brighter and brighter and revealing more of the underlying pattern as it was polished, but never finally reaching gleaming perfection. The writer Kate Summerscale, in her book *The Suspicions of Mr Whicher*, has defined detective investigations in these terms:

> Perhaps this is the purpose of detective investigations, real and fictional – to transform sensation, horror and grief into a puzzle, and then to solve the puzzle, to make it go away. 'The detective story,' observed Raymond Chandler in 1949, 'is a tragedy with a happy ending.' A storybook detective starts by confronting us with a murder and ends by absolving us of it. He clears us of guilt. He relieves us of uncertainty. He removes us from the presence of death.

And yet, the 'investigators' of the Druce affair across the decades – Chief Inspector Dew, J. G. Littlechild, the estate manager turned amateur sleuth Turner, myself many years after the event – all of us had polished the mirror of the past just a little more, revealing another detail of the underlying image. But to re-create it to perfection would be impossible. Worse than impossible, it would be a lie. Because it would imply that time can be recaptured in its entirety – that nothing is lost by the passage of years. But the past is always the past, and something is always lost; just as something is always pre-served; and, also, discovered.

In the case of the Druce affair, what had occurred in the past had not simply been lost owing to the natural erosion of time. It seemed, on the contrary, from my investigations, that there had been a deliberate – and partially successful – attempt to cut out entire events, to erase certain people whole-sale from the record, in order to facilitate the fighting of the case. The existence of Fanny Lawson and her brothers had been, effectively, hushed up in order to bolster a defence that the 5th Duke was incapable of fathering an heir. Even before the Druce claim was filed, the splitting of Fanny Lawson from her mother and brothers in early childhood was clearly an attempt to dilute the impact of their presence, so much more glaringly obvious if they had remained together as a family. It echoed the deliberate fragmenting of his first family that T. C. Druce accomplished, by telling his daughter Fanny that her mother was dead, and sending the Crickmer-Druce children on separate paths.

The Druce affair, in fact, was significant not so much because it was a fraud; or because it was started by a mad woman; or because it was an early example of a media sensa-tion. It was significant because of the light it shed on the lies, deceit and hypocrisy practised by society at the time, and their tragic consequences.

In the course of my investigations, I managed to track down a great-grandson of Fanny Lawson, and therefore putatively a direct lineal descendant of the 5th Duke of Portland. Tentatively, I wrote asking for an interview. The address was a suburban house, a world away from Welbeck Abbey. Several months later, I received a reply. After long and anxious deliberation, the letter stated, the respondent had concluded that he could not help me in my inquiries. He asked that I respect his privacy. Evidently, in one small corner of England, the pain of events that occurred more than a century and a half ago lives on to this day.

Some months after my return from Nottingham, I made my last research trip in relation to the Druce affair. It was a cold, wintry day, and the wind burned my cheeks as I made my way down the winding paths of Kensal Green cemetery. It took almost an hour, and the assistance of the cemetery keeper, before I found what I was looking for. It was the grave of the 5th Duke of Portland.

Despite being the largest plot in the cemetery, it was very difficult to find. When I finally succeeded in locating it, I found it to be extremely plain. It consisted of a pink Peterhead granite slab, surrounded by grey granite kerbs and posts. It, also, had been assailed by the forces of time: the tombstone had been damaged by bombing in the Second World War, and the bronze chains and fittings had been stolen in the 1950s. The inscription read:

SACRED TO THE MEMORY OF
THE MOST NOBLE
WILLIAM JOHN CAVENDISH BENTINCK SCOTT
FIFTH DUKE OF PORTLAND.
BORN 17TH SEPTEMBER 1800.
DIED 6TH DECEMBER 1879.

For a few minutes, I stood at the grave in contemplation. I could not help thinking that, with this plain and simple monument overgrown with the bushes that he ordered to be planted there, the 5th Duke had finally achieved his aim in life, which was to disappear completely from view. I was sure, too, that he would have been proud of his grandsons' distinguished careers in the service of their country, had he known about them, and equally pleased that his subsequent progeny had vanished from the public gaze, into the crowds of ordinary folk hurrying about their daily business. It was a fate the duke had always longed to share, but from which he had been precluded by accident of birth and fortune. I watched the sparrows hopping in the bushes, and listened to the wintry wind whistling in the long grass; and wondered how anyone could ever imagine unquiet slumbers, for the sleeper in that quiet earth.

POSTSCRIPT

In November 1907, two gentlemen named Calkin, one from Millville, New Jersey, and the other from New Zealand, announced themselves as claimants to the Portland estates. Nothing more was heard of them.

Letters in the Attic

Dorset, November 2014

Footfalls echo in the memory
Down the passage which we did not take
Towards the door we never opened
Into the rose-garden.

T.S. ELIOT
Four Quartets

It was a damp November morning, almost a year after I had – as I then thought – completed my investigation into the Druce affair. Since the hardback publication of The Dead Duke, His Secret Wife and the Missing Corpse in September 2014, I had been swamped with correspondence from people interested in the Druce-Portland case – descendants of the protagonists, historians and genealogists researching the history of the families involved. The most intriguing communication was the following Tweet:

@PiuEatwell hi, I have just got your book and this may be about my family as my great- grandad was G A Lawson son of Fanny very interesting.

Further correspondence established that the author of the Tweet was indeed the great-grandson of George Lawson, Fanny's elder son, and that George had written voluminous memoirs that were still in the possession of his descendants. I was also informed that there were photographs of Fanny in existence.

It was with a view to examining these memoirs and photographs that I now found myself rattling on an Intercity train from London to Dorset, where Fanny's descendants now lived. The house was in a small and unassuming village, nestling in the shadow of the grey ruins of Corfe Castle. When I arrived, I found that the whole family was gathered expectantly. Over copious cups of tea, they told me a tragic tale. Fanny had lived a hard life. Her husband, George Lawson Snr., had been a drunkard and ne'er-do-well. He had met a terrible end, cut in half when he fell under the wheels of a moving train while involved in a drunken brawl. Fanny had soldiered on alone, bringing up her two boys to grow into the fine men they were to become. Mysteriously, Fanny never seemed to have any obvious income – she appeared to survive on private means, but what these were nobody could ever establish. Her son George had frequently told his children and grandchildren that the family were descended from the 5th Duke of Portland, and that Welbeck Abbey had been the childhood playground of his mother. They had never believed the story. Until, that is, they read my book.

I had now come to the moment for which I had been waiting. With some ceremony, I was led to a room where – carefully arranged on a bed – were piles of letters, hand-written loose-leaf sheets and photographs. Here, in beautiful script, were George's memoirs – detailed records of his experiences in war and peacetime, of the ships he had commanded, and the battles he had fought. Whilst the bulk of the memoirs dealt with George's professional life, there were a few pages here and there that touched on other, more personal issues. One such passage related the story of how George had found out the identity of his true grandfather. It ran as follows:

My mother, when I was a small boy, wanted to tell me a story of her earliest days; but as this entailed the loss of playing time, it did not soak in. Years after, on looking for some information in an old Bible belonging to my Grandfather [i.e. George Ashbury], my mother's name was not there. This was very strange; for in those days, in every Family Bible, the names of all children were entered as soon as they were christened. The list was headed by Aunt Hannah, then should have been my mother Fanny, but there was no entry of her name; instead came Aunt Florrie, followed by the youngest, Lucy. On pointing this out to my mother, she told me the story she had wanted to tell me years before: a story that I now sincerely believed. It was the story of her connection with the Cavendish-Bentincks [...]

The 5th Duke of Portland, son of the 4th Duke, was William John Cavendish Bentinck Scott, and was born 18th September 1800. Died 6th December 1879. He married secretly and built the underground quarters at Welbeck Abbey where he and his bride resided, when staying at Welbeck. His only object in getting married was to have a son to continue the succession in the direct line. When the baby was born and it turned out to be a girl, he was furious and had it put out with foster parents. This baby, the only legitimate child of the 5th Duke, was named Fanny, and was put out with and adopted by the Duke's land overseer George Ashbury, who died in 1892. Fanny left the Ashburys when quite a young girl and lived with a family in Edinburgh named Crawford, who travelled a good deal on the Continent, taking Fanny with them. She married in Edinburgh and became my mother.

So, there it was. George had found out the truth about Fanny's parentage after noticing that her birth had not been recorded in the Ashbury Family Bible, and confronting her over this fact. Interestingly, it appeared that there was no note either of the boy William, who had been listed in the censuses as part of the Ashbury household in the 1860s. It seems, therefore, that George did not even know of his putative uncle's

As for the strange story related in George's memoirs of the 5th Duke's 'secret marriage', it was difficult to know what to make of it. I had already trawled through hundreds of files on the Druce case and the succession of the Portland dukedom at Nottingham University, the National Archives, and the Lord Chancellor's Department. There had certainly been rumours of a 'secret marriage' – indeed, such rumours had been part of the building blocks of the Druce claim – but there was no hard and fast evidence. And it was easy to see why Fanny might have fabricated such a tale, to cover up the shame of illegitimacy when relating the story of her parentage to her eldest son. Nor did George's memoirs contain any reference as to the identity of Fanny's mother.

The surviving photograph of Fanny turned out to be a tinted reproduction on glass. It revealed a handsome woman with piercing blue eyes and a refined, aquiline nose, uncannily reminiscent of the bust of the 5th Duke. Fanny's gaze was veiled, her demeanour stiff in her ruffled collar that was clasped tightly shut with an elegantly simple brooch. It was a face that revealed no secrets, but rather a reserved stoicism.

Taking my farewells of the family, I set off for the train to London. Perhaps, finally, I really was now turning my back on the Druce case.

> And deeper than did ever plummet sound
> I'll drown my book...

Those final words of Prospero in Shakespeare's *The Tempest* haunted me during the long journey home. Was this really the end of it? Prospero's final drowning of his book is an ironic act, the sea being the repository for things to be deposited, lost, found and returned, having experienced the ultimate transformation of a 'sea change'. I had already, figuratively speaking, 'drowned' this book once, only for it to re-surface with a new twist. Who knows, I pondered, but that it might float up again from the depths, transformed by yet another sea change?

For the moment, though, I turned my back reluctantly on the dust that re-settled on the ashes of the past, and turned my attention to other things.

NOTES

Key to abbreviations

- Records from the Nottingham University Portland (London) archives are referred to as 'NU', followed by the catalogue reference number (starting 'Pl').

- Records from the National Archives are referred to as 'NA', followed by the catalogue reference number.

- Records from the London Metropolitan Archives are referred to as 'LMA', followed by the catalogue reference number.

SCENE ONE

p. 3   *Description of the 6th Duke's arrival at Welbeck.* The description of the arrivals, of the people who took part and other details are taken from *Men, Women and Things: Memories of the Duke of Portland K.G., G.C.V.O.* by the 6th Duke of Portland, London: Faber & Faber, 1937, in particular the account of their arrival by the 6th Duke's half-sister, Lady Ottoline Morrell.

p. 3   *Great Central Railway Company.* Previously the Manchester, Sheffield and Lincolnshire Railway, the company had changed its name in August 1879.

p. 3   *After about three hours.* In 1879, three non-stop trains per day slipped their last coach at Worksop, allowing a faster journey time from King's Cross.

p. 4   *'The young duke! Did you see him?'* See the account of Lady Ottoline Morrell in *Men, Women and Things*, op. cit., p. 32.

p. 5   *The portrait of Bess.* After a 1592 portrait of Bess by Rowland Lockey, still in the Welbeck Collection.

p. 5   *One biographer says of her.* See Brian Masters, *The Dukes*, London: Pimlico, 2001, p. 138.

p. 7   *squirrel scampering through the frozen bracken.* The description of the approach to Welbeck Abbey and the landscape is taken from that given in the section on Welbeck Abbey in *Historic Houses of the United Kingdom; descriptive, historical pictorial*, London: Cassell & Company, 1892, chapter on Welbeck Abbey by C. Edwardes.

p. 8　*Description of Welbeck as at the 5th Duke's death in* 1879. See account of Lady Ottoline Morrell in *Men, Women and Things*, op. cit.

p. 9　*no coat of arms.* See proof of Thomas Keetley, the Duke's coachman, at NU Pl L1/2/7/99.

p. 9　*carriage… goods wagon.* See account of Lady Ottoline Morrell in *Men, Women and Things*, op. cit., p. 33.

p. 9　*his Grace's impatient voice from inside the carriage.* See *Daily Express*, 20 June 1903.

p. 9　*dead body housed in a box on the roof.* See Theodore Besterman, *The Druce-Portland Case*, London: Duckworth, 1935, p. 17.

p. 9　*two or even three overcoats (whatever the weather).* There are many testimonies to the 5th Duke's eccentric style of dress. See, for example, the evidence of estate worker, the engineer Mr James Rudd, reported in the *Lichfield Mercury*, Friday, 13 December 1907; also the *Daily Chronicle*, 15 March 1898.

p. 9　*vast umbrella.* See William Day, *Reminiscences of the Turf*, London: Richard Bentley & Son, 1886, p. 137.

p. 10　*on pain of immediate dismissal.* See obituary notice of the 5th Duke in *The Times*, 8 December 1897; also Charles J. Archard, *The Portland Peerage Romance*, London: Greening & Co. Ltd, 1907.

p. 10　*kindly and generous employer.* See obituary of the duke in *The Times*, 8 December 1879.

p. 10　*donkeys… umbrellas.* See account of Lady Ottoline Morrell in *Men, Women and Things*, op. cit., p. 36.

p. 10　*skating rink.* See account of Lady Ottoline Morrell in *Men, Women and Things*, op. cit., p. 36.

p. 10　*listening to the men singing.* See proof of Joseph Harvey at NU PL L1/2/6/4.

p. 12　*'no beauty in these rooms'.* See account of Lady Ottoline Morrell in *Men, Women and Things*, op. cit., p. 35.

p. 12　*'leaving… the lonely figure'.* See account of Lady Ottoline Morrell in *Men, Women and Things*, op. cit., p. 34.

p. 14　*Rugeley Poisoner.* See the memoirs of the politician and journalist Louis John Jennings (1836–1893).

p. 14   *several eye-witnesses at the inquest.* See *Daily Express*, 10 July 1903.

p. 15   *body laid out.* The 6th Duke notes in his autobiography that he never met his predecessor in life, although he saw him in death: *Men, Women and Things*, op. cit., p. 30.

p. 16   *Medici lace collar.* See Archard, op. cit.

p. 16   *'The City? I have only been here in processions.'* See *Chips: the Diaries of Sir Henry Channon*, ed. R. R. James, London: Weidenfeld & Nicolson, 1967, p. 468.

SCENE TWO

p. 18   *Proceedings of the 9 March 1898 consistory court hearing.* The dialogue in this chapter is taken from the record of the court proceedings in the London Consistory Court of 9 March 1898 and the interview with Mrs Druce and Dr Forbes Winslow reported in *Lloyd's Weekly Newspaper* of 13 March 1898.

p. 18   *Wellington Chapel of St Paul's Cathedral.* See Besterman, op. cit., p. 18. The description of the chapel here is based on the contemporary description given by the Rev. Arthur Dimock MA, *St Paul: An Account of the Old and New Buildings with a Short Historical Sketch*, London: George Bell & Sons, 1900.

p. 19   *A diminutive and portly figure.* Physical descriptions of Chancellor Tristram are taken from *Thomas Hutchinson Tristram: For Forty Years Chancellor of London: A Memoir*, London: Longmans, Green and Co., 1916, pp. 24–5.

p. 19   Smith and Others *v.* Tebbit and Others, 1867. See the account of this case in *Thomas Hutchinson Tristram: For Forty Years Chancellor of London: A Memoir*, op. cit., pp. 24–5.

p. 20   *middle classes fallen on hard times.* The physical description and clothing of Anna Maria Druce is taken from illustrations in newspaper reports of the time. She is referred to as having once been handsome in a number of newspaper reports, for example, in *Society*, 3 December 1898.

p. 24   *a fact that bothered the chancellor.* The chancellor in his judgments repeatedly referred to the significance of T. C. Druce's medical certificate not being signed by a doctor.

p. 26   *Dr Lyttleton Stewart Forbes Winslow.* The physical description of Forbes Winslow is taken from contemporaneous portraits and photographs.

SCENE THREE

p. 29   *gaunt figure in widow's weeds.* See the interview with Mr T. E. Bois (mis-named as 'Tu' Bois in some accounts), superintendent of Highgate Cemetery, reported in *Lloyd's Weekly Newspaper*, 13 March 1898. He states to the reporter that Mrs Druce had been 'worrying' him for some time.

p. 29   *She had even brought a mining engineer.* See *Lloyd's Weekly Newspaper*, 12 June 1898.

p. 30   *firm of undertakers.* See *Lloyd's Weekly Newspaper*, 13 March 1898.

p. 30   *'Depend upon it…'* Quoted in *Lloyd's Weekly Newspaper*, 13 March 1898 (as are Mr Bois' misgivings on the issue).

p. 33   *revelatory biography.* Tomalin, Claire *The Invisible Woman: The Story of Nelly Ternan and Charles Dickens*, London: Viking, 1990.

p. 33   *'official' account of Dickens' death in 1870 was a fabrication.* As argued by Tomalin in *The Invisible Woman*, op. cit.

p. 34   *Henry Wainwright.* The full story of the Wainwright saga is recounted in grisly detail in Judith Flanders' *The Invention of Murder*, London: HarperPress, 2011.

p. 35   *a 'certain impatient gaiety of disposition… profound duplicity of life'.* Robert Louis Stevenson, *Strange Case of Dr Jekyll and Mr Hyde* (1886): Norton Critical Edition, 2003, p. 48.

p. 36   *'high moral tone'.* Oscar Wilde, *The Importance of Being Earnest* (1895), Bantam, 2005, p. 465.

SCENE FOUR

p. 38   *to work as a salesman for old Mr Munns.* See statement of Josh Cooke, cabinet maker, at NU PI/LI/1/1/29.

p. 38   *The Pantheon Bazaar.* See Knight, Charles, *Knight's London*, London: Charles Knight & Co., 1841–44; also *Physiology of the London Idler*, Chapter IV – *Of the Pantheon, considered in relation to the Lounger*, in *Punch*, Jul–Dec 1842.

p. 40   *discreet brougham.* See statement of Josh Cooke, op. cit., NU PI LI/1/1/29.

p. 40   *the sight of red meat was abhorrent to him.* See the *Daily Express*, 22 June 1903.

p. 40   *a particular fondness for wigs.* See the *Daily Express*, 22 June 1903.

p. 40   *rose or flower in his buttonhole.* See NU Pl L1/1/1/29.

p. 40   *jaundiced appearance… brooked no contradiction.* See interview with former employee of Baker Street Bazaar, Mr Redgell, in the *Daily Express*, 26 June 1903.

p. 40   *'The old man… had an eye that could see right through you.'* See the deposition evidence given by George Druce's son Charles at NU PL L1/2/4/2/23/2.

p. 40   *underground passages… red curtains.* Interview with former employee of Baker Street Bazaar in *P. T. O.*, 2 February 1907. There was much dispute about whether Druce's office had curtains or not, but in the end Herbert Druce actually admitted as much in the perjury proceedings of 1908, as did Mrs Stoward, widow of the former partner of T. C. Druce (see NU Pl L1/4/2/12; NU Pl L1/2/6/12).

p. 41   *'sprung from the clouds… profound secret'.* Comments such as this were frequently made of T. C. Druce. See, for example, the *Daily Express*, 20 July 1903; *P. T. O.*, 2 February 1907; interview with J. G. Littlechild on 5 December 1898, NU Pl L1/9/1/2.

p. 41   *refusing to deal with all but his regular business acquaintances.* See, for example, the affidavit of James Smeaton of the horticultural engineers Gray & Ormson of Chelsea, filed in support of Mrs Druce's probate action, which states that Druce refused to meet him when the partner of the firm that he usually dealt with was sick (NU PI L1/1/2). Also interview with Smeaton in the *Daily Mail*, 30 August 1898.

p. 41   *Mill Hill… Holcombe House.* See 'Hendon: Growth before 1850', in *A History of the County of Middlesex: Volume 5: Hendon, Kingsbury, Great Stanmore, Little Stanmore, Edmonton Enfield, Monken Hadley, South Mimms, Tottenham*, eds T. F. T. Baker and R. B. Pugh, London: Victoria County History, 1976, pp. 5–11; also the statement of the cook employed at Holcombe House, Charlotte High, at NU Pl L1/11/6/799/2.

p. 42   *'Not even so much as a pair of gloves'.* See interview with former Baker Street employee Mr Redgell, in the *Daily Express*, 26 June 1903.

p. 43   *'I see him now, the dead man!'* See NU Pl L1/1/2/1.

p. 43   *Harcourt House.* Cited by Tim Knox in *Precautions for Privacy: The 'Mole Duke's' Secret Garden at Harcourt House, Cavendish Square*, in *The London Gardener*, volume 2, 1996–1997, 2:27–33.

p. 44   *circular path.* See Knox, op. cit.

p. 45   *Sir William Folkes.* See NU Pl L1/2/8/2/20.

p. 45   *farewell speech.* See summary of events in 5th Duke's life complied by Baileys, Shaw & Gillett at NU Pl L1/2/8/2/20.

p. 46   *contemporary newspaper report.* See summary of events in 5th Duke's life compiled by Baileys, Shaw & Gillett at NU Pl L1/2/8/2/20.

p. 46   *the old duchess never forgave Lord John.* See statement of the widow Mrs Bethia Hartley at NU Pl L1/2/6/13.

p. 46   *Hayter.* The incident of Hayter being recalled to Harcourt House to take away the pastels of Adelaide is recounted by Flora Northesk-Wilson, the painter's granddaughter. The pastels remained with Hayter for the rest of his life. On his death in 1895, they reverted to Welbeck Abbey, but the 6th Duke gave Hayter's daughter one of them as a gift (see letter from Flora Northesk-Wilson published in the *Daily Mail*, 20 December 1898).

p. 47   *Lady Londonderry.* Cited in Masters, op. cit., p. 162.

p. 47   *repressed homosexual.* See, for example, Gwyn Headley and Wim Meulenkamp, *Follies: Grottoes, Gardens and Buildings*, London: Aurum Press, 1999, p. 404.

p. 47   *carriage accident.* Details of the carriage accident were related in court depositions by the duke's close friends the Dowager Countess Manvers (NU Pl L1 2/4/22) and the Dowager Countess of Cork (NU Pl L1/2/4/29).

p. 48   *average height of the Victorian male.* See statistical analysis for the Galton Institute, by Gary E. Pittman in their December 1999 Newsletter: 'We see that the average height of an Englishman [in the Victorian age] is 5'6" and the range of heights is between 5'3" and 5'9". An Englishman less than 5'3" would be considered unusually short, and one taller than 5'9" would be unusually tall. You would expect to see only about one in a thousand Englishmen above or below the normal range.'

p. 48   *'unhealthy pallor'.* See proof of Charles Nevett at NU Pl L1/ 2/6/13.

p. 48   *a form of eczema.* See interview with the foreman of Truefitt & Co., *Daily Express*, 22 June 1903.

p. 48   *'intense irritation of the skin'.* Cited in A. S. Turbeville, *A History of Welbeck Abbey and its Owners*, London: Faber & Faber, 1934, p. 434.

p. 48   *Henry Powell, recollected.* See proof of Henry Powell at NU Pl L1/2/6/13.

p. 49   *averse to red meat.* See the *Daily Express*, 26 June 1903.

p. 49   *Descriptions of the 5th Duke's mode of dress.* Descriptions of the oddities of the 5th Duke's manner of dress are legion: see, for example, the *Daily Express*, 22 June 1903; also the *Daily Chronicle*, 15 March 1898.

pp. 49–50 *Particulars of clothes orders of duke from Messrs Batt & Co.* See interview with Mr Batt Jnr, son of the firm, in the *Daily Mail*, 26 August 1898. Several details given by Mr Batt – including the mysterious use of different initials on linen – are echoed by Lady Ottoline Morrell in her account of the 6th Duke's discoveries during their early days at Welbeck.

p. 50 *'inclemency of a Siberian winter'*. See Day, op. cit., p. 137.

p. 51 *quite bald*. See statement of the duke's coachman Thomas Keetley at NU Pl L1/2/7/99.

p. 51 *Wig-maker's visit to Harcourt House*. See interview with former foreman of Truefitt & Co., *Daily Express*, 22 and 26 June 1903. The description of the room honeycombed with wigs in pigeonholes at Harcourt House mirrors that of the description of a room at Welbeck Abbey given by Lady Ottoline Morrell and recounted in *Men, Women and Things*, op. cit.

p. 51 *Duke's handling of newspapers and coins*. See interview with former servant of 5th Duke of Portland in the *Daily Express*, 1 July 1903. Several accounts of servants and tradesmen refer to the peculiarity of coins having to be washed before the duke would touch them (see, for example, the interview with the duke's tailor, Mr Batt, in the *Daily Mail*, 26 August 1898, and also the proof of the valet William Kerridge at NU Pl L1/2/6/13).

p. 52 *letter boxes... As his own valet conceded*. See interview with duke's former valet in *P. T. O.*, 2 February 1907. William Day in his *Reminiscences of the Turf* (op. cit., p. 137) also remarks that, in later years, the duke would scarcely see anybody except a few of his old servants. The young Lady Ottoline had noticed the heavy brass letter boxes on the duke's door.

p. 53 *left Welbeck Abbey for the last time*. See proof of Thomas Hardwick at NU Pl L1/2/6/13.

SCENE FIVE

p. 54 *the best 'rummy go'*. The *Daily Mail*, 25 August 1898.

p. 56 Great Expectations. For an enlightening discussion of the meaning of the word 'gentleman' in Charles Dickens' *Great Expectations*, see Rupert Christiansen, 'What is a Gentleman?' in 'Charles Dickens'

Great Expectations: a new interpretation for students', http://exec.typepad.com/greatexpectations.

p. 57   *Boucicault,* London Assurance. See Dion Boucicault, *London Assurance*, stage adaptation by Ronald Eyre, London: Methuen & Co., 1971, Act Five, Scene I.

p. 57   Self-Help *by Samuel Smiles.* See Samuel Smiles, *Self-Help*, 1859, Project Gutenberg ebook.

p. 60   *letter... to the Home Office.* See NA X27066.

p. 61   *Memorandum of Edwin Freshfield.* See Memorandum of Freshfields to the Home Office dated March 1899, NA BT 31/12141/95200.

p. 62   *As one contemporary newspaper.* See *Lloyd's Weekly Newspaper*, 27 March, 1898.

p. 64   *private investigators.* The files of the private investigator concerned – J. G. Littlechild – are now part of the Portland (London) Collection at Nottingham University.

p. 64   *Duke and Herbert Druce collaboration.* The Portland (London) Collection includes extensive correspondence between Baileys, Shaw & Gillett (on behalf of the duke) and Freshfields (on behalf of Herbert Druce) and exchanges of evidence and information.

p. 65   *long vacation.* See the description of the long vacation in Charles Dickens' *Bleak House*, Chapter 19.

p. 66   *ghost of the unburied ducal tradesman.* The *Daily Mail*, 27 August 1898.

p. 66   *spiritualistic séance. The People*, 13 March 1898.

p. 66   *'the most interesting woman in England'.* The *Daily Mail*, 2 September 1898.

p. 66   *Serial on* The Double Duke. The *Daily Mail*, 29 August 1898. The series, *The Double Duke*, penned by the pot-boiler author Houghton Townley, ran 5 September–15 October 1898.

p. 66   *'I myself was a Miss Butler'.* See interview in *Lloyd's Weekly Newspaper*, 13 March 1898. Anna Maria's story was contradicted by Mr Stoward in an interview with J. G. Littlechild (see note below).

p. 67   *daughter of a humble Irish paperhanger.* See the private-investigator reports of J. G. Littlechild for the duke's solicitors, Baileys, Shaw & Gillett, interview with Mr Stoward (a partner and old acquaintance of T. C. Druce), NU PI LI/1/3/3. Anna Maria several times referred in newspaper reports to her birth in Ireland, and gave Ireland as her place of birth in the 1881 English census.

p. 67   *Caroline Graves.* See Lyn Pykett, *Wilkie Collins*, Oxford World's Classics, ebook 2005.

p. 67   *new, cannier, more upwardly mobile type.* See Kathryn Hughes, *The Victorian Governess*, London: Hambledon, 2001, Chapter 3.

p. 67   *Lady Elizabeth Eastlake.* From *Vanity Fair, Jane Eyre, and the Governess' Benevolent Institution*, *Quarterly Review*, 84 (December 1848), p. 176.

p. 69   *carriage and pair... Brighton.* Note of evidence of Anna Maria Druce in the consistory court proceedings, NU PI LI/1/1/5.

p. 69   *three children.* The 1871 census return shows Annie May at 43 Belsize Square with Florence, Walter and Bertha. Mr Stoward (see note below) refers to Walter being persuaded to leave Anna Maria and return to Belsize Park.

p. 70   *mystery about him... guarded her dead husband's secrets.* Note of evidence of Anna Maria Druce in the consistory court proceedings, NU PI LI/1/1/5.

p. 70   *Staffordshire.* The 1876 *Kelly's Directory of Stafford* gives Walter Druce as living in Little Haywood. The 1880 *Directory* gives him as living in Hopton Hall, Hopton. Both are in Staffordshire.

p. 70   *business failures.* The accountant and executor of T. C. Druce's will, Alexander Young, mentioned in his evidence during the proceedings in the probate court that Walter Druce had lost his legacy in failed farming ventures (NU PI/d/2).

p. 70   *relations with old Mrs Druce.* See interview with Anna Maria Druce in *Society*, 3 December 1898.

p. 71   *the workhouse.* The records of the Examinations for Settlement of the Marylebone Workhouse record an entry for Anna Maria Druce being examined for eligibility for entry to the workhouse in February 1884 (LMA ST/M/BG/165/10). The Creed Register for 1884 records the entry in February of Anna Maria and her children Margaret (Marguerite), Sidney, Walter and Nina. Florence was presumably out at work as a house servant at this point (see later note). Anna Maria described her time in the Marylebone Workhouse in an interview with *Society* on 3 December, repeating this story in an interview with the *Modern Detective* (30 March 1898). Mr Stoward in his interview with J. G. Littlechild stated that she had been 'living on the public' since 1881 (NU PI LI/1/3/3).

p. 71   *arrival at the workhouse.* This routine treatment of new arrivals at the workhouse is described in many contemporary accounts, such as the writer Charles Shaw's account of a temporary stay at the Wolstanton and Burslem Union Workhouse at Chell in 1842, in his autobiography *When I was a Child* (1903).

p. 71   *'workhouse stripe'.* The description of female inmates' garb is given by the master of Marylebone Workhouse, George Douglas, in his 1892 Report on the Management of the Workhouse, presented to the Workhouse Visiting Committee of the Guardians of the Poor (London Metropolitan Archives).

p. 71   *silent rows... scarlet-lettered anger.* See contemporary photo-graphs of meals taken in Marylebone and other workhouses in Peter Higginbotham, *The Workhouse Encyclopaedia*, Stroud: The History Press, 2012; photograph of the new casual ward in the Marylebone Workhouse designed by Henry Saxon Snell in 1867, featured in *The Illustrated London News*.

pp. 71–2 *Daily routine.* Based on the 1835 Poor Law Commissioners' daily routine for able-bodied inmates.

p. 72   *gossip and whisper tales.* See Shaw, op. cit.

p. 72   *the rest of Walter's family.* In the 1891 census, Florence is listed as a 'general servant' to a family in Willesden and Nina as an inmate of the Field Lane Industrial School for Girls in Church Row, Hampstead. According to the New South Wales Unassisted Passenger Lists, Sidney Druce arrived in Sydney, New South Wales, on 17 August 1895. According to the 1891 census return for Marylebone Rackham Infirmary, Walter Druce (aged fourteen) spent census night in April as a patient on the premises. He is described as a 'sailor seas'.

p. 72   *died there in 1891... buried in a pauper's grave.* In her interview referring to her time spent in the Marylebone Workhouse with *Society* on 3 December 1898, Anna Maria stated that she had a son who 'died there' and was buried in a pauper's grave. She repeated this story in an interview with the *Modern Detective* (30 March 1898). The Marylebone Workhouse Creed Register shows that a Walter Druce was admitted from the training ship *Exmouth* and discharged to the Rackham Street Infirmary on 4 March 1891 (LMA X095/913). There is an entry for a Walter Druce, aged fourteen, in the records of the Rackham Street Infirmary for the April 1891 census, showing he was still there at this point. The records of the London Borough of Kensington include the death certificate of one Walter Druce, aged fourteen, apprentice from the training ship *Exmouth*, who died on 13 June 1891 at the Marylebone Infirmary.

p. 73   *'That will be exhumation number two'*. Quoted in interview with Mrs Druce in the *Modern Detective*, 30 March 1898.

p. 73   *nine months' unpaid rent*. Mr Stoward, in his interview with Baileys, Shaw & Gillett of January 1899, mentioned that he had met a Mr Marler in court, who had stated that his wife was keeping Mrs Druce at Tavistock Square, and that she had not paid rent in nine months (NU PI LI/1/3/3).

p. 74   *offers to settle the case*. Anna Maria stated on several occasions that she had received offers to settle the case, from both the duke's and Herbert Druce's representatives, exceeding £60,000. See, for example, interview in the *Modern Detective*, 30 March 1898.

SCENE SIX

p. 75   *the Man from the* Star… *fog*. The December of 1898 was characterized by fog in London – see, for example, the *London Daily News*, 22 December 1898. The *Star* man's visit to Mrs Druce's offices which is recounted in this chapter is based on a real-life *Star* journalist's visit, reported in the *Star* of 23 December 1898, and the incidents described are as reported in this account.

p. 76   *All around… were newspaper offices*. The description of Fleet Street is based on the account of Charles Peabody, one-time reporter on the *Morning Post* and editor of the *Yorkshire Post*, in *English Journalism and the Men Who Have Made It* (1882).

p. 77   *preferred thrills to politics*. See Karen Roggenkamp, *Narrating the News: New Journalism and Literary Genre in Late Nineteenth Century Newspapers and Fiction*: Kent, Ohio: Kent State University Press, 2005; Dennis Griffiths, *Fleet Street: Five Hundred Years of the Press*: The British Library, 2006.

p. 80   Daily Mail… *loggerheads with the* News of the World. See the *Daily Mail*, 19 October 1898, and the *News of the World*, 23 October 1898.

pp. 80–1   *handwriting samples*. See the *Daily Mail*, 6 October 1898.

p. 81   *'one skilled in the science of the head'*. See the *Daily Mail*, 6 December 1898.

p. 84   *Marlow… John Sheridan*. Detective J. G. Littlechild, who was tailing Mrs Druce on behalf of the duke and Herbert Druce, followed her in the company of Marlow and Sheridan, and noted in a confidential report to his employers dated 10 August 1898 that Mrs Druce was 'mixing herself up with a queer lot of City men, Marlow setting the type, but what good they will be to her is questionable'. He also noted the background in relation to Sheridan and the Dreyfus affair (NU PI LI/9/1/1). Since Mrs Druce was being permanently tailed by journalists as well, it is likely that these rumours were current in Fleet Street at the time.

SCENE SEVEN

p. 88   *Then, cheering crowds… the queen had ascended the daïs.* See contemporary newspaper reports of the opening of the new Law Courts on the Strand by Queen Victoria on 4 December 1882. Also *Uncle Jonathan, Walks in and Around London,* 1895 (3rd edn).

p. 88   *Law Court Particular.* See George Augustus Sala, *London Up to Date, Ten-Thirty AM at the new Law Courts,* Pt I–II (1895).

p. 89   *'ghoulish women'.* See *Pall Mall Gazette,* 4 December 1890.

p. 90   *Description of central hall and corridors to probate, divorce and admiralty division.* See Sala, op. cit.; also the description of the entrance to the new Law Courts in Sir Henry Rider Haggard, *Mr Meeson's Will,* Chapter 19 (1888).

p. 91   *had hastily revised his view.* See letter from Forbes Winslow to *The Times,* 17 March 1898.

p. 93   *'a great sameness and simplicity about it'.* See J. E. G. de Montmorency, *John Gorell Barnes, First Lord Gorell: A Memoir,* London: John Murray, 1920, Introduction.

p. 94   *intimacy… 'loss of individuality'.* See de Montmorency, op.cit.

p. 94   *'Madam, you cannot have a Special Jury unless you can show that you are able to pay for it.'* While the full content of the proceedings has necessarily been truncated, the dialogue is transcribed directly from the copy of the short-hand notes taken in the probate court by the court reporter (NU PI/LI/d/2).

p. 101 *committed to a lunatic asylum… bought off by somebody.* The 'official' story given to the press was that Mrs Druce was committed to an asylum. However, in an interview with an agent of J. G. Littlechild on 10 July 1907, an informant told him that she was 'not in a lunatic asylum as reported but was living in opulence, which leads them to believe that she has been bought over, especially as her case finished in the way it did' (NU PI LI/9/4/61).

SCENE EIGHT

p. 106   *Unrest in Bury St Edmunds.* See David Addy, *St Edmundsbury Chronicle 2000*, St Edmundsbury Council millennial project.

p. 107   *St Matthew's Fair.* St Matthew's Fair — one of three traditional fairs at Bury — was also the most famous, taking place on the three days preceding and subsequent to St Matthew's feast on 21 September. It was abolished by the Fairs Act of 1871.

p. 107   *Reverend William Stocking, rector at the village of Tuddenham and reader at St James' Church in Bury.* See *Suffolk: Bury St. Edmunds — Biographical List of Boys Educated At King Edward 6th Free Grammar School, 1550–1900*: 'N.B.--Rev. William Stocking, father of this boy, was reader at St. James', Bury, 1810–29, rector of Tuddenham 1820–29. Died Mar 1829 aged 58.'

p. 107   *marriage licence.* The licence for the couple to marry was granted on 16 October 1816, three days before the wedding (Suffolk: Sudbury — Marriage Licences, 1815–1839; Book 12. The Hearth Tax. Charles 2nd). In order to obtain the marriage licence, Thomas Charles Druce was required to execute a bond certifying that there was no just cause for the couple not to be married without their parents' consent, thus certifying that the couple were of age (i.e., at least twenty-one years old). The exact ages of both T. C. Druce and Elizabeth Crickmer, however, remain something of a mystery, as no birth certificate has been found for either. The claimants in the Druce case always alleged that he was born about 1800, as indeed they had to, as that was the birth year of the 5th Duke of Portland. The year of birth of Elizabeth Crickmer, T. C. Druce's first wife, is given as 1795 in both her death certificate (Death Dec qtr 1851, St George, Southwark, vol. 4, p. 371) and in the record of her burial (LMA, Norwood Cemetery, Norwood Road, Lambeth, Transcript of Burials, 1851, DW/T Item, 0912; Call Number: DW/T/0912). However, in an interview given to J. G. Littlechild by T. C. Druce's granddaughter in 1898, she is stated to have been 'about seventeen' when she married, which would make her year of birth 1799 or 1800.

p. 107   *one of the most beautiful young women.* Many accounts stood testimony to the beauty of Elizabeth Crickmer: see, for example, the *Daily Express*, 29 June 1903.

p. 107   *attended by the reverend's own son.* See records of King Edward 6th Free Grammar School, op. cit. above.

p. 108   *She came from a prosperous family.* See the *Daily Express*, 29 June 1903.

Elizabeth Crickmer's parentage has never been traced with certainty and the figure of £7000 has not been confirmed. However, that she came from a prosperous family is evident from the style in which she and T. C. Druce lived in the four years after their marriage. G. H. Druce's publication *The Idler* of 18 January 1908 (a source that must be approached with caution as it embroiders many facts, but is generally reasonably reliable with reference to background on the Crickmer family) refers to Frances Elizabeth staying in Yarmouth with her 'cousins', the Burtons, one of whom – Samuel Burton – was later to become Mayor of Yarmouth. It appears from this statement and the records that Elizabeth's sister Mary Crickmer made an advantageous match in August 1819 to a gentleman named Samuel Burton. Their marriage was reported in *The Times* – further indicating that the Crickmers were a family of no small status. See register of marriage, Guildhall, St Andrew Holborn, Register of marriages, 1817–1820, P69/AND2/A/01/Ms 6672/3; also announcement in *The Times* dated 3 September 1819, in which Mary Crickmer is said to be 'of Ditchingham', a village next to Bungay.

p. 108   *apparently of good breeding.* See interview given by John Dalgety Henderson, husband to T. C. Druce's granddaughter, with J. G. Littlechild, 5 December 1898, NU PI L1/9/1/12: 'From his [i.e., T. C. Druce's] manners and habits he was evidently of good birth.'

p. 108   *'She ran away from school to get married.'* See NU Pl L1/2/11/3.

p. 109   *School at Southgate Street.* The exclusive boarding school, at nos 42 and 43 Southgate Street, was run by Miss Cooke at the time Elizabeth Crickmer would have attended it. By 1865, it had been taken over by a Miss Amelia Hitchins.

p. 109   *Inspiration for school in* The Pickwick Papers. There have been rival claims by the town of Rochester to being the source of the inspiration for the girls' boarding school in *The Pickwick Papers*.

p. 109   *impressive house on Great Market.* T. C. Druce is first referenced at the house in Great Market on 22 September 1816, about a month before his marriage, when he was obviously preparing a home for his wife. He remained a tenant of this house from 1816 until some time between September 1818 and June 1819, each succeeding assessment list containing his name. See the confirmation of entries in the rate books from Bury St Edmunds Corporation to Baileys dated 19 August 1907 at NU Pl L1/11/6/612; also certified entries of the rate books at Bury at NU Pl L1/2/12/2/7.

p. 109   *resident town portraitist.* See the *Daily Express*, 17 July 1903. It is possible that the portraitist in question was the painter James Canterbury Pardon (b. 1792) or a relative.

p. 110   *overseer of the poor.* See the confirmation of entries in the rate books from Bury St Edmunds Corporation to Baileys dated 19 August 1907 at NU Pl L1/11/6/612; also certified entries of the rate books at Bury at NU Pl L1/2/12/2/7.

p. 110   *admitted to a nunnery.* See account in *Society*, 3 September 1898; corroborated by a report of J. G. Littlechild, NU PI LI 9/1/1.

p. 110   *Benjafield... Payne.* See proof of Charles Benjafield at NU Pl L1/2/7/10.

p. 111   *rented a cottage in... Lower Baxter Street.* See the confirmation of entries in the rate books from Bury St Edmunds Corporation to Baileys dated 19 August 1907 at NU Pl L1/11/6/612; also certified entries of the rate books at Bury at NU Pl L1/2/12/2/7.

p. 111   *Childhood recollections of George Druce.* See *The Idler*, op. cit., 18 January 1908.

p. 111   *sent to Yarmouth to live with her cousins, the Burtons.* See *The Idler*, op. cit., 18 January 1908.

p. 111   *Applications to be excused from having to pay the poor rates.* See the confirmation of entries in the rate books from Bury St Edmunds Corporation to Baileys dated 19 August 1907 at NU Pl L1/11/6/612, also certified entries of the rate books at Bury at NU Pl L1/2/12/2/7.

p. 112   *William Druce.* The ostensible fifth child of Thomas Charles and Elizabeth Druce, William Druce was born at a time when, according to the available records, the couple were estranged.

p. 112   *Claim of George Hollamby that William was illegitimate.* See statement of Amanda Gibson to Walter Dew at NA Mepol 3/175.

p. 112   *Freshfields note stating that 'William is illegitimate'.* See NU Pl L1/2/10/90.

p. 112   *poorer area... Eastgate Street.* See the confirmation of entries in the rate books from Bury St Edmunds Corporation to Baileys dated 19 August 1907 at NU Pl L1/11/6/612; also certified entries of the rate books at Bury at NU Pl L1/2/12/2/7.

p. 113   *Elizabeth leaves Bury for Kennington.* See the *Daily Express*, 18 July 1903.

p. 113   *Confrontation between Druce and his wife.* The account of Elizabeth tracking down T. C. Druce and compelling him to maintain her is given in the *Daily Express*, 29 June 1903. It was confirmed in many newspapers and witness statements by other members of the Crickmer family.

p. 113   *12 shillings a week.* See interview with Mrs Clayton in the *Daily Express*, 30 June 1903.

pp. 113–14   *T. C. Druce's actions with respect to the Crickmer children.* See *The Idler*, 18 January 1908.

p. 114   *Mrs Gibbons... Mrs Whitwell.* Reference to Fanny being sent to these establishments is made in *The Idler* (18 January 1908). Mrs Gibbons' school appears in Pigot's Directory of 1839 and in the 1841 census, in which Mrs Whitwell is listed as a governess. Fanny is not listed at either address in the 1841 census; possibly because, as noted in *The Idler*, she left boarding school that year.

p. 114   *Letter from T. C. Druce to Fanny.* Cited in *The Idler*, op. cit., 18 January 1908. A sample of T. C. Druce's handwriting in the form of a letter signed 'your affectionate father' was handed to the *Daily Mail*, to compare with that of the 5th Duke of Portland.

p. 114   *assigned the lease.* See record of T. C. Druce's movements compiled by Freshfields at NU Pl L1/2/9/5.

p. 114   *Annie May introduced as aunt.* According to an account published in the magazine *The Idler* on 18 January 1908.

p. 115   *her father told her that Elizabeth had died.* See *The Idler*, 18 January 1908, supported by the interview of J. G. Littlechild with Fanny's daughter on 8 December 1898 (NU PI LI/9/1/2). G. H. Druce goes on to state in *The Idler* that Fanny continued to see her mother in secret (see also interview with Mrs Clayton in the *Daily Express*, 30 June 1903).

p. 115   *collecting her weekly allowance from her husband at her brother's house in Kennington.* See account of an interview with Elizabeth's nephew John Crickmer in the *Daily Express*, 29 June 1903; also Mrs Clayton in the *Daily Express*, 30 June 1903. Mary Ann Robinson recounted in a statement to police in June 1908 that John Crickmer had told her that he, or sometimes his father Charles, Elizabeth's brother, would collect her money from T. C. Druce at the Baker Street Bazaar (NA Mepol. 3/175).

p. 115   *Fanny continued to see Elizabeth... cast-off clothes.* See interview with Mrs Clayton in the *Daily Express*, 30 June 1903. The fact that Elizabeth made shirts to eke a living is borne out by the 1851 census, where there is an entry for an 'Elizabeth Douce, visitor', described as a 'shirt-maker', in the household of the Waller family at 8 East Street,

St George's, Southwark. Mary Waller, the wife of the household, is listed on Elizabeth's death certificate as the informant who was present at her death, at the same address.

p. 115   *Description of Elizabeth Crickmer.* See interview with Mrs Clayton in the *Daily Express*, 30 June 1903.

p. 116   *'appeared to be intoxicated'.* See Pl L1/2/6/9.

p. 116   *Elizabeth's real death in 1851.* See records of burials at Norwood Cemetery and Elizabeth's death certificate (ref: *London Metropolitan Archives, Norwood Cemetery, Norwood Road, Lambeth, Transcript of Burials,* 1851, *DW/T Item,* 0912; Call Number: *DW/T/*0912; 1851, 4th qtr, Southwark, Vol. 4, p. 371).

p. 116   *George and William… outbound ships to Australia.* George Druce married Mary Hollamby in Victoria in 1854; William Druce married Hannah Church in Paddington, New South Wales, also in 1854.

p. 116   *Charles Crickmer was to follow them.* A Mr C. Druce is listed in the Unassisted Immigrant Passenger Lists from Plymouth arriving in Sydney, New South Wales, on 24 February 1878, on the vessel *Lochee*.

p. 116   *marrying after her 'aunt's' death a butcher by the name of John Izard.* Eliza Tremaine died at the house in St John's Wood in 1857 (2nd qtr, 1857, St Marylebone, London, Vol. 1a, p. 307). Fanny married John James Izard, a butcher, on 14 September 1858, in the parish of St Marylebone (LMA, Saint Marylebone, Register of marriages, P89/MRY1, Item 231).

p. 117   *John Crickmer.* See account of an interview with the nephew of Elizabeth Crickmer, John, in the *Daily Express*, 29 June 1903.

pp. 117–18   *Letter from Mr Edney.* Cited in *The Idler*, 18 January 1908.

p. 118   *not been told the truth.* See report by J. G. Littlechild of interview with Fanny's daughter on 8 December 1898, NU PI LI 9/1/2.

p. 118   *no carriage in the funeral cortège having been provided for them. Charles Crickmer was present at the official reading of his father's will.* See interview of Fanny's daughter by J. G. Littlechild on 8 December 1898, NU PI LI/9/1/2.

SCENE NINE

p. 121   *born in a mining camp at Campbell's Creek, Victoria.* The details of George Hollamby's early life in Australia are taken from an interview given by him in the *Penny Illustrated Press*, 30 November 1907 (*My Life in Australia*).

p. 121   *Edward Hammond Hargraves.* For a full account of the now legendary discovery by Hargraves of gold in Ophir, see Nancy Keesing, ed., *History of the Australian Gold Rushes*, New South Wales: Angus & Robertson Publishers, 1967, pp. 11–14.

p. 124   '*That… was the start in life she gave me.*' See the *Penny Illustrated Press*, 30 November 1907, op. cit.

p. 124   *George Hollamby in the Australian bush.* The account of George Hollamby's experiences in the Australian bush is taken from his interview with the *Daily Express*, 8 July 1908.

p. 125   *younger brother Charles burst into the room.* The story is recounted by George's brother Charles in evidence given on deposition to the court in Australia at NU Pl L1/2/4/2/23/2.

pp. 127–8   *Letter from Mark Twain.* Letter from Mark Twain to Jesse M. Leathers, 5 October 1875, Mark Twain Papers, California Digital Library.

p. 130   *confidential offer of £50,000.* See statement of Francis Coles to Walter Dew, NA Mepol 3/175.

p. 131   *bankrupted on several occasions.* See the various petitions for bankruptcy filed by T. K. V. Coburn in the Victoria court at NU Pl L1/11/4/38/12.

p. 131   *J. Howden comment.* See NA PRO DPP 1/11, *R. v. Robinson*.

SCENE TEN

p. 133   *65 London Wall.* The offices once occupied by the Druce supporters at 65 London Wall in 1907 still exist today. The building retains many of its original period features.

p. 134   '*Second floor*'. The description of the location, people and events at the Druce offices at 65 London Wall in this chapter are taken from the two statements given by Amanda Malvina Gibson to Detective Chief Inspector Walter Dew in July 1908, unless otherwise stated (NA Mepol. 3/175).

p. 135   *30 shillings to £2 a week.* See statements of Amanda Malvina Gibson, NA Mepol. 3/175, op. cit.

p. 135   *had recently visited George Hollamby and Thomas Coburn.* See statements of Amanda Malvina Gibson, NA Mepol. 3/175, op. cit.

p. 135   *the New Thought movement.* See Beryl Satter, *Each Mind a Kingdom: American Women, Sexual Purity, and the New Thought Movement 1875–1920,* Oakland: University of California Press, 2001.

p. 136   *Amanda's book.* Amanda Gibson referred in her statement to Walter Dew (NA Mepol. 3/175) to bringing a novel with her to England in 1906, in the hope of finding a publisher. The completion date of *A Marriage of Souls* in 1906 (see Prologue) would suggest it was this novel that she brought with her. It was not in fact published until 1914, in Australia.

p. 136   *a central tenet of her own beliefs.* See Veni Cooper-Mathieson, *Australia! Land of the Dawning,* Sydney: Universal Truth Publishing Company, c.1904; also *A Marriage of Souls: A Metaphysical Novel,* Perth: Truth-Seeker Publishing, 1914.

p. 137   *Letters poured in daily.* See statements of Amanda Malvina Gibson, NA Mepol. 3/175, op. cit.

p. 141   *a 'short time between their births'.* See the statement of Mrs Fanny Hughes at NU Pl L1/11/4/33/2.

p. 141   *Agreement between George Hollamby and Charles Edgar:* see NU P1/ L1/2/4/13.

p. 143   *Case that Druce and the duke were one and the same person.* The correspondences between T. C. Druce and the 5th Duke of Portland that convinced Amanda Gibson are taken from *The Idler* pamphlet of 1905 entitled *Claim to the Portland Millions. Was Druce the Duke? Facts shortly stated,* which was privately circulated (see NU Pl L1/2/4/15–20).

p. 147   *Caldwell's story.* Caldwell's story as told to Amanda Gibson, along with those of Mary Robinson and Mrs Hamilton, are based on the witness evidence given by the three in the subsequent court hearing.

SCENE ELEVEN

p. 155   *sawdust, turpentine and cheese.* See the description of Great Grubby Street Police Court in George Augustus Sala, *London Up to Date,* 1895: *Ten AM at Great Grubby Street Police Court (Pt. I & II).*

p. 155   *'blue or black eyes of some goddess'.* See Alfred Chichele Plowden, *Grain or Chaff? The Autobiography of a Police Magistrate,* London: T. F. Unwin, 1903, p. 46.

p. 156   *sickly blue tiles.* See Plowden, *Grain or Chaff?* op. cit., p. 176.

p. 156 'so is the wig to a Judge'. See Plowden, *Grain or Chaff?* op. cit., p. 223.

p. 157 *leniency towards homosexuals.* See Matt Houlbrook, *Queer London: Perils and Pleasures in the Sexual Metropolis 1918–1957*, Chicago: University of Chicago Press, 2005, p. 252.

p. 157 '*Illegitimate?' etc.* The dialogue in this chapter, although necessarily abridged, is accurately reported from the court transcript of the perjury proceedings (NU PI L1/4/3).

p. 158 '*attenuated hands... mask-like face'.* See *A Judge of Distinction – The Life and Work of Horace Avory*, in the *Law Society Gazette*, 29 May 1991.

p. 159 *Notices had been posted in the newspapers.* See NA Mepol. 3/174.

p. 167 *Georgina Hogarth.* See letters and memorandum of interview with Miss Georgina Hogarth at NU Pl L1/11/6/568 and NU Pl L1/2/7/33/1.

p. 168 *Thomas Edward Crispe, KC.* For an account of Crispe's informal cross-examination of Mrs Hamilton and his conviction that she was telling the truth, see his memoir, *Reminiscences of a KC*, London: Methuen & Co., 1909, p. 179.

p. 174 *6th Duke of Portland's pressure on Herbert Druce to consent to open the grave.* See NU Pl L1/11/1/67/1.

SCENE TWELVE

p. 175 *a small group of men.* The description and circumstantial details of the exhumation are taken from the report in *The Times*, 31 December 1907.

p. 176 *a morbid obssession.* See Nicholas Connell, *Walter Dew: The Man Who Caught Crippen*, The History Press, 2013, ebook edition, Chapter 2 (citing Dew's memoir *I Caught Crippen*, London: Blackie & Son Ltd, 1938).

p. 176 *Born in humble circumstances.* See Connell, op.cit., Prologue.

p. 176 *nickname 'Blue Serge'.* See Connell, op.cit., Prologue.

p. 177 '"swell" mobman... Dew.' *Saturday Post*, 29 January 1916.

p. 178 *plot afoot surreptitiously to open the Druce grave.* See letter from Edmund Kimber to Superintendent Froest of Scotland Yard, 26 November 1907, NA Mepol. 3/174.

p. 178 *Dew had advised against it.* See internal CID report of Walter Dew dated 28 November 1907, NA Mepol. 3/174.

p. 179   *Was it not a coincidence.* See internal CID report of Walter Dew into the incident of the stolen diary dated 9 November 1907, NA HO. 45/10541 File/157177.

p. 180   *Russell and Whistler.* See account in *Black and White*, 19 August 1899, p. 230.

p. 181   *offered in excess of £1000.* See NU Pl L1/11/1/153.

p. 181   *different coloured handkerchiefs.* See memorandum from Edwin Freshfield to the Home Office dated 4 January 1908, NA Mepol. 3/174.

p. 182   *A tarpaulin was spread over a portion of the floor.* For this and the subsequent details of the procedure for opening the vault, see *The Times*, 31 December 1907.

p. 183   *approximately six feet five and a quarter inches in length.* See internal CID report of Walter Dew dated 31 December 1907, NA Mepol. 3/174.

SCENE THIRTEEN

p. 185   *fourteenth and last court hearing.* See documents relating to the proceedings of *R.* v. *Herbert Druce* at NU Pl L1/4.

SCENE FOURTEEN

p. 194   *warrant for Caldwell's arrest.* For this and the subsequent events at Albert Square, see the reports of Walter Dew at NA DPP 1/11.

p. 195   *A coded message.* See NA DPP 1/11.

p. 196   *hanging around his master's London residence.* See NU Pl L1/11/6/882–3.

p. 197   *Subterfuge by which the duke's coat was obtained from Harrington's daughter.* See the statement of Bertha Lambourn, daughter of John Harrington, at NU Pl L1/2/7/102.

p. 198   *'I have been on the track all day'.* See letter dated 8 December 1907 from T. W. Turner to Horseman Bailey, NU Pl L1/11/6/633/1.

p. 200   *Burning of Welbeck paintings.* See letter from Richard Goulding to Baileys, Shaw & Gillett dated 12 December 1907, NU Pl L1/11/3/102.

p. 201   *dismissed three workmen… caricature.* See the evidence of the mechanical engineer James Rudd for the prosecution in the Druce perjury case, NU PI L1/4/2/7; also the proof of John William Tinker at NU Pl L1/2/6/13.

SCENE FIFTEEN

p. 203   *Battle for Caldwell's extradition.* The account of the battle for Caldwell's extradition for trial in Britain on charges of perjury is taken from the Department of Public Prosecutions file on the subject at the National Archives, NA DPP 1. 11.

p. 204   *fellow passenger... daughter of the late Captain Joyce.* See statement of Robert Caldwell's fellow passenger Roulston at NU PI L1/4/2/17; also Dew's investigations into Captain Joyce at NA Mepol 3/174 and NA DPP 1.11.

p. 205   *'Woman just arrested.'* See telegram from J. G. Littlechild to Bailey dated 17 January 1908, NU Pl L1/11/6/960.

p. 206   *Account of Robinson's arrest.* The account of Mary Robinson's arrest is taken from the report submitted to Scotland Yard by Walter Dew dated 21 January 1908 at NA Mepol 3/176.

p. 207   *Kimber accused of perjury.* See *Leeds Times*, 7 November 1891.

p. 207   *Kimber representing the Tichborne claimant.* See *Manchester Evening News*, 13 September 1880.

p. 208   *Background of Mrs Robinson.* Dew's research into Mary Ann Robinson's background is contained in the National Archive police files on the case, in particular NA Mepol 3/176.

p. 209   *Royal Hotel.* Inspector Dew stayed at the Royal Hotel on his visit to Worksop in August 1908 (NU Pl L1/11/6/1199). It is therefore likely that he stayed there during his earlier visit that year, in January. The hotel stood on the old market square at Worksop, and has since been demolished.

p. 210   *'loose character in Worksop.'* NA MEPO 3/175.

p. 210   *Researches into Mary Robinson.* For these events during Inspector Dew's visit to Welbeck, see the letter from Turner to Baileys dated 24 January 1908, at NU Pl/L1/11/6/985/1-3.

p. 211   *Letter from Arthur Markham.* Markham's letter to Turner, along with Crowder's statement, is at NU Pl L1/11/6/769/2–3.

p. 211   *trouble with the local press.* See *Manchester Evening News*, 28 August 1902.

p. 212   *Joseph Burns*. See proof of Joseph Burns in *Druce* v. *Howard de Walden*, NU Pl L1/2/6/12.

p. 213   *Bernard Boaler*. See proof of Bernard Boaler in *Druce* v. *Howard de Walden*, NU Pl L1/2/7/14.

p. 213   *old teller of underwood cuttings*. See proof of William Ashberry of Holbeck Woodhouse in *Druce* v. *Howard de Walden*, NU Pl L1/2/6/13.

p. 214   *Henry Powell's evidence*. See proof of Henry Powell in *Druce* v. *Howard de Walden*, NU Pl L1/2/6/13.

p. 214   *truss for a rupture of the right side of the groin*. See letter from William Higgs to Baileys dated 10 December 1907, at NU Pl L1/11/6/845.

p. 215   *Message from Mary Robinson at Holloway Prison*. NA Mepol 3/176.

SCENE SIXTEEN

p. 217   *Mrs Robinson's confession*. The details of Mary Ann Robinson's confession are taken from the reports to Scotland Yard by Inspector Dew of a series of interviews with her in Holloway Prison during January and February 1908 (NA Mepol 3/176) and her official statement as submitted during her trial (NU Pl L1/6/1/10).

p. 223   *'Harry the Valet'... Conrad Harms*. Both cases were discussed by Dew in his autobiography, *I Caught Crippen*, op. cit.

pp. 223–4   *The 6th Duke also dismissed the idea... as ridiculous*. See letter to Baileys dated 24 January 1908, NU PL L1/11/6/935/1-2.

p. 224   *Letter penned by Mary Ann Robinson as one to her from the 5th Duke*. See NU Pl L1/6/2/1–11.

p. 225   *'Kimber and Coburn into our net'*. NU Pl L1/3646.

SCENE SEVENTEEN

p. 227   *the town of Kendal, in Westmorland*. The background story of Mrs Hamilton is taken from the private investigator reports of J. G. Littlechild at NU PI LI/9/1/3.

p. 227   *black ringlets*. See letter from Moser & Son to Baileys at NU Pl L1/11/6/942.

p. 229   *Mussabini and Littlechild*. See Jan Bondeson, *The Great Pretenders: The True Stories behind Famous Historical Mysteries*, London: W.W. Norton & Co., 2004, p. 251.

p. 230   *Mussabini's report back to Littlechild.* See letter from Mussabini to Littlechild dated 14 November 1901, at NU PI LI/9/2/1-16.

p. 231   *'tissue of lies'.* See letter from Moser & Sons to Baileys dated 9 January 1908, at NU Pl Lɪ/11/6/943/1.

p. 231   *wreath on the tomb.* See NU Pl Lɪ/11/1/12.

p. 232   *Thomas Wyatt.* See letter from Freshfields to Baileys dated 22 November 1907, NU Pl Lɪ/11/1/133.

p. 233   *Botten's statement.* See NU PI Lɪ/4/2/11, proof of Charles Louis Botten, Manager to Dickson & Rowe of 17 Walbrook (paper dealers) dated 19 November 1907.

pp. 234–5   *Statement of Edward Phillips.* See statement of Edward Phillips to Walter Dew at NA Mepol 3/175.

p. 236   *tuberculosis of the lungs and throat.* See notes of interview between Dew and Official Receiver's Office dated 18 March 1908, NU Pl Lɪ/11/6/1111.

p. 236   *amateur detective… professional plain-clothes policeman.* For the divergence in public perceptions, see the analysis by Lucy Worsley in *A Very British Murder*, BBC Digital, September 2013.

p. 239   *'all persons who should be brought to book'.* See NU Pl Lɪ/11/6/938.

p. 239   *'Coburn and the whole crew'.* See NU Pl Lɪ/11/6/1103/1.

p. 239   *recorder at Newcastle.* See letter from Turner to Baileys at NU Pl Lɪ/11/6/990/1.

p. 240   *Letter from Home Office dismissing investigation.* See NU Pl LI/11/6/1177.

SCENE EIGHTEEN

pp. 241–2   *Letter from Baileys to Home Office.* See NU Pl Lɪ/11/6/1178.

p. 242   *joint legal opinion.* See Opinion dated 4 June 1908, NU Pl Lɪ/2/1/60.

p. 245   *Sir Tatton and Lady Sykes.* The full eccentricities of Sir Tatton Sykes and the history of his spectacularly unhappy marriage to Jessie are set out in Christopher Simon Sykes' biography of the Sykes family and Sledmere House, *The Big House: The Story of a Country House and its family*, London: HarperCollins, 2005.

p. 246   *A vicar of Sledmere.* From the Sykes papers at the Brynmor Jones Library, University of Hull, DDSY /104/168.

pp. 247–8 *Sir Tatton Sykes' advertisement.* This advertisement appeared in *The Times*, the *Morning Post*, the *Standard*, the *Daily Telegraph* and the *Daily News* on 7 December 1896.

p. 249 *'left the matter alone'.* See NU Pl L1/11/6/217/1, NU Pl L1/11/6/2/2.

p. 249 *Mary Ann's account of meeting with Lady Sykes.* See statements of Mary Ann Robinson in Holloway Prison at NU Pl L1/6/1/10.

p. 251 *Oakland Tribune.* See *Oakland Tribune*, 20 January 1913.

p. 252 *Final fate of George Hollamby.* See Stratmann, Linda, *Fraudsters and Charlatans*, Stroud: The History Press, ebook, 2010.

pp. 252–3 *6th Duke's thanks to Dew and other officers.* See NU Pl L1/11/6/1204.

pp. 253–4 *Saturday Post.* See *Saturday Post*, 29 January 1916.

p. 254 *Dew's biographer Nicholas Connell.* See Nicholas Connell, *Walter Dew: The Man who Caught Crippen*, Stroud: The History Press, 2013.

SCENE NINETEEN

p. 256 *Thomas Mann citation.* © 1960, 1974 S. Fischer Verlag GmbH, Frankfurt am Main. All rights reserved.

p. 258 *Edwin Freshfield had referred to them in a letter to the Home Office.* See NU Pl L1/11/1/191.

p. 259 *Fire at Harcourt House.* See proof of Henry Powell at NU Pl L1/2/6/13.

p. 259 *'The late Duke well knew the opinion of the outside world concerning him'.* See proof of Joseph Burns at NU Pl L1/2/6/12.

p. 260 *record books split into double columns.* See, for example, NU Pl L1/2/9/5.

p. 261 *Action against the 6th Duke over census returns.* See NU Pl L1/8 – documents relating to *Haworth* v. *Portland* and another.

p. 262 *Kerridge's statement.* See proof of William Kerridge at NU Pl L1/2/6/13.

p. 263 *trade circular.* See NU Pl L1/11/3/108.

p. 263 *French Embassy in London... Albert, the Prince Consort.* See memorandum of former Druce employee Richard Smith at NU Pl L1/2/7/150/1.

p. 263 *Proofs of Leslie Ward and Henry Hope-Pinker.* See NU Pl L1/2/7/170 and NU Pl L1/2/6/13.

p. 265   *Lawledge statement.* See NU Pl L1/2/6/9.

p. 265   *Edward Swift.* See NA MEPOL 3/175.

p. 266   *Bernard O'Donnell.* See O'Donnell, *The Trials of Mr Justice Avory*, London: Rich & Cowan, 1935, pp. 93–4.

p. 267   *Plans and specifications for 'sub-way at Harcourt House'.* See NU PL L1/11/3/34.

pp. 268–9 *Letters from Fanny Lawson to Horace Avory.* See NU PL L1/11/6/1224/2, NU PL L1/11/6/1231.

SCENE TWENTY

p. 276   *Citation from* A Natural History of the Senses. Cited by kind permission of the author, Diane Ackerman.

p. 277   *police photographs of the Druce grave.* NA HO 45/10541/FILE/157177.

p. 279   *'a pompous-looking man with a moustache'.* See Masters, op. cit., p. 169.

p. 285   *'upset the applecart'.* See NU Pl L1/11/6/303.

p. 286   *Military service records of George and Bertram Lawson.* Register No 203497, Portsmouth Division, and Register No 9894, Chatham Division.

p. 288   *handwritten note of a meeting.* See NU Pl L1/2/10/37.

2014 POSTCRIPT

p. 295   *Four lines from* Four Quartets: Burnt Norton (1936) by T. S. Eliot, quoted with permission of Faber and Faber Ltd.

pp. 297–8 *My mother, when I was a small boy... She married in Edinburgh and became my mother.* Extracted from the unpublished memoirs of George Lawson, and cited by kind permission of Patricia Davies.

ACKNOWLEDGMENTS

This book could not have been written without reliance on the vast collection of documents housed at Nottingham University Manuscripts & Special Collections; in particular, the important Portland (London) Collection that is the primary source of unpublished material relating to the Druce–Portland case. To the patience and forbearance of the staff there, I owe much in the way of thanks. Other important collections are held by the National Archives at Kew and the London Metropolitan Archives, to whose staff I am likewise most grateful.

The task of researching this book has been truly enormous, and many people have generously stepped in with advice and assistance on the way. I am grateful to Norma Bulman for her painstaking photographing of literally hundreds of documents to facilitate my task, and also to Sue Newman for invaluable assistance on the genealogical research front. Gordon Ashbury generously provided vital clues to Fanny Lawson's Scottish connections, and Geoff Wright gave helpful pointers to the ultimate fate of George Hollamby. Forces War Records were of great assistance in retrieving the service records of George and Bertram Lawson, and Michael Goldschmidt provided detailed insights into their interpretation, bringing the invaluable benefit of his expertise as a military historian. Dr Lionel Thevathasan MB BS FRCS spared some time from a busy schedule to give medical advice. Thanks are also due to Charles Dalglish and Melvyn Tan, both of whom put me in touch with the right people. I am grateful also to Shelley Thevathasan, for her careful review of the manuscript.

To Derek Adlam, the curator at Welbeck Abbey, I owe an enormous debt. His generous allocation of time for a visit and guided tour, together with his passionate enthusiasm for the abbey and its occupants throughout time, made the story come alive in a way that would not have otherwise been possible. I also have him to thank for a careful scrutiny of certain passages relating to the incredibly complicated family history of the Cavendish-Bentinck family.

I should thank my incredible agent Andrew Lownie, and my best and severest critic, my editor Richard Milbank. I am also very grateful to Anne Newman for her fabulously rigorous copyediting. Love and thanks also to my mother Sarah Das Gupta and, as ever, to my husband, Nikolaï Eatwell. To my sons Alek, Oscar and Noah, I am perhaps the most grateful of all: for allowing their mother to sneak off, at times, to her double life.

SELECT BIBLIOGRAPHY

PRIMARY SOURCES

The primary (unpublished) sources for this book come from two principal archives:

The Portland (London) Collection at Nottingham University Manuscripts & Special Collections department. This important collection, consisting of several thousand documents, is the most comprehensive record of the Druce–Portland proceedings in existence. It includes all the court papers from the numerous hearings of the case, the correspondence of the 6th Duke's solicitors Baileys, Shaw & Gillett that related to it and the private-investigator reports of J. G. Littlechild, along with numerous press clippings. Detailed references to the Nottingham University Portland (London) archive are contained in the endnotes, and are prefaced by the reference NU. Files reviewed were:

Pl L1/1	Pl L1/8
Pl L1/2	Pl L1/9
Pl L1/3	Pl L1/11
Pl L1/4	Pl L1/12
Pl L1/6	

The National Archives. The National Archives contain important documents from the Home Office, Director of Public

Prosecutions, and Metropolitan Police files relating to the initial claims by Anna Maria Druce and the later perjury and conspiracy charges. A number of the files were classified until the 1980s. Detailed references to the National Archive files relating to the Druce case are contained in the endnotes, and are prefaced by the reference NA. Files reviewed were:

PRO BT 31/11183/85345
PRO BT 31/12175/95549
PRO DPP 1/11
PRO HO 45/10541/157177
PRO HO 144/1020/160196
PRO MEPO 3/174
PRO MEPO 3/175
PRO MEPO 3/176
PRO TS 18/272
BT31/12141/95200
HO45/10253/X27066
J14/560

In addition, there are references to documents in the London Metropolitan Archives, particularly relating to nineteenth-century workhouse records, which are prefaced by the reference LMA. References to birth, marriage and death certificates, together with census records, are identified by the appropriate source reference.

SECONDARY SOURCES

Adlam, Derek:

    – *Miss Butler Remembers: A Laundry Maid's Recollections of the 5th Duke of Portland*, Florida: The Pineapple Press, 2003.

    – *Tunnel Vision: The enigmatic 5th Duke of Portland*, Harley Gallery, Welbeck, 2013 (reissue).

    – *The Great Collector: Edward Harley, 2nd Earl of Oxford*, Harley Gallery, Welbeck, 2013.

Archard, Charles J., *The Portland Peerage Romance*, London: Greening & Co. Ltd, 1907.

Baker, T. F. T. and Pugh, R. B., eds, *A History of the County of Middlesex: Volume 5: Hendon, Kingsbury, Great Stanmore, Little Stanmore, Edmonton, Enfield, Monken Hadley, South Mimms, Tottenham*, London: Victoria County History, 1976.

Besterman, Theodore, *The Druce Portland Case*, London: Duckworth, 1935.

Boston, Ray and Evans, Harry, *The Essential Fleet Street*, London: Cassell Illustrated, 1990.

Boucicault, Dion, *London Assurance*, stage adaptation by Ronald Eyre, London: Methuen & Co., 1971.

Bradbury, David J., *Welbeck and the 5th Duke of Portland*, Nottinghamshire: Wheel, 1989.

Braddon, Mary Elizabeth, *Lady Audley's Secret* (1862), London: Wordsworth Classics, 1997.

Brontë, Charlotte, *Jane Eyre* (1847), London: Wordsworth Classics, 1992.

Bryson, Bill, *Notes from a Small Island*, London: Black Swan, 1996.

Cavendish-Bentinck, William John Arthur Charles James, 6th Duke of Portland, *Men, Women and Things: Memories of the Duke of Portland K.G., G.C.V.O.*, London: Faber & Faber, 1937.

Chancellor, E. Beresford, *The Private Palaces of London Past and Present*, London: Kegan, Paul, Trench, Trübner & Co., 1908.

Christiansen, Rupert, 'What is a Gentleman?', in 'Charles Dickens' *Great Expectations: A New Interpretation for Students*', Christiansen, 2013, http://exec.typepad.com/greatexpectations.

Clarke, William M., *The Secret Life of Wilkie Collins*, Chicago: Ivan R. Dee, 2004.

Collins, Wilkie:

– *The Woman in White* (1859), London: Penguin Classics, 2012.

– *Armadale* (1866), London: Penguin Classics, 1995.

Connell, Nicholas, *Walter Dew: The Man who Caught Crippen*, Stroud: The History Press, 2013.

Cooper-Mathieson, Veni:

– *Australia! Land of the Dawning*, Sydney: Universal Truth Publishing Company, 1904.

– *A Marriage of Souls: a Metaphysical Novel*, Perth: Truth Seeker Publishing Company, 1914.

Cox, Jane, *Hatred Pursued Beyond the Grave*, London: Stationery Office, 1996.

Crispe, Thomas Edward, *Reminiscences of a KC*, London: Methuen & Co., 1909.

Day, William, *Reminiscences of the Turf*, London: Richard Bentley & Son, 1886.

Dew, Walter, *I Caught Crippen*, London: Blackie & Son, 1938.

Diamond, Michael, *Victorian Sensation*, London: Anthem Press, 2004.

Dickens, Charles:

– *The Pickwick Papers* (1836), Ware: Wordsworth Classics, 1993.

– *Bleak House* (1853), Ware: Wordsworth Classics, 1993.

– *Hard Times* (1854), London: Penguin Classics, 1995.

– *Great Expectations* (1860), London: Penguin Classics, 2004.

Dimock, Rev. Arthur MA, *St Paul: an account of the old and new buildings with a short historical sketch*, London: George Bell & Sons, 1900.

Eastlake, Lady Elizabeth, *'Vanity Fair', 'Jane Eyre', and the Governess' Benevolent Institution*, Quarterly Review, 84 (December 1848), p. 176.

Flanders, Judith, *The Invention of Murder: How the Victorians Revelled in Death and Detection and Created Modern Crime*, London: HarperPress, 2011.

Freeman-Keel, Tom and Croft, Andrew, *The Disappearing Duke: The Improbable Tale of an Eccentric English Family*, New York: Avalon Publishing Group, 2003.

Graham, Clare, *Ordering Law: The Architectural and Social History of the English Law Court*, Surrey: Ashgate Publishing, 2003.

Griffiths, Dennis, *Fleet Street: Five Hundred Years of the Press*, London: The British Library, 2006.

Haw, George, *From Workhouse to Westminster: The Life Story of Will Crooks, MP*, London: Cassell & Co., 1907.

Headley, Gwyn, and Meulenkamp, Wim, *Follies, Grottoes, and Garden Buildings*, London: Aurum Press Limited, 1999.

Herdman, John, *The Double in Nineteenth Century Fiction*, London: Palgrave Macmillan, 1990.

Higginbotham, Peter, *The Workhouse Encyclopaedia*, Stroud: The History Press, 2012.

Historic Houses of the United Kingdom; descriptive, historical, pictorial, London: Cassell & Co., 1892.

Houlbrook, Matt, *Queer London: Perils and Pleasures in the Sexual Metropolis 1918–1957*, Chicago: University of Chicago Press, 2005.

Hughes, Kathryn, *The Victorian Governess*, London: Hambledon, 2001.

Hume, Fergus, *The Mystery of a Hansom Cab* (1886), Melbourne: Text Classics, 1999.

James, R. R., ed., *Chips: The Diaries of Sir Henry Channon*, London: Weidenfeld & Nicolson, 1967.

Keesing, Nancy, ed., *History of the Australian Gold Rushes by Those Who were There*, New South Wales: Angus & Robertson Publishers, 1971.

Kelly's Directories for the 1800s.

Knight, Charles, *Knight's London*, 1841.

Knox, Tim, *Precautions for Privacy: The 'Mole Duke's' Secret Garden at Harcourt House, Cavendish Square*, in *The London Gardener*, Volume 2, 1996–1997, 2:27–33.

Lang, Gordon, *Mr Justice Avory*, London: Herbert Jenkins, 1935.

Mason, Walter, *Sister Veni Cooper-Mathieson: Pioneer Thinker and Metaphysical Teacher*, in *New Dawn Magazine*, November–December 2013, pp. 69–70.

Masters, Brian, *The Dukes*, London: Pimlico, 2001.

Montmorency, de, J.E.G., *John Gorell Barnes, First Lord Gorell: A Memoir*, London: John Murray, 1920.

O'Donnell, Bernard, *The Trials of Mr Justice Avory*, London: Rich & Cowan, 1935.

Peabody, Charles, *English Journalism and the Men Who Have Made It*, London: Cassell, 1882.

Pigot's Directories, 1800s.

Plowden, Alfred Chichele, *Grain or Chaff? The Autobiography of a Police Magistrate*, London: T. F. Unwin, 1903.

Pykett, Lyn, *Authors in Context: Wilkie Collins*, Oxford: Oxford World's Classics, 2005.

Rider Haggard, Sir Henry, *Mr Meeson's Will* (1888), London: The British Library, 2010.

Roggenkamp, Karen, *Narrating the News: New Journalism and Literary Genre in Late Nineteenth Century Newspapers and Fiction*, Kent, Ohio: The Kent State University Press, 2005.

Sala, George Augustus, *London Up to Date*, London: A. and C. Black, 1894.

Satter, Beryl, *Each Mind a Kingdom: American Women, Sexual Purity, and the New Thought Movement 1875–1920*, Oakland, California: University of California Press, 2001.

Shaw, Charles, *When I was a Child*, London: Methuen, 1903.

Slinn, Judy, *A History of Freshfields*, Freshfields, 1984.

Smiles, Samuel, *Self-Help*, 1859, Project Gutenberg ebook.

Stead, William Thomas, *Works*, The Perfect Library ebook, 2013.

Stevenson, Robert Louis, *Strange Case of Dr Jekyll and Mr Hyde* (1886), New York: Norton Critical Edition, 2003.

Stratmann, Linda, *Fraudsters and Charlatans: A Peek at Some of History's Greatest Rogues*, Stroud: The History Press, 2012.

Sykes, Christopher Simon, *Big House: The Story of a Country House and its Family*, London: HarperCollins, 2005.

Thackeray, William Makepeace, *Vanity Fair* (1843), Ware: Wordsworth Classics, 2001.

Thomas Hutchinson Tristram: For Forty Years Chancellor of London: A Memoir, London: Longmans, Green and Co., 1916.

Tomalin, Claire, *The Invisible Woman: The Story of Nelly Ternan and Charles Dickens*, London: Viking, 1991.

Turbeville, A. S., *A History of Welbeck Abbey and its Owners*, London: Faber & Faber, 1939.

Twain, Mark:

    – *Adventures of Huckleberry Finn* (1884), London: Penguin Classics, 2003.

— *The American Claimant* (1892), Project Gutenberg ebook, 2006.

— *Uncle Jonathan, Walks in and Around London*, London: Charles H. Kelly, (1895), 3rd edn.

Whittington-Egan, Molly, *Dr Forbes Winslow: Defender of the Insane*, Capella Archive, 2000.

Wilde, Oscar, *The Importance of Being Earnest* (1895), London: Bantam, 2005.

Woolcock, Helen R., *Rights of Passage: Emigration to Australia in the Nineteenth Century*, London: Tavistock Publications, 1986.

A large number of newspaper reports, journal articles and pamphlets are also referred to in the book, identified individually in the Notes. Local information such as descriptions of buildings, roads and train timetables comes from contemporary guides and maps; weather conditions on specific days from the newspaper weather reports.

A NOTE ON MONEY

As the contemporary value of money is sometimes relevant
to the story, in order to give the reader a rough idea of
how much quoted sums were worth at the time, I have
used the historic inflation calculator of Associated News-
papers/'This is Money', which uses official UK inflation data
to show how prices have changed, and what money used to
be worth: http://www.thisismoney.co.uk/money/bills/
article-1633409/Historic-inflation-calculator-value-money-
changed-1900.html

PICTURE CREDITS

16. The *Idler*, 1907

17. The *Idler*, 1907

18. Bridgeman Images

19. London News Agency, from *Mr Justice Avory* (1935) by Gordon Lang.

20. Wikimedia Commons

21. The *Penny Illustrated Paper*, 30 November 1907

22. The *Penny Illustrated Paper*, 30 November 1907

23. The *Penny Illustrated Paper*, 30 November 1907

24. The *Penny Illustrated Paper*, 30 November 1907

PAGE 275

Police photograph of the coffin of T. C. Druce: The National Archives